STAR WARS

THE RISE OF SKYWALKER

™

THE VISUAL DICTIONARY

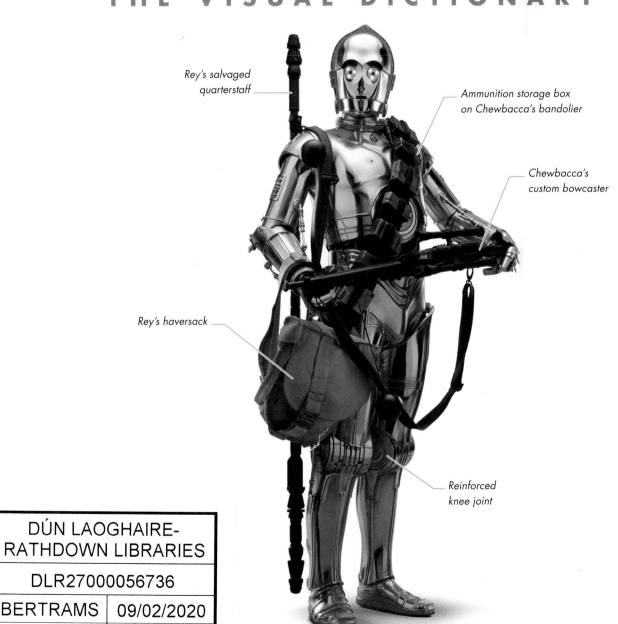

Rey's salvaged quarterstaff

Ammunition storage box on Chewbacca's bandolier

Chewbacca's custom bowcaster

Rey's haversack

Reinforced knee joint

C-3PO

Photoreceptor

Repurposed astromech
dome from obsolete model

Treaded
foot pod

0-LT UTILITY DROID

Heavy-duty
power cable

T-70 X-WING STARFIGHTER

Yellow markings denote past
service in Xantho Squadron

Repulsorfield
conductor ring

Torque-impelling jaws

REY'S QUARANTINE SUSPENSOR

BABU FRIK'S MAGNASPANNER

Processor
plane calibrator

Sleeves cover
taste-receptor hairs

Visualization
display shroud

Cracks welded with
Sarrassian iron

Insulated
hand grip

Shielded
ion trap

**RIOT CONTROL
ELECTROPROD**

WIZZICH MOZZER

**KYLO REN'S
HELMET**

**QUANTUM COMPUTER
DIAGNOSTICS LABORATORY**

STAR WARS

THE RISE OF SKYWALKER

™

THE VISUAL DICTIONARY

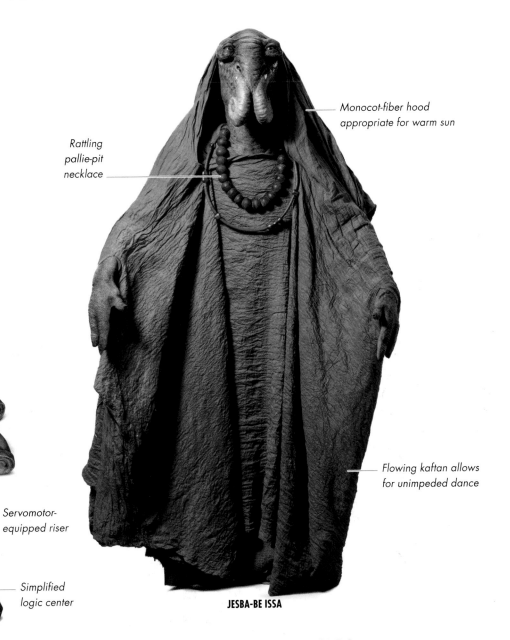

Monocot-fiber hood appropriate for warm sun

Rattling pallie-pit necklace

Flowing kaftan allows for unimpeded dance

JESBA-BE ISSA

FESTBOX DRUM MALLETS

Servomotor-equipped riser

Simplified logic center

"BOOST-BOT" BFB-7

WRITTEN BY PABLO HIDALGO

CONTENTS

FOREWORD

As a former literature major, I would like to say that the most well-worn book in my library is *War and Peace* or *Moby Dick*. The truth is that the distinction belongs to a book called *The Return of the Jedi Sketchbook*, a 1983 paperback that I looked at just about every night before bed from age 6 to age 10.

Return of the Jedi was the first movie I ever saw—and saw and saw. My parents gamely, if wearily, submitted to my demands to be driven to the cinema every Saturday for an entire summer to watch (and rewatch and rewatch) the third installment of the *Star Wars* trilogy. When I wasn't watching the film, I would pore over the *Jedi Sketchbook*. Even at that age, I could not believe that it was someone's job— some adult's job—to sit at a sketchpad and imagine the *Star Wars* galaxy: to create a sail barge fit for a Hutt, or the sticks-and-stones warfare of the Ewoks, or the unlikely verticality of a B-wing fighter.

Thirty-odd years later, I had the astonishing luck to be asked by J.J. Abrams to work with him on crafting the script for the end of the Skywalker saga, and I'm still not convinced that I have not been dreaming for the last two years.

Imagine how the heart of a lifelong *Star Wars* fan leapt upon seeing the concept drawings of Kevin Jenkins, or hearing the shamanic ideas of Rick Carter, as we spent hour after hour with Kathy Kennedy, Michelle Rejwan, and our friend and captain J.J., puzzling over how we would conclude the central myth of our lives.

Imagine trying to contain yourself when ushered into a cramped workshop to see Neal Scanlan's visionary creature designs for the first time. Or standing on the deck of a Star Destroyer, looking at a green screen but imagining the worlds that Roger Guyett and his team of wizards would eventually conjure outside the viewport window.

There was never a shooting day when I didn't make sure that six-year-old me was standing alongside forty-year-old me, both of us lost in the galaxy where we would both happily spend the rest of our lives.

The Rise of Skywalker: The Visual Dictionary, written by one of this planet's great *Star Wars* authorities, Pablo Hidalgo, allows readers to share the experience of living in the worlds created for the film: the characters, the creatures, the planets, the ships, the weapons.

This book shows us a place where novelty and legacy meet to create dreamscapes that feel both entirely new and utterly true to the galaxy George Lucas dreamed up more than 40 years ago. I hope there are six-year-olds and sixty-year-olds who will wear it out.

Chris Terrio

CHRIS TERRIO
CO-WRITER, *STAR WARS: THE RISE OF SKYWALKER*

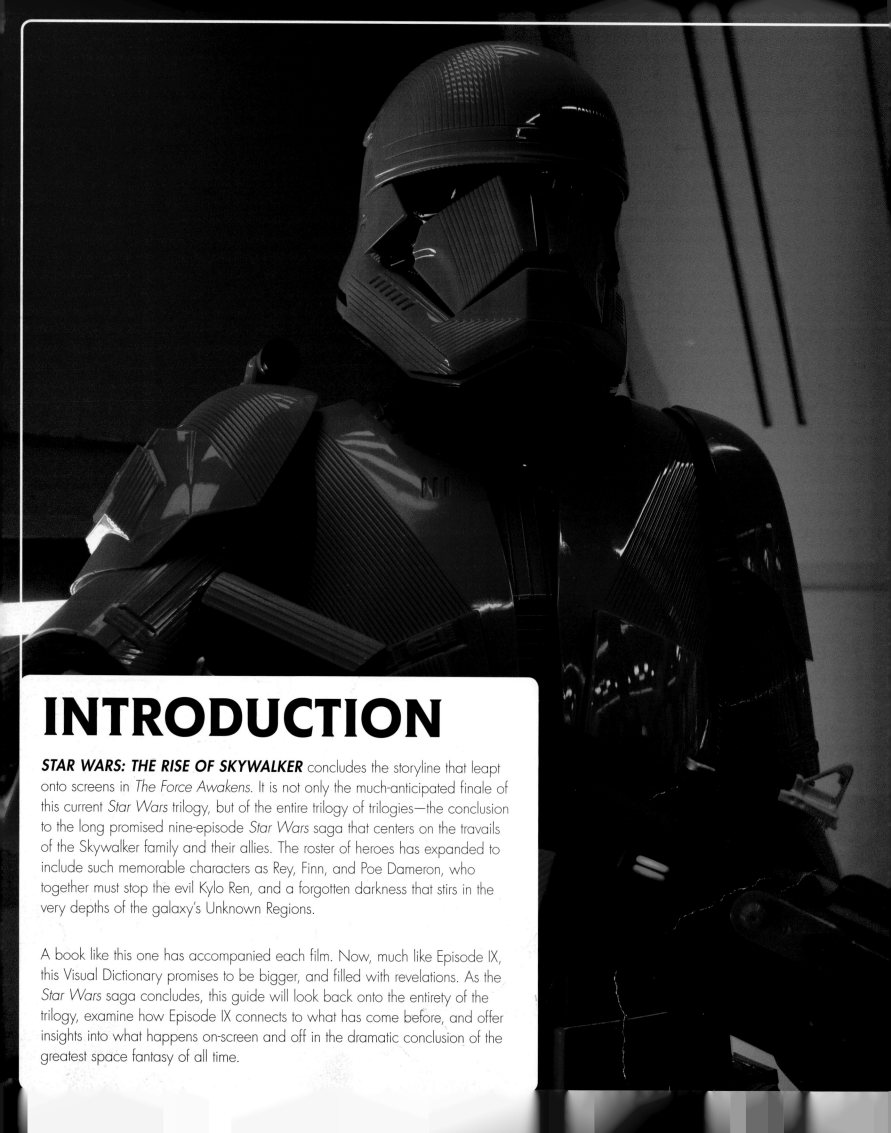

INTRODUCTION

STAR WARS: THE RISE OF SKYWALKER concludes the storyline that leapt onto screens in *The Force Awakens*. It is not only the much-anticipated finale of this current *Star Wars* trilogy, but of the entire trilogy of trilogies—the conclusion to the long promised nine-episode *Star Wars* saga that centers on the travails of the Skywalker family and their allies. The roster of heroes has expanded to include such memorable characters as Rey, Finn, and Poe Dameron, who together must stop the evil Kylo Ren, and a forgotten darkness that stirs in the very depths of the galaxy's Unknown Regions.

A book like this one has accompanied each film. Now, much like Episode IX, this Visual Dictionary promises to be bigger, and filled with revelations. As the *Star Wars* saga concludes, this guide will look back onto the entirety of the trilogy, examine how Episode IX connects to what has come before, and offer insights into what happens on-screen and off in the dramatic conclusion of the greatest space fantasy of all time.

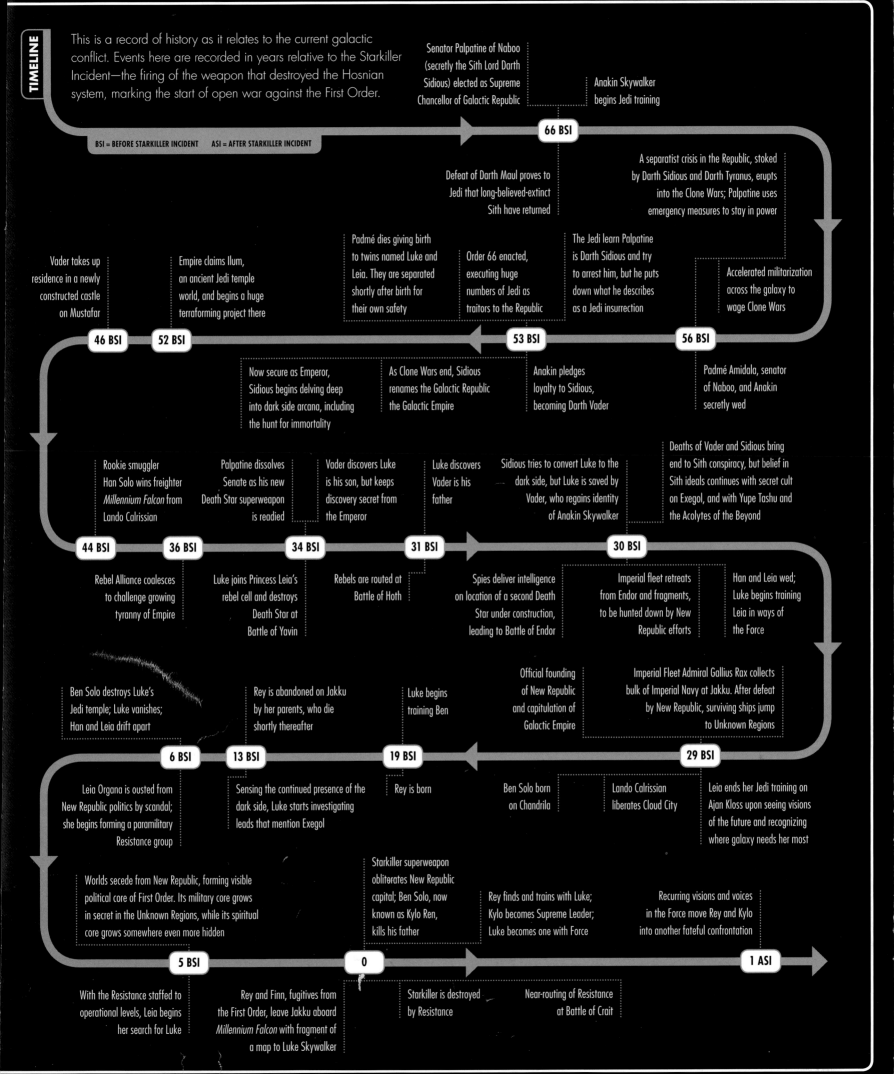

TIMELINE

This is a record of history as it relates to the current galactic conflict. Events here are recorded in years relative to the Starkiller Incident—the firing of the weapon that destroyed the Hosnian system, marking the start of open war against the First Order.

BSI = BEFORE STARKILLER INCIDENT   ASI = AFTER STARKILLER INCIDENT

Senator Palpatine of Naboo (secretly the Sith Lord Darth Sidious) elected as Supreme Chancellor of Galactic Republic

Anakin Skywalker begins Jedi training

66 BSI

A separatist crisis in the Republic, stoked by Darth Sidious and Darth Tyranus, erupts into the Clone Wars; Palpatine uses emergency measures to stay in power

Defeat of Darth Maul proves to Jedi that long-believed-extinct Sith have returned

Padmé dies giving birth to twins named Luke and Leia. They are separated shortly after birth for their own safety

Order 66 enacted, executing huge numbers of Jedi as traitors to the Republic

The Jedi learn Palpatine is Darth Sidious and try to arrest him, but he puts down what he describes as a Jedi insurrection

Accelerated militarization across the galaxy to wage Clone Wars

Vader takes up residence in a newly constructed castle on Mustafar

Empire claims Ilum, an ancient Jedi temple world, and begins a huge terraforming project there

46 BSI   **52 BSI**   **53 BSI**   **56 BSI**

Now secure as Emperor, Sidious begins delving deep into dark side arcana, including the hunt for immortality

As Clone Wars end, Sidious renames the Galactic Republic the Galactic Empire

Anakin pledges loyalty to Sidious, becoming Darth Vader

Padmé Amidala, senator of Naboo, and Anakin secretly wed

Rookie smuggler Han Solo wins freighter *Millennium Falcon* from Lando Calrissian

Palpatine dissolves Senate as his new Death Star superweapon is readied

Vader discovers Luke is his son, but keeps discovery secret from the Emperor

Luke discovers Vader is his father

Sidious tries to convert Luke to the dark side, but Luke is saved by Vader, who regains identity of Anakin Skywalker

Deaths of Vader and Sidious bring end to Sith conspiracy, but belief in Sith ideals continues with secret cult on Exegol, and with Yupe Tashu and the Acolytes of the Beyond

44 BSI   **36 BSI**   **34 BSI**   **31 BSI**   **30 BSI**

Rebel Alliance coalesces to challenge growing tyranny of Empire

Luke joins Princess Leia's rebel cell and destroys Death Star at Battle of Yavin

Rebels are routed at Battle of Hoth

Spies deliver intelligence on location of a second Death Star under construction, leading to Battle of Endor

Imperial fleet retreats from Endor and fragments, to be hunted down by New Republic efforts

Han and Leia wed; Luke begins training Leia in ways of the Force

Ben Solo destroys Luke's Jedi temple; Luke vanishes; Han and Leia drift apart

Rey is abandoned on Jakku by her parents, who die shortly thereafter

Luke begins training Ben

Official founding of New Republic and capitulation of Galactic Empire

Imperial Fleet Admiral Gallius Rax collects bulk of Imperial Navy at Jakku. After defeat by New Republic, surviving ships jump to Unknown Regions

6 BSI   **13 BSI**   **19 BSI**   **29 BSI**

Leia Organa is ousted from New Republic politics by scandal; she begins forming a paramilitary Resistance group

Sensing the continued presence of the dark side, Luke starts investigating leads that mention Exegol

Rey is born

Ben Solo born on Chandrila

Lando Calrissian liberates Cloud City

Leia ends her Jedi training on Ajan Kloss upon seeing visions of the future and recognizing where galaxy needs her most

Worlds secede from New Republic, forming visible political core of First Order. Its military core grows in secret in the Unknown Regions, while its spiritual core grows somewhere even more hidden

Starkiller superweapon obliterates New Republic capital; Ben Solo, now known as Kylo Ren, kills his father

Rey finds and trains with Luke; Kylo becomes Supreme Leader; Luke becomes one with Force

Recurring visions and voices in the Force move Rey and Kylo into another fateful confrontation

5 BSI   **0**   **1 ASI**

With the Resistance staffed to operational levels, Leia begins her search for Luke

Rey and Finn, fugitives from the First Order, leave Jakku aboard *Millennium Falcon* with fragment of a map to Luke Skywalker

Starkiller is destroyed by Resistance

Near-routing of Resistance at Battle of Crait

CHAPTER 1:
THE STORY SO FAR...

The Galactic Civil War has passed into history. On countless worlds, the broken debris of legendary battles lies silently rusting, forgotten by a galaxy that wishes to move on from its painful past. For most, the heroic Rebellion against the Empire is now just a dramatic tale; a story told to children and grandchildren.

But for some, thirty years is merely the blink of an eye. Hidden in the shadows of the Unknown Regions, the descendants of the Empire have been watching, waiting to reclaim what they see as their rightful rule over the galaxy. Few see this threat for what it is, and those that do are shunned, derided as fantasists and warmongers.

Leia Organa can sense that conflict is inevitable, and she has created a small force of armed partisans, which she has dubbed the Resistance. But she knows all her preparation will be for nothing without the help of her brother, the last Jedi. In this most desperate hour, she sends one of her most trusted officers on a secret mission to find Luke, and gain his help in the new war that threatens to engulf the galaxy...

THE FIRST ORDER

The First Order is the result of a vast conspiracy decades in the making. Seemingly unrelated events and their consequences can now, with the benefit of hindsight, be seen to be part of an elaborate plan with a shadowy mastermind at its center. The First Order as a regime became known to the wider galaxy as a result of a separatist schism, which seceded a bloc of star systems that wanted a more centralized style of government than that offered by the New Republic. What was dismissed as merely political games by some was actually cover for a military expansion that, following years of preparation, brought the return of tyrannical fascism and deadly militarism to the galaxy.

The firing of the Starkiller weapon is specifically engineered—through spacetime-bending quintessence physics—to be seen across the galaxy as a horrifying example of the First Order's might. It is meant to encourage surrender with a single shot. For many undefended worlds, it works.

FIRST ORDER SYMBOL

FIRST ORDER LEADERS

The vanguard of First Order leadership is strikingly young; a new generation of adherents to the ideals of the old Empire, who never experienced that regime firsthand. These commanders—Kylo Ren, General Hux, and Captain Phasma—bring a zeal that makes up for their lack of experience or the wisdom of age. Far from the front lines, elder leaders who had been part of the Empire watch approvingly. Farther still, veiled in secrecy, is the true leadership, driven by the tenets of the dark side of the Force and the ancient ways of the Sith.

Shrouded and masked visage to impose fear, in the tradition of Darth Vader

Precision tailored military uniform evokes Imperial imagery

Salvaged Imperial-era chromium

CAPTAIN PHASMA   **KYLO REN**   **GENERAL ARMITAGE HUX**

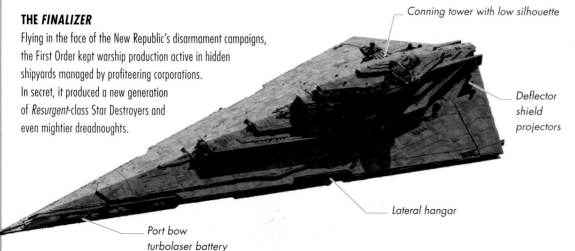

The image of endless legions of white-armored troopers was a symbol of galactic salvation during the Clone Wars; the First Order has appropriated this heritage.

THE *FINALIZER*
Flying in the face of the New Republic's disarmament campaigns, the First Order kept warship production active in hidden shipyards managed by profiteering corporations. In secret, it produced a new generation of *Resurgent*-class Star Destroyers and even mightier dreadnoughts.

Conning tower with low silhouette

Deflector shield projectors

Lateral hangar

Port bow turbolaser battery

FACT FILE

> The First Order stormtrooper program developed by the late Brendol Hux (Armitage's father) centered on training potential soldiers from early childhood.

> Each world newly annexed by the First Order in its expanding territories becomes a source of new "recruits" to the cause.

THE COMING OF A SUPREME LEADER

In time, Imperial-era leaders like Grand Admiral Rae Sloane, General Brendol Hux, and Allegiant General Pryde would make way for the rise of Supreme Leader Snoke, heir apparent to the contingency crafted by Emperor Palpatine before his demise. Snoke gave no indication as to his origins, but possessed the knowledge and Force-ability that made him undisputed heir. Strangely, he made no designs on the old title of Emperor, and his Force abilities were not explicitly of the Sith heritage that Palpatine embodied as Darth Sidious. Snoke seemed content to focus on spiritual matters, ceding control of the military to generals, and the shaping of the First Order's public image to propaganda masterminds. Some, like Pryde, came to peer behind the veil and realized that Snoke himself was subservient to an unseen force.

Extensive scarring and twisted build confound attempts to identify Snoke's species

SUPREME LEADER SNOKE

Golden khalat robes are an eccentric symbol of Snoke's power

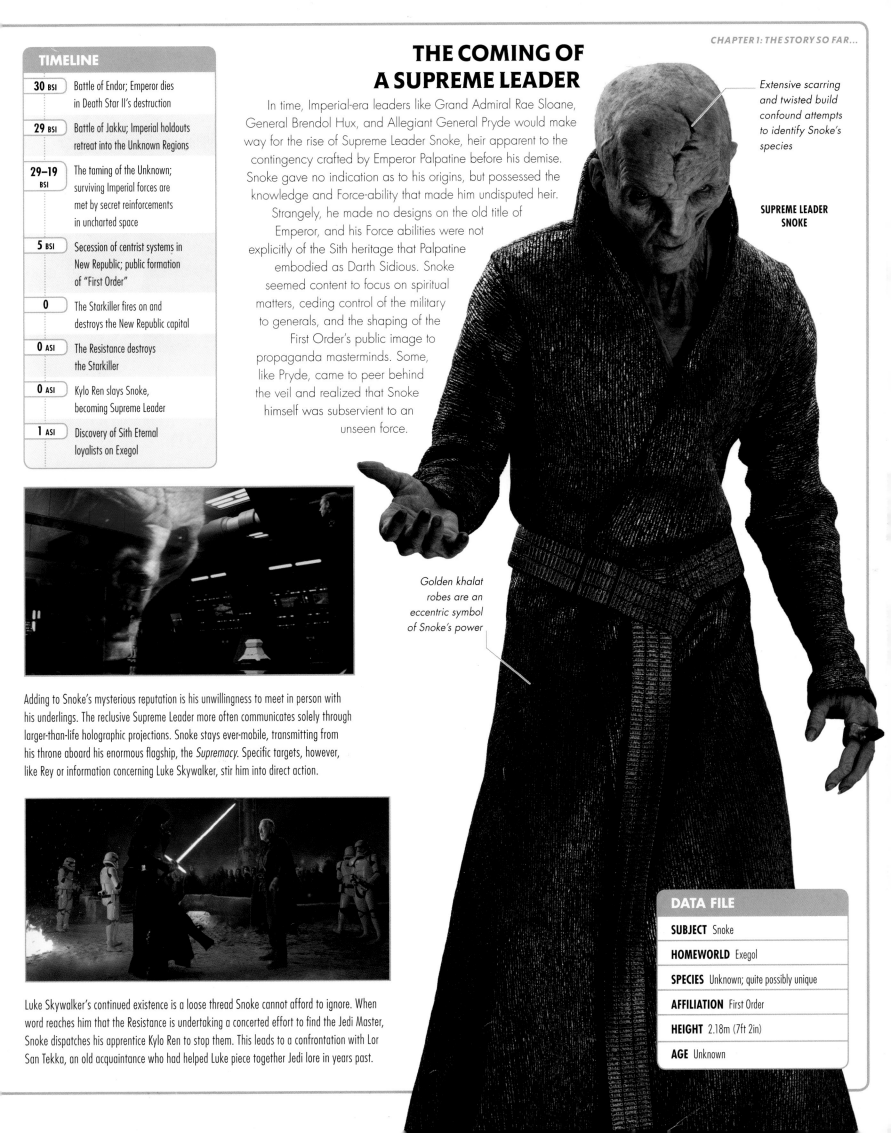

Adding to Snoke's mysterious reputation is his unwillingness to meet in person with his underlings. The reclusive Supreme Leader more often communicates solely through larger-than-life holographic projections. Snoke stays ever-mobile, transmitting from his throne aboard his enormous flagship, the *Supremacy*. Specific targets, however, like Rey or information concerning Luke Skywalker, stir him into direct action.

Luke Skywalker's continued existence is a loose thread Snoke cannot afford to ignore. When word reaches him that the Resistance is undertaking a concerted effort to find the Jedi Master, Snoke dispatches his apprentice Kylo Ren to stop them. This leads to a confrontation with Lor San Tekka, an old acquaintance who had helped Luke piece together Jedi lore in years past.

DATA FILE

SUBJECT	Snoke
HOMEWORLD	Exegol
SPECIES	Unknown; quite possibly unique
AFFILIATION	First Order
HEIGHT	2.18m (7ft 2in)
AGE	Unknown

THE RESISTANCE

Surplus New Republic flight suit dyed to match old Rebel Alliance colors

BB-series astromech

It seemed like Leia Organa alone saw the coming storm. The movements of political players across the New Republic, and the subsequent secession of worlds to become the territorial heart of the First Order, seemed too sculpted to be happenstance. She was also politically compromised at a time when she could have been most effective, and ousted from the New Republic Senate by the scandalous revelation that Darth Vader was her father. Events that were intended to sideline her instead gave her the freedom to operate outside the confines of New Republic protocol. She set to work building the Resistance.

The new generation and the old work side-by-side on Resistance operations. Poe Dameron grew up hearing tales of Admiral Ackbar's military career and is honored to serve beside him.

POE DAMERON AND BB-8

D'QAR BASE

The Resistance established its primary base in the Ileenium system. The role her family played in the early Rebel Alliance gave Leia access to secret planetary information: lists of worlds with the potential to become rebel bases. She dusted off these old records and found D'Qar, an unpopulated verdant world.

RESISTANCE COMMAND

The upper command of the Resistance originally consisted of veterans of the Rebel Alliance personally recruited by Leia. In secret entreaties, she laid out her concerns regarding the First Order's militarization and the New Republic's inability to deal with it. Though some refused her invitation, others were stirred by her words. Gial Ackbar, Caluan Ematt, Ushos Statura, and Nien Nunb were among the earliest. Others, like Wedge Antilles, Carlist Rieekan, and Lando Calrissian, would take more time to stir from retirement. Few realized that before the First Order was even known to be a threat, many of the old commanders had been specifically targeted—either assassinated outright or emotionally hobbled by tragedies that ripped them from their military careers.

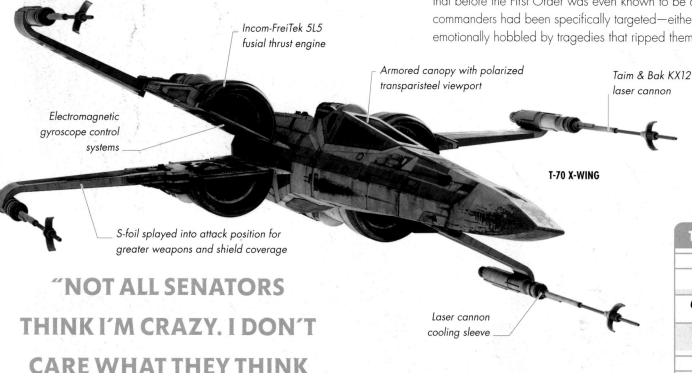

Incom-FreiTek 5L5 fusial thrust engine

Armored canopy with polarized transparisteel viewport

Taim & Bak KX12 laser cannon

Electromagnetic gyroscope control systems

T-70 X-WING

RESISTANCE SYMBOL

S-foil splayed into attack position for greater weapons and shield coverage

Laser cannon cooling sleeve

"NOT ALL SENATORS THINK I'M CRAZY. I DON'T CARE WHAT THEY THINK ABOUT ME AS LONG AS THEY TAKE ACTION."

—LEIA ORGANA

RESISTANCE SHIPS

The Resistance is a perpetually lean operation, underfunded and understaffed. It has to make do with the equipment available, and this often means outdated surplus cast aside by others. The T-70 X-wing fighters, though cutting edge compared to the T-65s of the previous generation, are outdated compared to the standard set by the New Republic's T-85s.

TIMELINE	
6 BSI	Leia Organa leaves New Republic politics
6–5 BSI	Leia forms Resistance to operate separately from the New Republic
5 BSI	Centrist worlds secede from the New Republic
5–0 BSI	Cold war between New Republic and First Order
0 ASI	Open war between Resistance and First Order

DATA FILE

SUBJECT	Leia Organa
HOMEWORLD	Alderaan
SPECIES	Human
AFFILIATION	Resistance
HEIGHT	1.55m (5ft 1in)
AGE	54 standard years

Functional collar can be drawn up to protect against the elements

The Resistance takes care not to collect its meager resources into a single target for the First Order. During the Starkiller crisis, only its starfighter launch base on D'Qar is ready to act, while the Resistance fleet and bomber craft—ships that would have been useful in the attack—are on missions elsewhere. They arrive just in time for the D'Qar evacuation.

HOLDING THE LINE

Though the destruction of the Starkiller is an undeniable victory over the First Order, General Organa has no time for celebration. The battle is a costly one, and among the casualties is her husband, Han Solo. That such personal family tragedy continues to be intertwined with galactic upheaval is a recurring quality of the Skywalker lineage. Leia's strength leads the Resistance through their harried evacuation of the D'Qar base, but pursuit continues as the First Order hounds the Resistance fleet. Leia is grievously wounded and must spend time recuperating. It is during these dark days that the next generation of Resistance leadership must emerge, for Leia will not always be there to guide them.

Having finally pieced together the location of the first Jedi temple, Leia sends Rey on a mission to recruit Luke Skywalker to the cause.

Alderaanian signet ring

FACT FILE

> The Starkiller crisis becomes a final reunion for Leia Organa and Han Solo, who had become estranged following their son's fall to the dark side.

> Solo's brash plan of flying through First Order shields at lightspeed gives the Resistance access to Starkiller Base.

REY
AN AWAKENING

In her nineteenth year, Rey's life radically changes from one of endless toil and monotonous routine to an adventure that will span the galaxy. Eking out an arduous existence in the sun-scorched junkyards of Jakku, Rey sees herself as a "nobody"—an anonymous drudge picking through the bones of grand galactic history. She has heard the legends of great heroes and villains of the past, and though tales of Luke Skywalker, Han Solo, and Princess Leia fuel her imagination, she sees them as distant, unknowable icons far beyond her reach.

Rey brings her scavenged and polished wares to Unkar Plutt, the odious "Junk Boss" of Niima Outpost. Plutt has known Rey for most of her life, serving as a mean-spirited guardian to the abandoned girl. This is not due to any sense of compassion on his part—Plutt saw potential profit in a scavenger small enough to fit inside the most compact wreckage.

LIFE ON JAKKU

What passes for an economy on Jakku consists of raiding the hulking ruins left after the Battle of Jakku nearly 30 years earlier, stripping them of salvageable machinery. Rey becomes very well versed in technology, intrinsically understanding how pieces work together to make a greater whole. By reactivating long-dormant flight simulators within canted, dust-encrusted Star Destroyer decks, she hones her piloting skills to a fine point, unknowingly bolstered by an innate connection to the Force.

"Borrowed" flight jacket from Resistance ace, Poe Dameron

Though Rey has piloted suborbital craft in the past, prior to her encounter with Finn she has never flown beyond Jakku's atmosphere. Her reluctance to depart the desert world stems from the hope that her family will someday return for her. This choice is stripped from her after a run-in with a Resistance droid and a stormtrooper deserter.

Rey's encounters with first BB-8 and then a mysterious man named Finn unlock the mental cage that has trapped her on Jakku. Both BB-8 and Finn desperately need to get off the desert planet and make contact with the Resistance, as the droid carries valuable information. The compassionate Rey feels she has no choice but to help them.

FN-2187, STORMTROOPER DESERTER

FACT FILE

> The *Millennium Falcon* has been in Unkar's possession for years, though it has not flown for some time before Rey powers it up for flight.

> After Rey leaves Jakku, her meager possessions—her speeder and her abandoned AT-AT home—are claimed by competing scavengers.

"I KNOW ALL ABOUT WAITING. FOR MY FAMILY. THEY'LL BE BACK, ONE DAY."

—REY

Military-grade polarized lenses cut down on glare

GOGGLES (MADE FROM STORMTROOPER HELMET)

Determined salvager's gaze scans surroundings for dangers and opportunities

Salvaged insulated power conduit turned into quarterstaff

Rey is extraordinarily dexterous

Bindings keep out sun and sand

DATA FILE

SUBJECT	Rey
HOMEWORLD	Jakku
SPECIES	Human
AFFILIATION	Resistance, Jedi
HEIGHT	1.7m (5ft 7in)
AGE	20 standard years

Though Rey has heard tales of the Force and the Jedi, she finds it easier to believe they are fanciful myths than something real to hope for.

TIMELINE

19 BSI	Rey born on unknown world
13 BSI	Rey abandoned on Jakku to Unkar's custody; she still remembers the *Bestoon Legacy* flying away
10 BSI	Rey's education in technology begins as she becomes one of Unkar's most reliable scavengers
0 BSI	Rey meets Finn, leaves Jakku, and encounters Han Solo and General Leia Organa
0 ASI	Rey trains under Luke Skywalker and makes a sworn enemy of Kylo Ren
1 ASI	Rey continues her training in the ways of the Jedi under Leia Organa

"WHO ARE YOU?"

Rey's greatest weakness stems from her lack of identity. Having seen fellow scavengers work a fruitless lifetime in the Jakku deserts, she has never dared hope for an existence of greater meaning. Kylo Ren's probing of her mind reveals these fears to him, and he bludgeons her with harsh words that strike at her greatest dread: that she was abandoned as trash by indifferent parents who are long dead. The sting of these words makes the truth behind them hard to judge. As time passes, she comes to recognize Kylo's gambit as a cruel one, and struggles to focus on the family she has now, as opposed to the one she never knew.

TAKODANA

Rey and Finn's escape from Jakku aboard the *Millennium Falcon* is a short trip, thanks to sensors long-attuned to listen for the *Falcon's* telemetric cry. The wanted starship is scooped aboard the *Eravana*, an immense freighter piloted by Han Solo and Chewbacca, who have been scouring the spacelanes to find their beloved *Falcon*. Rey and Finn, assuming Solo to have Resistance contacts, inform him that BB-8 carries a map to Luke Skywalker. Solo reels from his past catching up with him, but takes the *Falcon* to Takodana in the hope of handing the youngsters and their data to Maz Kanata, who will surely pass them along to his estranged wife, Leia Organa.

> Han must first shake the pursuit of rival gangsters from Kanjiklub and the Guavian Death Gang before leaving with the *Falcon*.

> Han instantly relates to Rey, an impoverished orphan with no family name, who is gifted with mechanical and piloting abilities.

In a dank cellar storeroom of Maz's castle, Rey comes in contact with Anakin Skywalker's old lightsaber, and is instantly hit by visions from the Force. The lightsaber acts as a vergence, granting her insights into past events.

The Skywalker lightsaber: Maz promises to someday tell the story of how she acquired it

The respite on Takodana is interrupted by the First Order's destruction of the Hosnian system, and the arrival of Kylo Ren following a tip-off from a spy that BB-8 is present at Maz's castle. Ren lands an invasion army to capture his quarry.

As First Order invaders spill over the rubble of Maz's castle, Finn ignites the Skywalker lightsaber, recalling his combat training with melee weapons. Finn has an instinctive feel for the Jedi weapon and defends himself against a riot-control stormtrooper.

FIRST ENCOUNTER WITH DARKNESS

Distraught at the visions the Force has shown her—including a flashback to her abandonment on Jakku—Rey flees into the forest. She feels too small and unimportant to be connected to the glimpses of power she has seen. But Kylo Ren specifically seeks her out, at the behest of his master, for her awakening in the Force is a portent of something much bigger. Kylo uses his Force ability to freeze her in her tracks. He knocks her unconscious, carries her back to his shuttle, and returns with her to his flagship, the *Finalizer*. Since she has seen the map to Skywalker, Kylo is confident he can extract it from her mind.

Variable-strength corrective
lenses on spring arms

In the castle tavern, Maz Kanata takes pointed interest in both Rey and Finn. She has delved into Force lore and knows something of the significance of a pair in the Force, wondering if it may be these two. In Finn's eyes she sees fear; a compulsion to run from danger and duty. Finn balks at this assessment.

MAZ KANATA

More than a thousand years old, Maz has witnessed the rise and fall of civilizations and the changing balance of light and dark in the Force. Though wise beyond measure, Maz nonetheless lives a life of pleasure and fleeting comforts, for no matter how long a span fortune may grant you, she reasons, it will always be too short. Maz is mostly known as a pirate legend, a sympathetic ear, and a source of refuge and resources for the law-bending galactic fringe. She's helped out Han and Chewbacca many times and forged a solid friendship with Leia Organa. Maz has seen the extended Skywalker family weather profound tragedies, but has faith that the light will persevere.

Belt pouch
filled with hard
confectionary

Beckon call
transmitter
connected to her
ship, Epoch Swift

Bracelet of ancient
Uphradean volcanic ore

TIMELINE

1,007 BSI	Maz Kanata born
30 BSI	On Ord Mantell, Maz helps Leia Organa acquire the Ubese armor for her Boushh disguise
29 BSI	Han Solo meets an Imperial defector at Maz's castle to get information that will help in the liberation of Kashyyyk
0 BSI	Rey, Finn, and Han Solo come to Maz on Takodana seeking help
0 ASI	Maz's castle destroyed by the First Order
0 ASI	While distracted by a labor dispute, Maz helpfully offers the Resistance a contact on Canto Bight—the Master Codebreaker
1 ASI	Maz serves as advisor to Leia Organa at the Resistance base on Ajan Kloss

DATA FILE

SUBJECT Maz Kanata

HOMEWORLD Unknown

SPECIES Unknown

AFFILIATION Independent

HEIGHT 1.24m (4ft 1in)

AGE 1,008 standard years

The prevalence of spies in Maz's castle means both doom and salvation. Though the First Order is tipped off about BB-8's presence, so too are the Resistance by an informant loyal to their cause. Poe Dameron leads a squadron of X-wings to chase off the First Order invaders, though they are too late to prevent the destruction of Maz's castle.

STARKILLER BASE

The Empire's military technologists continued their research into apocalyptic energy weapons even after the regime had surrendered. After retreating into the Unknown Regions, Imperial survivors found fragments of experiments undertaken by the Empire that could be combined and refined into an unthinkable weapon. The tapping and storage of quintessence energy; the expulsion and amplification of that energy through hyperspace; the construction of a platform large enough to support such a weapon—these elements became Starkiller Base. It took decades to perfect, and many uncharted worlds in the unknown were cored and sacrificed in pursuit of this knowledge. The Starkiller fires only once, but its single blast wipes out the New Republic capital, undeniably demonstrating the First Order's power.

DECAPITATION STRIKE

The solarvac array in the Starkiller uses the gravitational lens of a nearby star to collect quintessence energy, storing and amplifying it within a hyperspatial field generated by the kyber crystalline core. The weapon array of the Starkiller punches a hole through hyperspace, sending the torrent of energy to a target light years away. Upon emergence in realspace, the energy follows spacetime curvature into planetary gravity wells, forking at extreme velocities to destroy every planet in a star's orbit. This is the fate of the worlds of the Hosnian system.

Having infiltrated the Starkiller, Finn holds Captain Phasma at gunpoint, ordering her to deactivate the weapon's protective shields. Phasma complies, far more interested in her own survival than loyalty to the First Order.

FIERCE MACHINE

Properly energized, kyber crystals create containment fields that hold and amplify power to incredible levels. The Empire controlled several kyber-rich worlds, funneling their resources into the Tarkin Initiative's Death Star development. One unique world in the Unknown Regions, Ilum, had a kyber crystalline core. Most of its more easily accessible deposits were scoured, but there were even larger crystals buried deeper beneath the surface. The First Order continued its excavations and gradually transformed Ilum—a revered Jedi world since antiquity—into an instrument of unfathomable destruction.

Chewbacca and Han Solo place pyron denton explosives throughout vital areas of the Starkiller's critical machinery. From a lofty vantage point, Chewbacca watches helplessly as Han confronts his son, Kylo Ren.

FACT FILE

> Although the Starkiller is several times larger than the Death Star, it is considered smaller than a dwarf planet in astronomical scales.

> Its concentration of kyber deposits gave Ilum unique and exploitable characteristics for a planet of its tiny size.

"ALL REMAINING SYSTEMS WILL BOW TO THE FIRST ORDER!"

—GENERAL HUX

TIMELINE

END OF THE STARKILLER

With the Starkiller's shields deactivated and the planted explosives tearing a hole in the oscillator's armor, the weapon is left vulnerable to Resistance starfighter attack. The oscillator's destruction causes a cascading failure of the planet's energy storage system, and the accumulated stellar mass begins seeping out of its hyperspatial pocket. On the planet's crumbling surface, Kylo Ren crosses lightsaber blades with Finn and Rey.

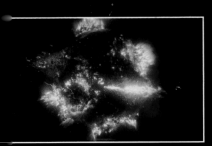

The micro-star hyperspatial singularity that now burns at the Starkiller's gravesite has been unofficially named the Solo

Finn tries his best to hold off Kylo Ren, but the dark swordmaster bests the young stormtrooper and brands him a traitor.

Poe Dameron soars his X-wing through a meltwater runoff trench, leading to the breach in the oscillator's wall. He squeezes past the Starkiller's armor, strafing the oscillator's vulnerable interior. The damage to the superweapon proves fatal.

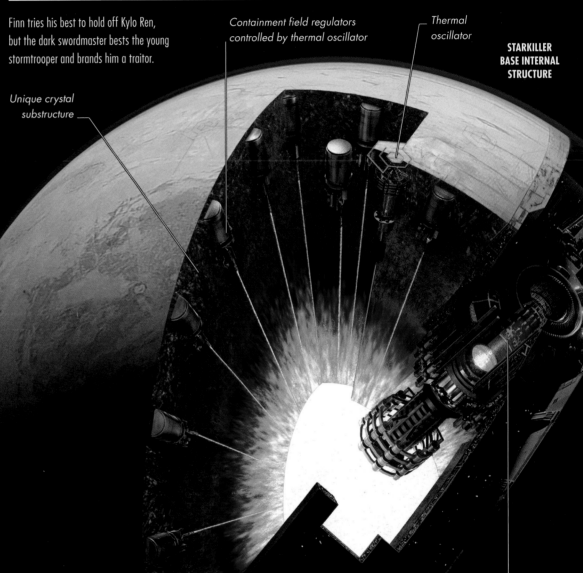

Containment field regulators controlled by thermal oscillator

Thermal oscillator

STARKILLER BASE INTERNAL STRUCTURE

Unique crystal substructure

DARK ENERGY CANNON
Dark energy surrounded by a halo of stellar fire bursts from the heart of the Starkiller.

RESISTANCE RETREAT

The victory over Starkiller Base is short lived, since the Resistance headquarters on D'Qar has been compromised and a hasty evacuation is in order. The meager Resistance fleet of four capital ships—called during the Starkiller crisis—arrives to find the Starkiller already vanquished, and immediately begins loading troops and supplies for the hurried exodus. First Order reinforcements drop out of hyperspace in the form of Star Destroyers escorting a massive siege dreadnought, the *Fulminatrix*. As the warship powers up its planet-scorching weaponry, Commander Poe Dameron flies a foolhardy solo mission to distract the First Order, buy time for the evacuation effort, and initiate a costly counterattack.

The last loadlifter to leave D'Qar, commanded by Lieutenant Kaydel Connix and Flight Officer Huetrin Jones, narrowly outruns the blossoming fireball of an orbital strike. The *Fulminatrix*'s siege cannons obliterate the jungle landscape, leaving no trace of the Resistance base. The hurried retreat leaves behind vital fuel stores.

Armored flight deck and viewport

Deflector shield generator

Rear gunner turret ball

TIE fighters swarm the bombers of Crimson and Cobalt Squadrons, with well-placed hits detonating entire bomb magazines in fiery waves of destruction.

Shipboard artificial gravity starts bomb descent

MG-100 STARFORTRESS HEAVY BOMBER

BATTLE OF D'QAR

Poe Dameron leads the attack to disable the First Order dreadnought, an unmistakable fleet killer bristling with huge cannons. He flies ahead to singlehandedly take out the many anti-starfighter defenses on the dreadnought's hull, while squadrons of X-wings and A-wings escort bomber craft into their drop zones. The ponderous bombers are vulnerable to enemy fighters and many are destroyed by TIE craft. Poe's decision to continue the attack results in the loss of all but one bomber, which delivers its entire payload onto the dreadnought's reactor. The *Fulminatrix* erupts in flames and the Resistance fleet jumps to lightspeed.

General Organa reprimands Poe for his costly and ill-thought-out tactics. While the fleet is able to outrun the First Order and claim victory over the dreadnought, many pilots die and irreplaceable ships are destroyed in the effort.

Osmium tiara

VICE ADMIRAL HOLDO

After Leia is severely injured in a First Order attack, command falls to Vice Admiral Amilyn Holdo of the cruiser *Ninka*, whose unconventional style and secretive nature draw Poe's suspicion and distrust.

Gatalentan somatohue earrings

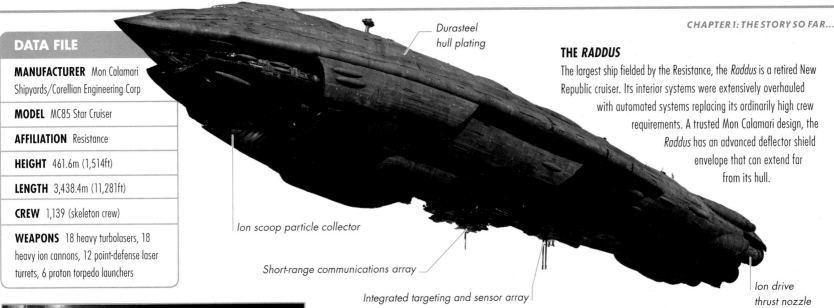

Durasteel hull plating

Ion scoop particle collector

Short-range communications array

Integrated targeting and sensor array

Ion drive thrust nozzle

DATA FILE

MANUFACTURER Mon Calamari Shipyards/Corellian Engineering Corp

MODEL MC85 Star Cruiser

AFFILIATION Resistance

HEIGHT 461.6m (1,514ft)

LENGTH 3,438.4m (11,281ft)

CREW 1,139 (skeleton crew)

WEAPONS 18 heavy turbolasers, 18 heavy ion cannons, 12 point-defense laser turrets, 6 proton torpedo launchers

THE *RADDUS*

The largest ship fielded by the Resistance, the *Raddus* is a retired New Republic cruiser. Its interior systems were extensively overhauled with automated systems replacing its ordinarily high crew requirements. A trusted Mon Calamari design, the *Raddus* has an advanced deflector shield envelope that can extend far from its hull.

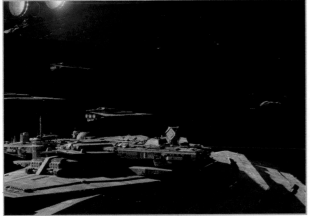

FLEET PURSUED

The Resistance leadership is stunned to discover the First Order can track their fleet through hyperspace—supposedly an impossible feat without an implanted tracking device. Rather than burn through its fuel with a useless jump, the Resistance fleet engages its sublight drives at an ever-accelerating rate, attempting to stay out of First Order weapons range.

Aboard the *Supremacy*, General Hux monitors the fuel supply of the doomed Resistance fleet.

Unaware of Vice Admiral Holdo's endgame—a plan she has kept secret for operational security reasons—Poe stages a mutiny to wrest command from her. The revolt is put down by a recovered Leia Organa.

When the First Order starts targeting the Resistance escape craft, Holdo sacrifices herself to protect their passage to Crait. The sole person aboard the *Raddus*, she prepares an unsurvivable hyperspace jump.

Forward viewport with photochromatic filters

Starboard deflector shield generator

U-55 ORBITAL LOADLIFTER

ESCAPE TO CRAIT

The initial lightspeed jump from D'Qar placed the Resistance fleet within sublight range of Crait, an unlisted mineral world that once served as an Alliance base. This is the ultimate refuge for the Resistance survivors, who have been whittled down to a few loadlifters'-worth of personnel after the harried pursuit by the First Order's flagship. These few ships make planetfall and the Resistance prepares for a last stand.

AHCH-TO

A partial map pieced together with R2-D2's memory archive points the way into the Unknown Regions, where the ancient world of Ahch-To rests. It is here that the first Jedi temple was built tens of thousands of years ago, a place that Luke Skywalker spent years questing to find. Rey and Chewbacca fly the *Millennium Falcon* to the oceanic world, where Rey hopes to deliver Leia Organa's request for help and return Luke's lightsaber, lost decades before on Cloud City. Rey grew up hearing legends of Luke Skywalker, and regards him as a larger-than-life hero. To find someone so defeated and so human takes Rey aback.

> "DO YOU THINK I CAME TO THE MOST UNFINDABLE PLACE IN THE GALAXY FOR NO REASON AT ALL?"
>
> —LUKE SKYWALKER

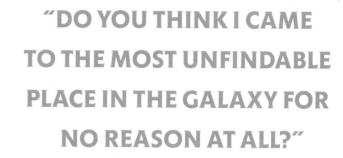

Water-shedding woolen cloak

Pinniped-skin leather glove protects artificial hand

Rey wordlessly greets Luke Skywalker standing at a cliffside on Ahch-To and delivers the lightsaber. Emotions roil over Luke's face as he takes the proffered weapon… and tosses it off the cliff.

RELUCTANT TEACHER

Luke's hard-learned lessons make him hesitant to teach another apprentice. His first apprentice, his sister Leia, stopped her training upon seeing another path she felt she must take. Unsure of his grounding in Jedi lore, Luke spent many years piecing together the lost history of the Order before he felt capable of taking on other students. Ben Solo was his most gifted apprentice, and Luke spent years teaching his nephew. Ben's betrayal hit Luke hard.

With reservation, Luke begins training Rey in the Force. Upon opening her mind in meditation, she is instantly drawn to the dark side.

FACT FILE

> Ahch-To's inquisitive seabirds, the porgs, have now spread remarkably far thanks to stowaways on the *Millennium Falcon*.

> Ahch-To has twin suns, but orbits at a great enough distance to be temperate, unlike the desert world of Tatooine.

NIGHT OF FIRE

For Luke, it was a moment of instinct—a flash of defensiveness in response to a dark vision of his loved ones in anguish. For Ben, it was an unspeakable betrayal that confirmed every worst fear he had about his family. But this singular moment was a culmination of mistakes and misunderstandings that had built up over years. In protecting his nephew from the darkest of truths, Luke isolated Ben—and in that isolation a dark voice twisted Ben's fears into reality.

Rey's overly energetic practice of lightsaber drills (called *cadences* in ancient lore) results in her accidentally splitting an ancient rock formation named the "Windwailer" by the natives. Though she has energy, she lacks control.

Symbolizes the duality of the Force

EAGER APPRENTICE

Rather than think herself a remarkable heir to a mystical power, Rey once attributed her skills to luck and intuition. She has come to realize that the Force has always been with her, but with the full awakening of her abilities, she has begun to feel doubts and fears regarding her darker inclinations. Rey seeks the wisdom of a mentor to guide her past such pitfalls, but finds little encouragement in Luke, who states the Jedi Order must end.

Loose openweave tabard in Jedi tradition

BORROWED LIGHTSABER
When Luke rejects his old lightsaber, Rey's scavenger instincts cause her to retrieve it and claim it as her own.

JEDI TEMPLE
Built atop a high ledge overlooking the ocean, the first Jedi temple is empty save for some timeworn meditation plinths and a remarkably intact mosaic of the Prime Jedi in meditation.

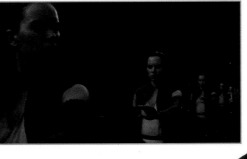

In a dark side vergence deep inside a cave, Rey sees a vision of the Force marked by endless versions of herself.

MUCH TO LEARN

Luke's isolation on the island has led him to the terrible conclusion that the Jedi are locked in an endless cycle of destruction and rebirth that takes the galaxy with it. He feels the Jedi Order needs to end, and seeks to destroy the first temple and its ancient lore. From the spectral form of Yoda, however, he comes to learn that these roots of the past do not preordain the future, and that a new generation of students must always grow beyond what has come before. Though Rey leaves Luke feeling lost, he will find her again.

The spectral form of Yoda joins Luke beside a burning ancient Uneti tree to contemplate the nature of the Force through generations. Though Yoda understandably calls Luke "Young Skywalker," they sit together as Jedi Masters.

KYLO REN
DESCENT INTO DARKNESS

The heir to the Skywalker legacy has succumbed to the darkest traits that have marked the bloodline. Kylo Ren—born Ben Solo—sees himself as carrying on the tradition embodied by his fallen grandfather, Darth Vader, although Ren's understanding of Anakin Skywalker's history has been twisted by a dark mentor. Supreme Leader Snoke's piercing perception of Ben's mind, his clear view of Ben's fears and insecurities, let him poison the Jedi apprentice with the dark side. By the time his family came to recognize the depths of Ben Solo's darkness, it was too late.

Ben adopted the title and look of the marauding Knights of Ren, casting aside his Jedi robes. His temperamental command style caused many a First Order underling to dread his unpredictable presence.

Sliding activation switch

Diatium power cell cradle

BEN SOLO'S JEDI LIGHTSABER

FALL OF A JEDI PADAWAN

The expectations of being a Skywalker—the nephew of the last Jedi and the grandson of a prophesized Chosen One—weighed heavily on Ben Solo. Though his parents tried to build a normal childhood for Ben, when the Force awakened in him it became apparent he needed guidance. Luke Skywalker took young Solo as an apprentice, and the two traveled the galaxy uncovering ancient Jedi arcana. In time, Luke's Jedi training temple grew. With Skywalker's attention now split among multiple students, Ben's focus wandered into dark corners of Force knowledge, and, like his grandfather before him, he fell under the sway of a dark master.

In his mind probe of Rey, Kylo Ren feels an innate connection to the scavenger, unaware that they form a prophesized "dyad" in the Force. The connection intractably bridges their minds.

Unbeknownst to Ben, one Sith trial of ascendancy requires the sacrifice of a loved one to unlock newfound depths of dark power. Ben carries this out with the shocking murder of his father, Han Solo.

The future that Snoke promised to Ren had him as the heir to the Force, with no Jedi to stand in his path. He reacts with fury to a challenge from Finn brandishing a lightsaber.

Ren's power costs him dearly, isolating him from all he once loved. As Snoke's enforcer he lives a friendless existence between a hated master and underlings he does not trust.

FACT FILE

> Ren inherited Force ability from his mother, but also amazing reflexes and piloting ability from his father.

> Kylo modified his lightsaber upon falling to the dark side, channeling dangerous amounts of power through a cracked kyber crystal.

KILLING THE PAST

With Kylo's power consistently held in check, first by Skywalker and then by Snoke, his frustration boils into a destructive worldview: the past needs to die, by his own hand if necessary. A lifetime spent living in the shadows of powerful mentors fosters in Kylo a need to determine his own destiny and discover his own path. Having usurped the title of Supreme Leader with his killing of Snoke, Kylo now has unprecedented freedom and power, and yet still feels shackled to a fate he is only just beginning to understand. Kylo's search for answers and direction has led him to learn that the past— particularly the ancient era of the Sith—will not die.

DATA FILE

SUBJECT Kylo Ren

HOMEWORLD Chandrila

SPECIES Human

AFFILIATION Knights of Ren, First Order

HEIGHT 1.89m (6ft 2in)

AGE 30 standard years

Static-damping fabric

Kylo questions the gifts given to him by Snoke, recognizing them as cages and leashes designed to keep him obedient under the Supreme Leader's rule.

TIMELINE

29 BSI	Born on Chandrila to Leia Organa and Han Solo
6 BSI	Ben falls to the dark side, and destroys Luke's Jedi temple
0 ASI	Kylo Ren kills Han Solo, but is defeated by Rey
0 ASI	Ren kills Snoke, and ascends to rank of Supreme Leader
1 ASI	Ren discovers Exegol and its Sith secrets

Quillon blades vent excess power of kyber crystal

Plasma blade in ragged kyber field due to cracked crystal

Kylo keeps his culpability in Snoke's death a secret, lest anyone should question his claim to the title of Supreme Leader. He forces his hated rival General Hux to kneel before him and pledge fealty.

FALL OF SNOKE

The ever-changing patterns of the Force converge so that Rey and Kylo stand before Supreme Leader Snoke at the same instance a Resistance infiltration team attempts to deactivate the *Supremacy*'s hyperspace tracker. This coincides with a last-ditch effort by the Resistance to make planetfall on Crait, and Vice Admiral Holdo's daring effort to buy them time via a cataclysmic hyperspace collision. The *Supremacy* is cleaved in two by the Resistance cruiser *Raddus*. Kylo betrays Snoke and invites Rey to join him. And the Resistance infiltrators battle their way out of the stricken *Supremacy*'s blazing hangar bay. The fallout of these actions is immediate: Rey and Kylo become sworn enemies, Kylo ascends to the rank of Supreme Leader, and the battle for the Resistance's very survival moves onto the sodium surface of Crait.

ABOARD THE *SUPREMACY*

With the codebreaking help of an untrustworthy slicer known only as DJ, Finn and Rose Tico infiltrate the *Supremacy*. Dressed as First Order officers, they navigate the mazelike interior of the enormous Mega-Destroyer, finding the experimental hyperspace tracker that has allowed the First Order to shadow the Resistance fleet's every move. Unfortunately, the group is intercepted by Captain Phasma and a crack security team before they are able to deactivate the device. DJ buys his freedom from the First Order by betraying the Resistance.

Star Destroyer
docking bay

THE *SUPREMACY*

An enormous wing-shaped Mega-Destroyer, the *Supremacy* is the one-of-a-kind flagship and mobile command headquarters of Supreme Leader Snoke. Its span measures 60 kilometers, and its crew numbers in the millions. Its interior serves as an enormous factory for other warships and combat vehicles.

Terraced sprawl structure
that houses crew space

Forward artillery
escarpment

Electro-plasma filament
in bilari chain-whip

Composite armor
helmet conceals identity

Vice Admiral Holdo perfectly times a devastating point-blank hyperspace jump so that her massive warship, the three-kilometer long *Raddus*, intersects the mass of the *Supremacy* at lightspeed before her ship fully enters hyperspace. The resulting collision cuts the *Supremacy* in half.

DATA FILE

SUBJECTS	Praetorian Guards
HOMEWORLD	Mobile, aboard the *Supremacy*
SPECIES	Presumably human
AFFILIATION	First Order
AVERAGE HEIGHT	1.8m (5ft 10in)

Magnetic
field-bolstered
armor

Symbolic red
armorweave

FACT FILE

> Aboard the battered *Supremacy*, Finn confronts his former commander, Captain Phasma. She perishes in the chaos.

> The Resistance takes to calling Holdo's unconventional but effective sacrifice "the Holdo Maneuver."

PRAETORIAN GUARD

Loyally serving as the final shield in Supreme Leader Snoke's formidable defenses is a cadre of elite protectors, his Praetorian Guards. The eight anonymous warriors are highly trained martial artists wielding specialized melee weapons and covered in sleek, advanced armor. Their red hue evokes the Royal Guard of the Old Empire, a resemblance all the more resonant given the scarlet Sith symbology found on Exegol.

THE SUPREME LEADER IS DEAD

Snoke's entire existence has been built for this moment: to be the final test of Kylo Ren. The Supreme Leader has tested Ren's worthiness as a disciple and—unbeknownst to all—his capacity to inherit the Sith legacy. Snoke is no Sith, but his role has been designed by the Sith Eternal cultists to act as a final crucible, to groom and mold Ren into a master not only of attack, but also cunning. Ren uses Snoke's reliance on reading his every thought, twisting it to his own advantage. Kylo outmaneuvers Snoke in an encounter engineered to misdirect the Supreme Leader's attention, and slays him, bisecting him with the Skywalker lightsaber.

SNOKE'S THRONE

Snoke's throne room has a suitably commanding view of the *Supremacy*'s upper hull. The chamber is wrapped in a brilliant red curtain that adds a heightened sense of theatricality to the Supreme Leader's quarters. It is from his throne that Snoke broadcasts his enormous holographic form to his underlings.

Snoke gloats in his success of gathering Rey and Ren before him, for it proves without a doubt that they share a unique bond in the Force; something that features so prominently in the lore of the Sith Eternal cult.

Singular focus, imposed by his unseen master

With Snoke's surprise death, his Praetorian Guards spring into action. Having failed to protect their master, they do all they can to stop his killer. Rey and Ren fight side by side, their abilities mirroring and amplifying each other. Their Force-bond strengthens with every passing moment.

Vulnerable midsection, soon to be parted

BATTLE OF CRAIT

Crait becomes the last stand of the Resistance, as the fleet survivors barricade themselves within an old rebel base. Unable to bombard it from orbit, the First Order lands an invasion force armed with a superlaser cannon to crack open the base's shielded door. To hold off these attackers, Poe Dameron leads a squadron of decrepit ski speeders, but they are simply not powerful enough to stop the First Order's inexorable march. Just when all appears lost, an unexpected figure steps out from the tunnels of the base: Jedi Master Luke Skywalker.

Resistance soldiers take cover in trenches cut into the crimson crystalline ground by rebel engineers decades earlier. They power up Spiezoc v-120 and v-232 cannons, which have never before been fired in combat.

Twin medium laser cannons

Repulsorfield thrust vector ring and rudder

Auxiliary power generator access port

Halofoil mono-ski

SKI SPEEDERS

The rebel-era V-4X-D ski speeders are wobbly repulsorcraft that are in fact repurposed recreational vehicles. They use a surface-skimming halofoil to stabilize their low-altitude flight. These vehicles are lightly armored—any more weight would compromise their maneuverability—and are armed with laser cannons.

Acceleration-compensating chair in open cockpit

BATTLE LINES

The First Order marches forward in a line of heavy armor—massive AT-M6 walkers flanked by upgraded AT-ATs, all in classic Veers formation. These lumbering machines escort an enormous superlaser siege cannon towed into position by AT-HH walkers. The miniaturization of Death Star superlaser technology has been an ongoing project for the First Order. So well defended is the weapon that the Resistance can't land a disabling hit on it. TIE fighter air support wipes out many Resistance ski speeders, until the First Order starfighters are lured away by the *Millennium Falcon*. Learning his lesson regarding too-costly victories, Poe orders a retreat.

The halofoils carve red lines into the salt covering the Crait battlefield.

The Resistance survivors retreat deeper into the base caverns and are led to freedom by Rey, who uses her complete faith in the Force to telekinetically lift a barricade of boulders.

SKYWALKER RETURNS

Luke Skywalker takes to the battlefield and is seemingly untouchable by First Order artillery. Kylo Ren rages against his former master, unable to strike Skywalker down. In truth, Luke's presence exists only in the Force, a projection through a Fallanassi technique chronicled by ancient Masters in the sacred texts as *Similfuturus*. This discipline requires extreme concentration and focus, as Luke essentially pours his living Force presence into the all-encompassing cosmic Force, bridging incredible distances. The transition is so complete that Luke gives his all into the Force, finding serenity in this final mortal moments and becoming one with the great beyond. This is inexplicable to First Order witnesses, who see an indestructible Jedi Master vanish before their eyes. Word of this miracle spreads far beyond Crait.

DATA FILE

SUBJECT	Luke Skywalker
HOMEWORLD	Tatooine
SPECIES	Human
AFFILIATION	Jedi Order
HEIGHT	1.72m (5ft 8in)
AGE	53 standard years (at time of disappearance into the Force)

Luke's appearance matches Kylo Ren's last memories of him

The woven Jedi robes Luke wore for a time during Ben Solo's training

Traditional Jedi belt buckle

Kylo Ren's single-minded determination to destroy Skywalker causes him to overlook inconsistencies in his old master's appearance, and he is duped by Skywalker's illusion. This buys the Resistance the time needed to escape.

"THE REBELLION IS REBORN TODAY. THE WAR IS JUST BEGINNING. AND I WILL NOT BE THE LAST JEDI."

—LUKE SKYWALKER

In his final moments in the living Force, Luke witnesses a binary sunset on Ahch-To, just like the ones he experienced as a youth on Tatooine many decades earlier.

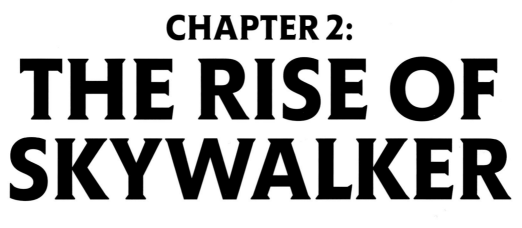

CHAPTER 2:
THE RISE OF SKYWALKER

The First Order reigns triumphant. After decapitating the New Republic in a single, spectacular strike, it has emerged as the dominant power in the galaxy. Worlds aligned to the First Order's vision of dominance, or those cowed by its destructive demonstrations of power, capitulate to this new rule. The fledgling Resistance, led by General Leia Organa, is vastly outnumbered by the might of the First Order.

But the spark of hope refuses to gutter. In his last stand against the mechanized might of the First Order, Jedi Master Luke Skywalker proved that it is possible to stand defiant against the dark tide. Word of this moment has spread, and General Organa has spent months rebuilding the decimated Resistance while in hiding.

Rey, the heir to the Jedi, continues her studies in the ways of the Force, though her path grows more uncertain. Kylo Ren, who has usurped the title of Supreme Leader, has uncovered secrets regarding the First Order's origins. Both must probe the shadows of the past to shed light on a clouded future…

A GALAXY AT WAR

The explosive emergence of the First Order's war machine at first seemed to be the culmination of a decades-old plan to avenge the defeat of the Galactic Empire. The truth goes deeper and darker than even the highest echelons of the First Order suspect. The regime's mighty Star Destroyers and stormtrooper legions are but the tip of a spear that originates in the depths of the Unknown Regions, hoisted by an ancient enemy long unseen in the galaxy—an enemy that has been patiently amassing a terrifying military might.

THE FIRST ORDER

The First Order now rules large swathes of the galaxy. At Supreme Leader Kylo Ren's decree, all Resistance collaborators and subversives opposed to First Order rule are to be crushed. Ren himself has become distracted, however, following a trail of clues regarding the mystery of the First Order's origins.

THE SITH ETERNAL

In the impassable depths of the Unknown Regions, on the dark world of Exegol, Sith cultists continue to venerate the efforts of the late Darth Sidious to bring about a New Empire. Shipyards have continued production for decades, creating a vast fleet ready to launch.

THE RESISTANCE

Nearly wiped out at the Battle of Crait, the Resistance eventually regrouped under General Leia Organa's leadership. Recruitment efforts were aided by the growing myth of the last Jedi among its ranks. The Resistance must now take the fight to the First Order once again.

THE GALAXY

Exegol

UNKNOWN REGIONS

Jedha

Jakku

Ahch-To

Batuu

Takodana

Ring of Kafren

Endor and Kef Bir

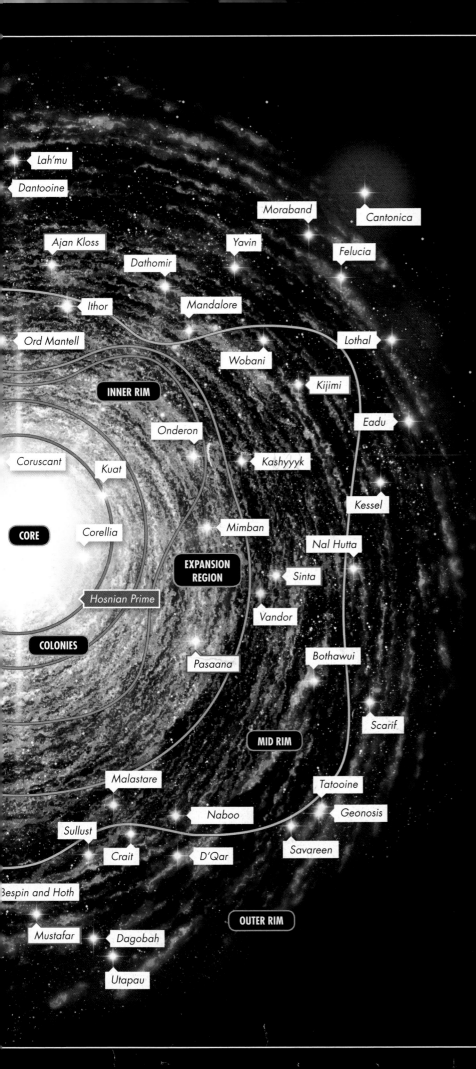

Lah'mu

Dantooine

Moraband

Cantonica

Ajan Kloss

Yavin

Felucia

Dathomir

Ithor

Mandalore

Lothal

Ord Mantell

Wobani

INNER RIM

Kijimi

Onderon

Eadu

Kashyyyk

Coruscant

Kuat

Kessel

CORE

Corellia

Mimban

Nal Hutta

**EXPANSION
REGION**

Sinta

Hosnian Prime

Vandor

COLONIES

Bothawui

Pasaana

Scarif

MID RIM

Malastare

Tatooine

Naboo

Geonosis

Sullust

Crait

D'Qar

Savareen

Bespin and Hoth

OUTER RIM

Mustafar

Dagobah

Utapau

AJAN KLOSS

Ajan Kloss is the current home of
the Resistance. A verdant world
covered in primeval jungles, like
many Resistance sanctuaries it
was originally scouted as a base
for the Rebel Alliance.

MUSTAFAR

A volcanic planet in the Outer Rim
Territories, Mustafar is known to history
as the one-time home of Darth Vader.
In the decades since his death, the
molten world has fallen into obscurity.

EXEGOL

Hidden deep in the Unknown Regions
behind veils of nearly unnavigable
space, Exegol is a planet steeped in
the dark side of the Force. This Sith
stronghold dating back to antiquity
holds many dark secrets.

PASAANA

Pasaana is a desert world far from
the center of affairs. Home to the
gregarious Aki-Aki people, it is
famous for its joyous Festival of
Ancestors that attracts visitors from
surrounding sectors.

KIJIMI

Kijimi is an old, frigid planet, once home
to mountaintop monasteries. These have
since been settled by outlaws, pirates,
and notorious spice runners, and the First
Order has stepped in to brutally crack
down on the rampant lawlessness.

KEF BIR

An oceanic moon in the Endor
system, Kef Bir was pelted with
debris from the second Death Star
after the battle station's destruction.
It is now home to a hill tribe with
origins tied to the First Order.

AJAN KLOSS

Prior to the outbreak of the Galactic Civil War, Alderaanian scouts charted—but deliberately hid from the Imperial Senate—the world of Ajan Kloss, located in a patchily explored stretch of space off the Celanon Spur. It was short-listed, along with nearby Yavin 4 and Dantooine, as a potential home for a rebel base, though the shifting battlefront against the Empire meant it was ultimately not used during the conflict. At Leia Organa's suggestion, Ajan Kloss did serve as a secluded outpost in the year after the Battle of Endor, becoming a training ground for Luke Skywalker and his first Jedi apprentice. Three decades later, it serves a similar function, as Rey continues her journey along the Jedi path.

The Resistance base is still in its early stages. General Organa's landed command ship, the *Tantive IV*, serves most of the functions—generator, barracks, meeting space—that a more established headquarters would provide.

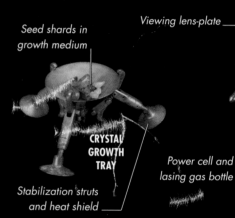

Seed shards in growth medium

Viewing lens-plate

CRYSTAL GROWTH TRAY

Stabilization struts and heat shield

Power cell and lasing gas bottle

REY'S WORKBENCH

A compact area of the Resistance cave is set aside for Rey to flex her mechanical skills and read through the Jedi texts. With the knowledge imparted by the ancient tomes, she has dissected the shattered Skywalker lightsaber, found the means of healing the broken crystal within, and repaired the weapon for her continued use.

Tuning readout

NANOFORGE

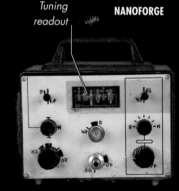

HARMONICS COUNTER

Convection bulb

NEW RESISTANCE BASE

Whenever possible, the old Rebellion avoided settling on planets with indigenous populations so that the wrath of the Empire would not be brought down on innocent bystanders. Ajan Kloss fits that category: although it teems with life, no civilizations dot its fertile surface. There is evidence of former inhabitants though, as some of the forest hollows appear to have been cleared by unknown hands centuries ago. The current Resistance settlers refer to these ancients as the Kloss, and scholar Beaumont Kin speculates that the Resistance's cave hideout was once, fittingly, some sort of refuge or storage cache.

Spin-adjusting quarkdriver with insulated grip

Grounding base

TOOL CADDY

HEATING PEDESTAL

"YOU'RE THE BEST FIGHTER WE HAVE. WE NEED YOU OUT THERE, NOT HERE."

—POE DAMERON TO REY, ON AJAN KLOSS

DATA FILE

REGION Cademimu sector, Outer Rim Territories

DIAMETER 11,353 km (7,054 miles)

TERRAIN Broadleaf forests, overgrown cliffs and valleys, grottos and oceans

MOONS 2 (note that Ajan Kloss is itself a moon of a larger planet)

POPULATION No permanent settlements

RESISTANCE CAVE
The Resistance hunker down within a vast limestone cave, in an area of jungle they call the Klosslands.

Mesocyclone supercell in formation, developing into a high-precipitation thunderstorm

During the night, plantlife draws sustenance from faint sunlight reflected by the Ajara gas giant

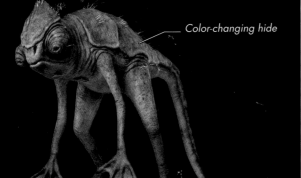

Color-changing hide

ARBOREAL ZYMOD

FACT FILE

> Its relative lack of large predators makes Ajan Kloss a welcoming environment, but dangers include fungal and insect infestations and unpredictable weather systems.

> Ajan Kloss orbits the gas giant Ajara, which shields it from cosmic radiation with an intense magnetic field.

> Resistance technicians work extended shifts to moisture-proof their delicate electronics from the humid Ajan Kloss environment.

> The overgrown jungle environment resonates with life through the Force, making it an ideal training ground for new Jedi.

REY

Rey's journey through the Force has proven challenging. Her first "awakening" to the greater power that binds the galaxy together came from a vision sparked by contact with an old Jedi lightsaber, showing her images of pain and destruction. This stirring in the Force alerted Supreme Leader Snoke and Kylo Ren to her presence, making her a prime target in their bid to rule the galaxy. Snoke knew that Rey and Kylo were linked through the Force, a prophesized "dyad" connecting two individuals across space and time. Though this connection and her long isolation caused Rey at first to sympathize with Kylo, his dark actions and sinister machinations prompted her to withdraw.

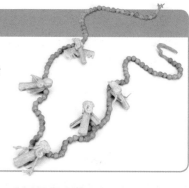

THE LAST JEDI

Rey journeyed to the lost world of Ahch-To, site of the first Jedi temple, where Luke Skywalker had withdrawn to contemplate the very future of the Jedi. Rey's conviction that the galaxy needed a hero like Skywalker eventually persuaded Luke to teach her in the ways of the Force, but he warned her of history's cruel cycle. Rey's greatest advantage was a deeply held faith in the power of the Force and her connection to it. But as her abilities grow, she has opened herself to more doubt, as dark voices and images spring unbidden into her mind.

Rey's compassionate nature and admiration of inner strength cause her to revere General Leia Organa.

High-energy plasma blade in kyber-powered permeable suspension field

Ring tuning flange

Magnetic stabilizing ring and emitter

Weld marks

Blade length adjust

Kyber crystal inside healed using techniques gleaned from Jedi scripture

Lower hand directs blade, upper hand grips and serves as fulcrum

Leather wrist strap repurposed to bind broken shaft

Rubberized grip ribbing

Refitted activation matrix

SIDE VIEW

THE SKYWALKER LIGHTSABER

Originally Anakin Skywalker's lightsaber, built at the onset of the Clone Wars, this weapon was long thought lost on Cloud City. It was salvaged from the mining colony's industrial depths and eventually found its way into Maz Kanata's possession. After it was used to kill Snoke, the lightsaber was split in two in a Force tug-of-war between Kylo Ren and Rey.

Rey demonstrates her supernatural agility and timing as she is pursued by Kylo Ren's TIE whisper in the badlands of Pasaana. She perfectly times a spectacular leap that catapults her above the craft.

Holstered LPA NN-14 blaster pistol, one of several found aboard the Millennium Falcon

"THE FIRST ORDER HAS ONE GOAL: TO BRING ME THE SCAVENGER!"

—KYLO REN

REY'S TRAINING

After Luke Skywalker became one with the Force, it fell to Leia Organa to continue Rey's training in the ways of the Jedi. It was a path that Leia herself had gone down 30 years earlier, before deciding that her future lay in a different direction. In a fitting bit of serendipity—or perhaps the invisible hand of the Force—Rey's training happens on the very same world where Leia took her first steps into the Force, in the jungles of Ajan Kloss. The primeval rainforests form a natural obstacle course to challenge Rey's physical and mental skills. Leia has even uncovered some of the old tools Luke used to hone her skills: training helmets and practice remotes that have lain unused for years.

Outstretched hand helps visualize projection of the Force

Leather arm band covers scars from previous skirmishes

Retracted plasteel blast shield

Repurposed KSE-H44 A-wing pilot helmet from Alliance surplus

Atmospheric seals lock in place if compatible breathmask is detected

TRAINING HELMET (VISOR RAISED)

Synthetic foam-padded interior

Ear cuff ordinarily houses comlink (deactivated)

TRAINING HELMET (VISOR LOWERED)

TRAINING EQUIPMENT

A trio of training remotes test Rey's evasion and deflection skills by zipping about her on repulsorfields, firing sting-beams to distract her. A typical training regime concocted by Leia involves Rey capturing colored ribbons tied to trees that are defended by color-coded remotes. The red remote is the most persistent and annoying, needling at Rey's temper with infuriating precision.

Shock-ray emitter

Color-coded duraplast helps Rey identify otherwise identical remotes

Tracking sensor

Maneuvering air jet

Lightweight synthetic capelet evokes Alderaanian style

MARKSMAN-H COMBAT REMOTE

Padded knee for athletic exercise

JEDI SCRIPTURE

The sacred texts are words of wisdom dating back to the dawn of the Jedi Order, contained within eight bound books—an exceedingly rare format in a galaxy that has wholly embraced electronic information systems. They describe tenets, history, and specific guidance to those studying the path of the Jedi. With foresight, the Masters of old encouraged future students to amend and add to the books as the millennia passed, so they are not just a single snapshot of history, but rather an evolving tapestry describing the Jedi Order. Luke Skywalker collected the volumes in his travels across the galaxy, and now they are in Rey's care.

HIDDEN DEPTHS

Separating myth from history proves difficult in the ancient language of Jedi scripture, which leans heavily on metaphor. This page from the texts describes the Force as a twisted ribbon lining the perimeter of all reality. Transit to any point across the cosmos is made possible by traversing this path through "the Netherworld of Unbeing."

Omniscient "eye" is from the Fourth Precept, a poem that describes gods battling in the primeval universe

Cover is "clay" pressed from reddish interstellar gases found in the Unknown Regions

Uneti wood spine and pages

THE *RAMMAHGON*

The *Rammahgon* is a well-known and influential work. The original was thought destroyed over 5,000 years ago, but was found by Master Skywalker during his exploration of the subterranean ruins on Ossus. It collects four varied (and conflicting) origin stories for the cosmos and the Force, and the precepts derived from those tales.

REY'S LIBRARY

It was Luke Skywalker's conviction that the library on Ahch-To should be destroyed, as the Jedi Order had been locked in a ruinous cycle of galactic upheaval since its very inception. Rey—perhaps driven by her innate scavenger instincts—left with the books before they could be burned, hiding them aboard the *Millennium Falcon* without her Master's knowledge. Though she recognizes the truth of the Force lies not within these pages, she nonetheless values their place in history and loses hours to fascinating readings on esoteric Force techniques and meditative practices. Rey keeps the books on a shelf in her workshop on Ajan Kloss, contained within the active field of a dehumicoil to prevent the moisture of the rainforest air from damaging the ancient pages.

Sturdy organo-silicon hide cover etched with decorative pattern

AIONOMICUM II (OR *THE SECOND VOLUME*)

Double-spine suggests second volume expanded to twice its original size during compilation

THE *AIONOMICA*

Jedi Master and historian Ri-Lee Howell collected many of the earliest accounts of explorations and codifications of the Force in the *Aionomica*: a two-volume combination of codex, correspondence, and scrapbook. Though much of its contents would later be stored in holocrons (which have since been lost), the physical books have passages written in the hands of the original sages, carefully preserved by Howell.

AIONOMICUM I (OR *THE FIRST VOLUME*)

> The sturdiest of the eight books have pages made of Uneti pulp, which came from Force-sensitive Uneti trees. This has preserved them for over a thousand generations.

> Rey has had R2-D2 scan and store the scripture in his memory core for future safekeeping.

> A rumored third volume of the *Aionomica* was the subject of a forgery scandal 300 years prior to the fall of the Jedi Order.

Rey is fascinated by the arcane healing techniques described in the *Chronicles of Brus-bu*, and uses the underpinnings of such teachings to heal the broken kyber crystal in her lightsaber.

DECIPHERING ANCIENT WISDOM

Very little of the Jedi scripture is readily legible—it must first be translated from archaic languages into modern Galactic Basic. Using simple translation programs available on most datapads, Rey can follow the words, though she recognizes this approach sacrifices nuance. She must trust her feelings when it comes to translating less concrete, more metaphysical concepts, of which there are many. Beaumont Kin, a historian and linguist in the Resistance ranks, offers his expertise on some of the densest sections of obscure, technical text. C-3PO is always eager to help, but is likely to spend as much time detailing the rules of grammatical construction and proper tense as he is explaining the meanings of the words he uncovers.

Vertical Tionese writing by Jedi Master Mott Corbet, expounding on his dictum, "what is, is without"

Unattributed visualization of the Chain Worlds Theorem, also known as the World Between Worlds, or Vergence Scatter

A description of notable beasts of Tython

Lightsaber diagrams

The Unsolved Thorpe Theorem, a hyperspace plotting conundrum posed to Padawan learners

Worn edges from millennia of use

Markers and notes from Jedi librarians from across centuries

Hand-drawn "Phases of Mortis" solution to the Unsolved Theorem of Master Thorpe

Annotations added by later authors (in this case, Jedi Master Odan-Urr)

MUSTAFAR

A molten world in the Outer Rim Territories, Mustafar has long been gripped by destructive, invisible forces of nature. Caught in a gravimetric tug-of-war between the planet Jestefed and the gas giant Lefrani, Mustafar roils like a wound that cannot heal. Such instability has churned valuable ores to its surface, making Mustafar a mineral trove for galactic mining conglomerates. Only within the last few decades have patches of the planet's angry surface started to cool. Offworlders are now drawn to the hellish planet for reasons far less tangible than precious metals. Some believe the world's nature is shaped by spiritual forces, a belief borne out by the planet's ancient mystical history, as well as its more recent reputation as the home of the Sith Lord Darth Vader.

Kylo soon outpaces his stormtrooper escorts as he cuts a swathe of destruction through the Alazmec, who attempt to block his path to Vader's castle—or rather, its crumbling ruins. Kylo enters the castle grounds with purpose, and finds an ark containing an artifact that will lead him to answers. The name "Exegol" burns in his mind, and he knows that at the source of this mystery he will find immense power.

Wide-set goggles protect eyes from blowing ash

Impact bolts

Sodium silicate-dusted protective clothing

Ironwood branch

IMPROVISED CLUB

CX-55 scatterblaster

ALAZMEC COLONIST

CULT COLONISTS

Since the death of Darth Vader, his legend has grown and cults have arisen that venerate his power. Fragmented tales of Vader's exploits and origins have been twisted by the faithful, who voyage to Mustafar in pilgrimage, seeking to tap into the powers that supposedly fueled him. One of the most tenacious sects is the Alazmec of Winsit, whose members are drawn to the Corvax Fen, an unlikely bog of fertile soil said to be soaked by the Lady Corvax's tears. The Alazmec are devoted to protecting the fen, planting a thin forest of irontrees around it in a futile attempt to reinvigorate the glen that covered the land centuries earlier.

LEGACY: MUSTAFAR'S DARK HISTORY

Ancient legends describe Mustafar as a garden world, home to Lady Corvax, a powerful Force-user obsessed with immortality. The unleashing of enormous energies in her pursuits pushed Mustafar from its original, safe orbit to a treacherous new path and caused irrevocable destruction. These legends brought the ancient Sith, seeking the same secrets of eternal life. They erected a shrine on Mustafar that would be discovered by Darth Vader early in his Sith apprenticeship. Vader—himself forever scarred by the fires of Mustafar—chose to build his castle there, within view of the site of his greatest defeat. The fortress was intended to act as a focal lens of Force power, but has long since fallen into ruins.

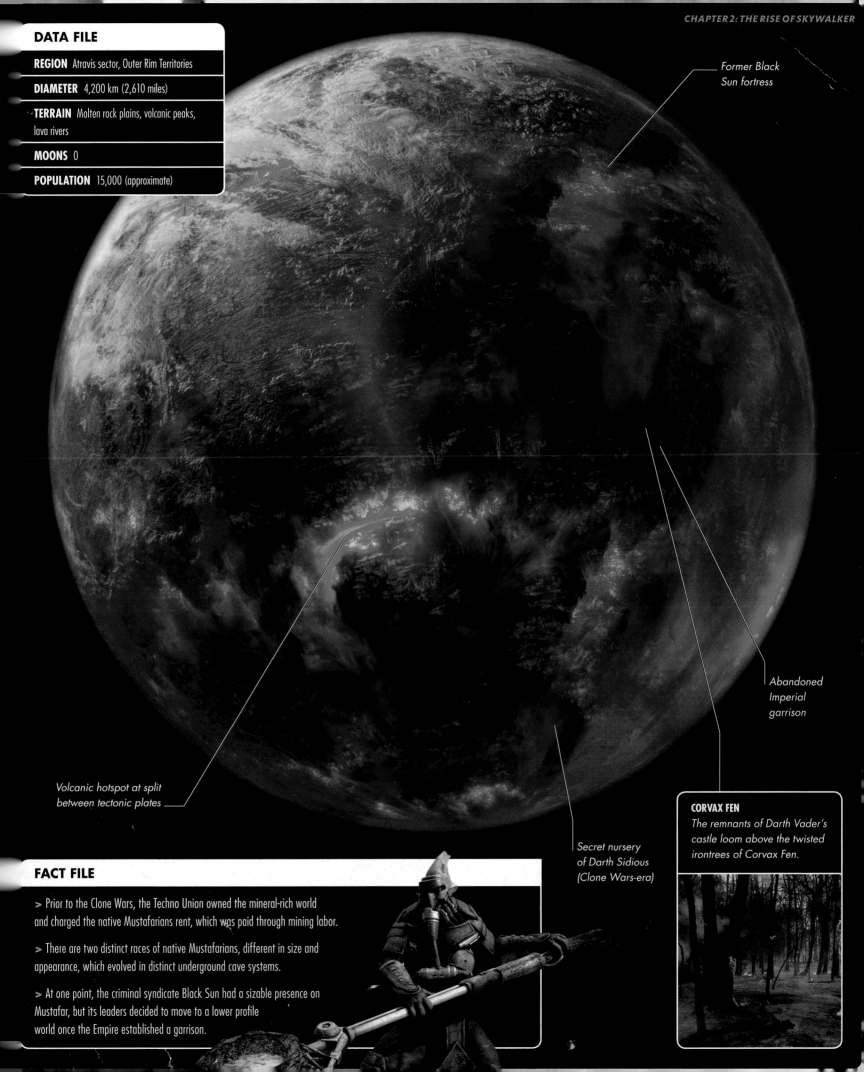

DATA FILE

REGION Atravis sector, Outer Rim Territories

DIAMETER 4,200 km (2,610 miles)

TERRAIN Molten rock plains, volcanic peaks, lava rivers

MOONS 0

POPULATION 15,000 (approximate)

Former Black
Sun fortress

Abandoned
Imperial
garrison

Volcanic hotspot at split
between tectonic plates

Secret nursery
of Darth Sidious
(Clone Wars-era)

CORVAX FEN
The remnants of Darth Vader's
castle loom above the twisted
irontrees of Corvax Fen.

FACT FILE

> Prior to the Clone Wars, the Techno Union owned the mineral-rich world
and charged the native Mustafarians rent, which was paid through mining labor.

> There are two distinct races of native Mustafarians, different in size and
appearance, which evolved in distinct underground cave systems.

> At one point, the criminal syndicate Black Sun had a sizable presence on
Mustafar, but its leaders decided to move to a lower profile
world once the Empire established a garrison.

KYLO REN

Kylo's reign as Supreme Leader has been marked by a fierce crackdown on any star systems exhibiting signs of independence or defiance. The persistent tale of his defeat by a "legendary Jedi" at the Battle of Crait proves a difficult fable to quash. Ren declares any worlds showing such disloyalty as "subversive" and dispatches stormtrooper patrols or even his dreaded Knights of Ren to root out malcontents and crush spirits. During this campaign of terror, visions in the Force as well as scraps of arcane lore uncovered in Snoke's old bases lead him to an ancient mystery. It becomes clear Snoke was not the apex of the First Order's dark side pyramid.

> "HE'S GONE MAD.
> FLAMES OF REBELLION
> BURN ACROSS THE GALAXY
> AND REN CHASES A GHOST."
> —GENERAL HUX

Reforged helmet strengthened through Sith alchemy

Silver visor frame cracked but rejoined

FACT FILE

> A gifted pilot, Ren is never satisfied with the speed and responsiveness of his craft, and pushes First Order engineers to outdo their best efforts.

> Throughout his life, Kylo has heard a dark voice. He long assumed it to be Snoke. With Snoke dead, it is evident he was wrong.

Crown fragment in magnetic forceps

Poseable arm mechanism

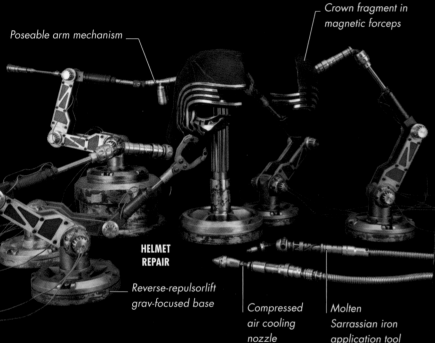

HELMET REPAIR

Reverse-repulsorlift grav-focused base

Compressed air cooling nozzle

Molten Sarrassian iron application tool

Magnification electro-goggles

Sensitive ears can tell the heat of metal from the tone it makes when struck

Dexterous, steady hands

Treated cloak is flame retardant

MYSTERIES OF THE SITH

Kylo's journeys to Mustafar and Exegol reveal to him that belief in the Sith tradition has continued, despite the demise of the last Sith Lord. Loyalists seeking to resurrect the tradition have coupled technology and the occult to bring forth unnatural embodiments of the dark side. Kylo comes to learn that he is heir to a vast Empire waiting to be unleashed from the depths of the Unknown Regions. He takes this mantle, but he knows there is still much work to be done.

ALBREKH, SITH ALCHEMIST

Unstable saber blade causes ragged wounds

MASKED RULER

After breaking free of Snoke's rule, Kylo redons the helmet marking him as a Knight of Ren, but this time on his own terms. The reforged helmet carries the luminous webwork of Sith alchemy—its fused shards mirror the breaking and rebuilding of Kylo's own identity.

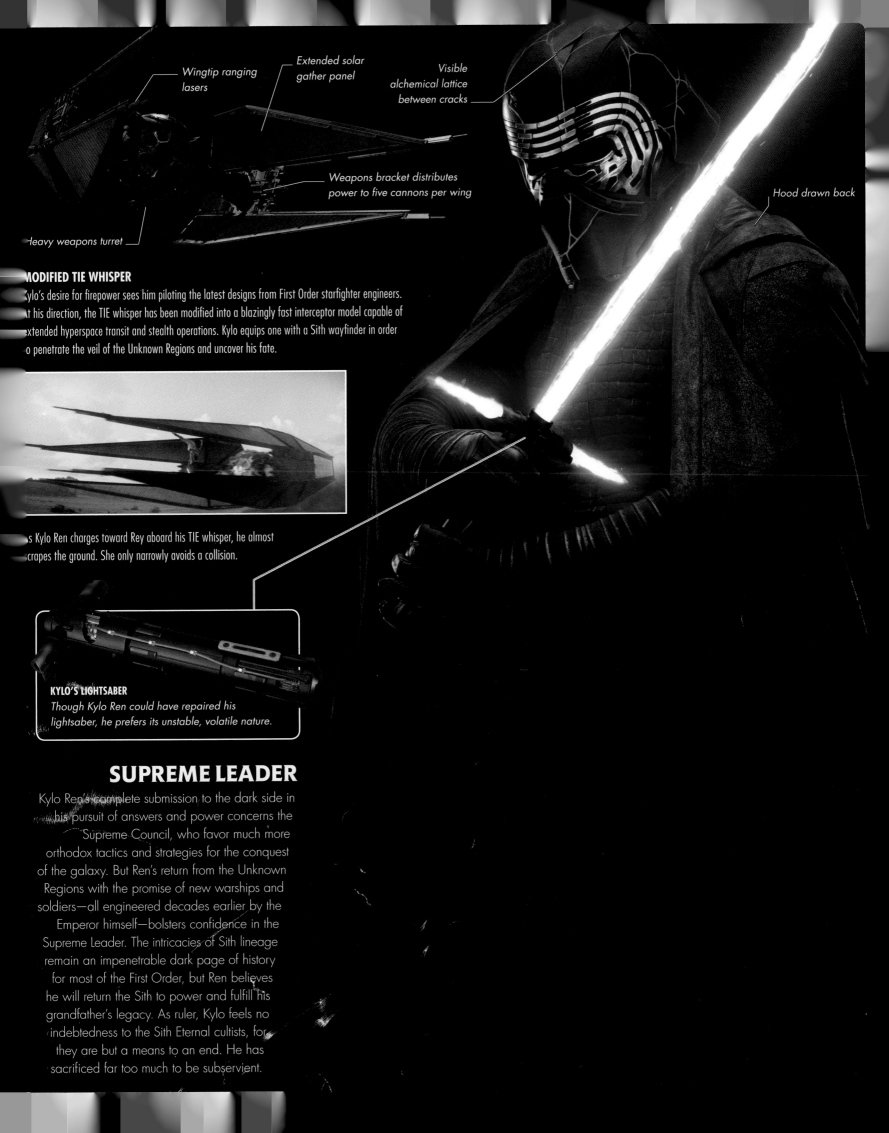

Wingtip ranging lasers

Extended solar gather panel

Visible alchemical lattice between cracks

Hood drawn back

Weapons bracket distributes power to five cannons per wing

Heavy weapons turret

MODIFIED TIE WHISPER

Kylo's desire for firepower sees him piloting the latest designs from First Order starfighter engineers. At his direction, the TIE whisper has been modified into a blazingly fast interceptor model capable of extended hyperspace transit and stealth operations. Kylo equips one with a Sith wayfinder in order to penetrate the veil of the Unknown Regions and uncover his fate.

As Kylo Ren charges toward Rey aboard his TIE whisper, he almost scrapes the ground. She only narrowly avoids a collision.

KYLO'S LIGHTSABER
Though Kylo Ren could have repaired his lightsaber, he prefers its unstable, volatile nature.

SUPREME LEADER

Kylo Ren's complete submission to the dark side in his pursuit of answers and power concerns the Supreme Council, who favor much more orthodox tactics and strategies for the conquest of the galaxy. But Ren's return from the Unknown Regions with the promise of new warships and soldiers—all engineered decades earlier by the Emperor himself—bolsters confidence in the Supreme Leader. The intricacies of Sith lineage remain an impenetrable dark page of history for most of the First Order, but Ren believes he will return the Sith to power and fulfill his grandfather's legacy. As ruler, Kylo feels no indebtedness to the Sith Eternal cultists, for they are but a means to an end. He has sacrificed far too much to be subservient.

THE STING OF REJECTION
Having once again confronted Rey and invited her to succumb to the dark side, Kylo Ren is thwarted by the efforts of Rey's comrades. The *Millennium Falcon*—itself a symbol of Ren's hated origins—blasts the hangar bay with the wash of its overpowered ion engines as it facilitates Rey's escape. Stormtroopers are tossed aside like ragdolls, but Ren secures his footing with help from the Force.

CHAPTER 3:
THE FIRST ORDER

Decades of peace have led to complacency. A demilitarized galaxy was not prepared for the unified, mechanized threat of the First Order's fleet and army. Worlds that have long depended on coalitions for protection find their allies surrendering, and without the New Republic to coordinate defense, more and more worlds are capitulating to Supreme Leader Kylo Ren's rule. Even more devastating, the First Order's discovery of untapped military assets on Exegol reveals at long last the full scope of the Emperor's contingency. With these fighting forces combined, the First Order threatens to be unstoppable as it transforms into a New Empire built on an ancient heritage.

GENERAL HUX

Hair coiffed to Hux's exacting standards

As the First Order geared up for its explosive debut on the galactic stage, the New Republic capital of Hosnian Prime in its crosshairs, General Armitage Hux was determined to become the face of this new regime. With the support of Supreme Leader Snoke, Hux proudly took the reins of the Starkiller Base project, vaunting its unparalleled technological might. That was the last time Hux felt certain about anything. Snoke's unforeseen demise has ruined Hux's career trajectory, and the years the young general spent jockeying for power against Kylo Ren now work against him, as Ren has assumed the title of Supreme Leader.

CHANGING FORTUNES

After the Star Destroyer *Finalizer* sustained major damage from a run-in with Resistance forces over Batuu, Kylo Ren transferred his command to his new flagship, the *Steadfast*. Ren brought Hux with him; the distrustful Supreme Leader will not lower his guard around someone as devious as Hux. Aboard the *Steadfast*, Hux serves below Allegiant General Pryde, having little independent authority without supervision. Ren gives assignments to Pryde or even to the Knights of Ren before entrusting Hux with anything of importance. Though Hux seems content to sit in the shadow of Pryde and Ren for now, it is unlikely he has completely abandoned his scheming nature.

At attention as per protocol, though not in spirit

LEGACY: RISE OF THE FIRST ORDER

The First Order is the combination of several separate elements of Palpatine's New Order. Few in the galaxy were aware that there was a contingency plan to meld the Empire's political, military, and spiritual survivors into a new regime. Hux is firmly part of the military branch, the heir of an Imperial officer who fled into the Unknown Regions. After much hardship in the galactic wilderness, the fleet and army survivors who refused to surrender to the New Republic uncovered dormant production facilities and resource-rich worlds, where they began forging a new fighting force.

GENERAL PRYDE

A veteran of the Imperial military, Allegiant General Pryde has patiently bided his time for decades, waiting for the authoritarian grip of order to return to the galaxy. He was part of a second wave of leadership kept in reserve by Supreme Leader Snoke during the unveiling of the Starkiller. After Snoke's demise, Pryde is left as one of the most senior officers in the First Order High Command. It is a privileged position, for Pryde knows far more about Snoke and the late Palpatine's machinations than many of his cohorts, and uses such insights to cement his own power.

Having roughed it in the galactic wilderness since the disastrous rout at Jakku, Pryde longs to return to the trappings of the "High Human" culture and civilization that once encased Coruscant. He wistfully recalls the pageantry and splendor of Empire Day parades of years past.

Swaggerstick connects to Alsakan military riding traditions

LACQUERED EBONWOOD SWAGGERSTICK

MILITARY TRADITION

Pryde's ideology allows him to tolerate the more macabre aspects of the First Order, which he would ordinarily disdain. While the mysticism of Snoke and Ren are alien to him—as are the arcane rituals of the Sith Eternal cult on Exegol—he accepts them as the eccentric by-products of a hunger for power. He knows this spiritual undercurrent dates back to the Galactic Empire, for when he was a young fleet officer he personally witnessed Darth Vader in action. Unlike less prudent military careerists, he knows better than to openly disrespect these beliefs. Pryde focuses instead on the material benefits they offer to the military.

Triple pleats denote unique rank and station

Officer gloves with electro-sensitive fingertips for touch-screen activation

FACT FILE

> Rebuilding his command after the destruction of the *Supremacy* and the death of Snoke, Kylo Ren discovered the reserve forces under Pryde's leadership and brought him to the fore.

> The rank of allegiant general is akin to that of a grand marshal—a commander of both ground and space-based forces. It is a title that Hux once aspired to.

TIMELINE

61 BSI	Born on Alsakan
45 BSI	Advanced placement in Alsakan Academy
40 BSI	Posting aboard Star Destroyer *Steadfast*
29 BSI	*Steadfast* destroyed in Battle of Jakku; Pryde flees into Unknown Regions
6 BSI	Snoke issues Pryde command of new Star Destroyer, named *Steadfast* in honor of his old vessel
0.5 ASI	Kylo Ren transfers his command to *Steadfast*

Double rank sash

DATA FILE

SUBJECT	Enric Pryde
HOMEWORLD	Alsakan
SPECIES	Human
AFFILIATION	First Order
HEIGHT	1.88m (6ft 2in)
AGE	62 standard years

WAYFINDERS

Wayfinders are ancient pieces of technology whose workings are not fully understood. They act as hyperspatial lodestones, showing safe paths through navigationally challenging stretches of space, and were essential for some of the earliest hyperspace exploration when navicomputers were still in their infancy. The construction of wayfinders was inspired by the study of the brains and carcasses of purrgil—spaceborne megafauna that can travel through hyperspace naturally. Wayfinders effectively reverse engineer the abilities of these faster-than-light titans. The Jedi and Sith of old somehow infused their devices with a presence in the Force.

FINDING HIDDEN WORLDS

A cosmic bramble of hyperspace anomalies has long prevented exploration along the galaxy's western edge, with a precipitous drop-off of known worlds beyond the Western Reaches. This barely understood barrier is as old as galactic civilization and hyperdrive technology. Rare exploratory missions have found some navigable worlds in this space—Csilla, Ilum, and Rakata Prime, for example—that are reachable by cautiously stepped hyperspace jumps into the wilderness. Through methods lost to time, the ancient Sith and Jedi were able to find worlds in the Unknown to serve as staging grounds or temples. Transit to such worlds would later be afforded by compasses and wayfinders.

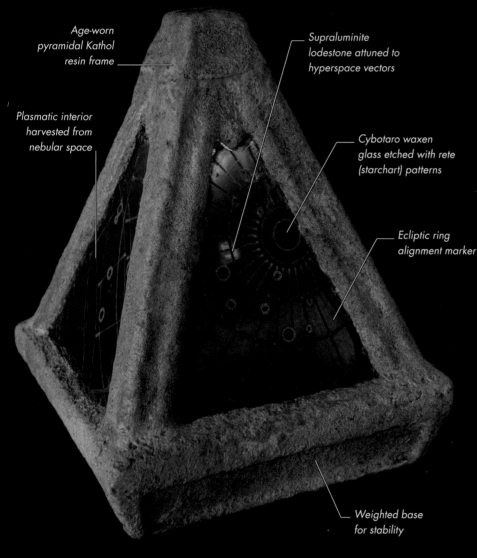

Age-worn pyramidal Kathol resin frame

Plasmatic interior harvested from nebular space

Supraluminite lodestone attuned to hyperspace vectors

Cybotaro waxen glass etched with rete (starchart) patterns

Ecliptic ring alignment marker

Weighted base for stability

"I KNOW HOW REN FOUND EXEGOL."

—REY

According to Skywalker's notes, a wayfinder would have to be used at least once to find a chartable path through the Unknown Regions to Exegol; the route could then be saved within a standard navicomputer for future use.

SITH WAYFINDER

As the last Dark Lords of the Sith, Darth Vader and Darth Sidious were each holders of ancient Sith wayfinders that could point the way to Exegol. Kylo Ren finds Vader's wayfinder stored in the ruins of his castle on Mustafar. Ren modifies his TIE whisper's astrogational systems to accept Vader's wayfinder as a signal source, and the ancient device sends out simplified binary signals that the ship's hyperdrive interprets as jump coordinates. In this way, the craft weaves a viable—if dangerous—path through the Unknown Regions. The Emperor's wayfinder proves to be a much tougher find.

FACT FILE

> An inert wayfinder said to have originally pointed the way to the Alderaan system was on display in the Royal Museum of Aldera at the time of the planet's destruction.

> Some alien species, like the Gree and the Aing-Tii, exhibit neural activity that very much resembles the motion and reactions of the plasma within wayfinders.

Skywalker's inserted notes describing his concerns

Translucent insert of wayfinder shape combinations and configurations

Protobesh cartouche containing the name "Exegol"

Aurodium clasp

Cascading Coremaic text regarding the Galactic Barrier

Astromeridian etch lines

Plasma-encased supraluminite lodestone

Graduated bezel

Detailed wayfinder illustration is at least 4,000 years old

Skywalker's illustrated studies of the wayfinder

Coremaic text warning of deep space dangers

LOST IN THE *RAMMAHGON*

When word of Ren's journey to Exegol reaches the Resistance, courtesy of a spy within the First Order ranks, Rey instantly knows how the Supreme Leader undertook such a voyage. She had read about wayfinders within the pages of the Jedi texts, specifically the red-covered *Rammahgon*, which had been annotated by Luke Skywalker. Master Skywalker had chronicled his efforts to find the Emperor's wayfinder, while tracking down fleeting mentions of Exegol during his explorations of the galaxy. Luke had grown concerned that the troves of Sith and Jedi artifacts hoarded by the Emperor in his various vaults could now be the target of nefarious agents. Luke especially feared what might happen if a Sith wayfinder fell into the wrong hands.

JEDI COMPASS

Luke Skywalker discovered an ancient Jedi star compass in the Emperor's storehouse on Pillio. It functions in a manner similar to the wayfinders. The lodestone, encased in a sphere of plasma, is attuned to specific points in hyperspace. Skywalker's study of it helped him uncover a path to Ahch-To, site of the first Jedi temple.

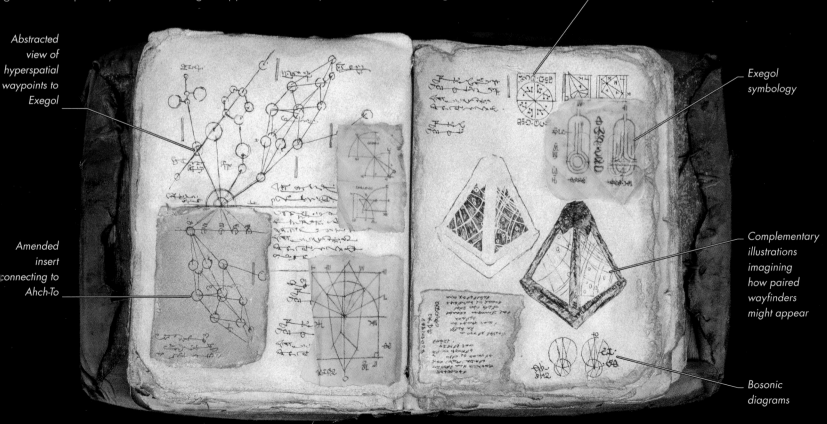

Abstracted view of hyperspatial waypoints to Exegol

Starchart extrapolations

Exegol symbology

Amended insert connecting to Ahch-To

Complementary illustrations imagining how paired wayfinders might appear

Bosonic diagrams

EXEGOL

The darkness at the heart of the Galactic Empire was unknown to most galactic citizens. Though its extreme militarization and authoritarian rule seemed to stem from a desire for security, they were actually fueled by a dark agenda over a thousand years old. The Sith, an ancient offshoot of the Jedi Order that had, in times past, ruled the galaxy, were once more ascendant. Sith Lords occupied positions of power until the Empire's defeat at the Battle of Endor. Secreted in the depths of the Unknown Regions, however, was the planet Exegol, a Sith redoubt. There, loyalists longing for the return of the Sith kept the flames of their sinister worship burning as they waited, building a force on Exegol that would not emerge for a generation.

MORABAND

SITH WORLDS

The greatest Sith fortress was once the cursed world of Moraband, known to antiquity as Korriban. Long since abandoned, its location is known to enough students of history to render it unsuitable as a base for the revived order. Exegol, by way of contrast, is shielded in the impenetrable veil of the Unknown Regions, providing Sith loyalists with a safe haven far from prying eyes. Other noteworthy Sith worlds that were quarantined in the time of the Republic include Malachor, Ziost, Jaguada, and Rhelg. Some worlds have had their Sith affiliations scrubbed so thoroughly from history that their denizens walk across avenues that were once ancient battlegrounds or sacred temple sites none the wiser about their dark history.

MALACHOR

SITH CITADEL

A thousand years before the fall of the Galactic Republic and the rise of the Empire, the galaxy had been ruled by the Sith. Exegol is one of the oldest Sith bastions, home to a massive citadel filled with ancient, crumbling statuary.

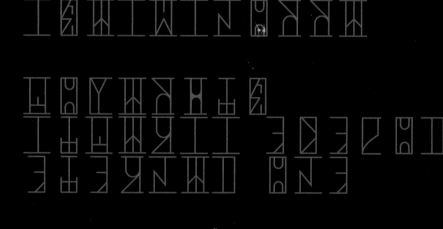

"DZWOROKKA YUN; NYÂSHQÛWAI, NWIQÛWAI. WOTOK TSAWAKMIDWANOTTOI, YUNTOKHYARUTMIDWANOTTOI."

—TRANSLATION OF SITH RUNES

OLD SITH RUNES

This Sith Eternal incantation carved in the Old Tongue denotes the nature of the dyad, a pairing in the Force. Curiously, it is nearly identical to text describing the Rule of Two—a Sith doctrine that there could only be two living Sith Lords—but inflection marks and line breaks change specific meaning in certain words.

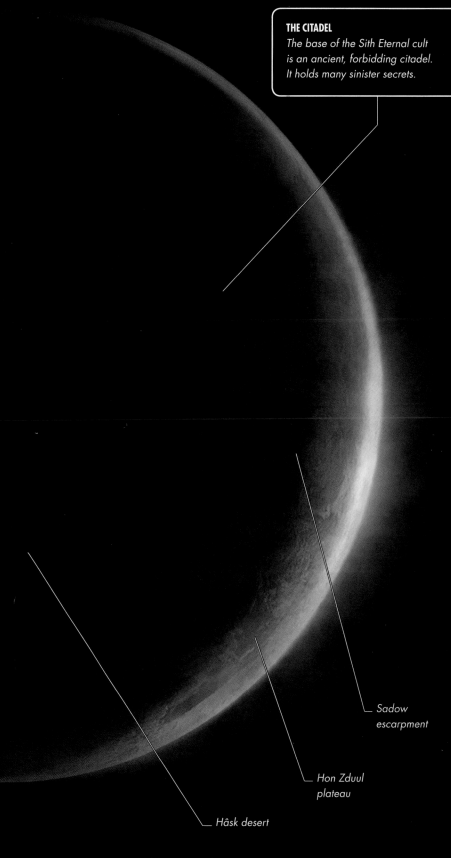

DATA FILE

REGION Unknown Regions, unincorporated space

DIAMETER 13,649 km (8,481 miles)

TERRAIN Barren rock and desert flats

MOONS 0

POPULATION Unknown; no native life, and total Sith and First Order forces have not been tabulated

THE CITADEL
The base of the Sith Eternal cult is an ancient, forbidding citadel. It holds many sinister secrets.

Sadow escarpment

Hon Zduul plateau

Hâsk desert

FACT FILE

> The dry conditions of Exegol and rubbing of dust particles in its atmosphere create enormous static discharges.

> A thick cloud of red gas and dust forms a navigational barrier to the planet. It is littered with the preserved remains of ancient space-faring megafauna.

> Enormous fissures reach deep into the planet's crust. They were excavated by Sith loyalists in centuries past, in a bid to reach a transportative vergence they believed to be hidden in the rock.

"FIND THE WAYFINDER, GET TO EXEGOL... AND BRING AN END TO THIS CONFLICT ONCE AND FOR ALL."

—REY, QUOTING LUKE SKYWALKER'S WRITINGS

KNIGHTS OF REN

The scattered settlements of the Unknown Regions and adjacent border territories tell cautionary tales of dangers lurking in unmapped space. Local folklore has warned for centuries of marauders known as the Knights of Ren. Since the rise of the First Order, myth has become reality. Whether or not this gang of dark warriors are truly connected to that ancient tradition or are wrapping themselves in the name and reputation of legends is not known, nor consequential, for whatever their origins they are a force to be reckoned with. The Knights were gifted to Ben Solo by Snoke, who promised the fallen Jedi apprentice powerful followers if he proved worthy. After a grueling trial, Kylo Ren emerged to lead them.

Case-hardened pastillion ore helmet

Annealed phrik scythe blade

Coat made from skin of unknown, monstrously large reptile

VICRUL

Vicrul sees himself as the harvester, the reaper of the fallen, and the targeter of souls. Every unfortunate victim to fall to his weapons augments his power. The dark side, though it may be muted by his lack of Force-training, surges in him with each hateful strike. Vicrul relishes this, and prefers to eliminate his targets at close range, though he keeps a blaster pistol at the ready in case he should need it. Vicrul's latent Force abilities manifest themselves in heightened reflexes and the power to magnify fear in his prey, though these abilities come unbidden and uncontrolled.

CARDO

While most of the Knights of Ren strike with exacting precision, Cardo's approach leaves wide swathes of destruction. His hefty arm cannon packs more than enough firepower for a single warrior. A wide-bore flamethrower launches jets of burning naphthex gel, burning down obstacles and any enemies using them as cover. A vented plasma bolt launcher has limited ammunition but fires explosive charges over 200 meters. Cardo's obsession with weapon modification makes him the best armorer of the Knights. He also carries a compact, expedient blaster pistol.

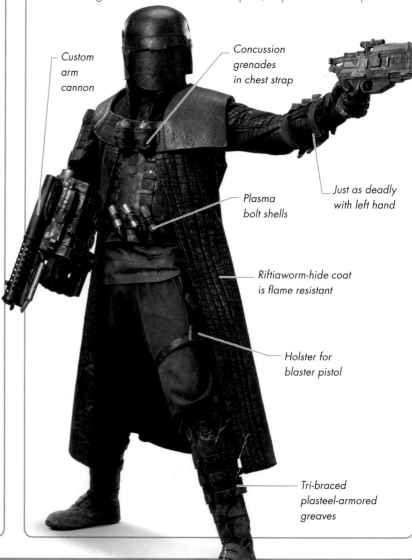

Custom arm cannon

Concussion grenades in chest strap

Just as deadly with left hand

Plasma bolt shells

Riftiaworm-hide coat is flame resistant

Holster for blaster pistol

Tri-braced plasteel-armored greaves

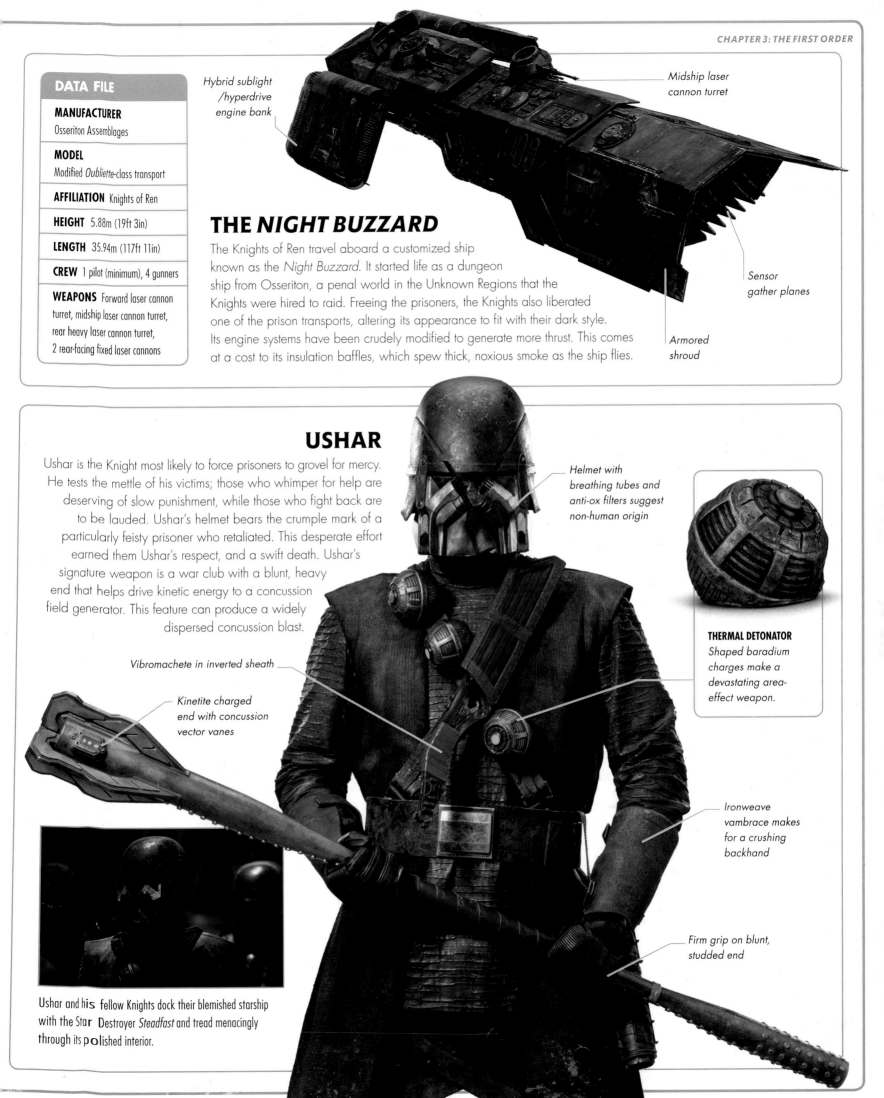

DATA FILE

MANUFACTURER
Osseriton Assemblages

MODEL
Modified *Oubliette*-class transport

AFFILIATION Knights of Ren

HEIGHT 5.88m (19ft 3in)

LENGTH 35.94m (117ft 11in)

CREW 1 pilot (minimum), 4 gunners

WEAPONS Forward laser cannon
turret, midship laser cannon turret,
rear heavy laser cannon turret,
2 rear-facing fixed laser cannons

Hybrid sublight /hyperdrive engine bank

Midship laser cannon turret

Sensor gather planes

Armored shroud

THE *NIGHT BUZZARD*

The Knights of Ren travel aboard a customized ship
known as the *Night Buzzard*. It started life as a dungeon
ship from Osseriton, a penal world in the Unknown Regions that the
Knights were hired to raid. Freeing the prisoners, the Knights also liberated
one of the prison transports, altering its appearance to fit with their dark style.
Its engine systems have been crudely modified to generate more thrust. This comes
at a cost to its insulation baffles, which spew thick, noxious smoke as the ship flies.

USHAR

Ushar is the Knight most likely to force prisoners to grovel for mercy.
He tests the mettle of his victims; those who whimper for help are
deserving of slow punishment, while those who fight back are
to be lauded. Ushar's helmet bears the crumple mark of a
particularly feisty prisoner who retaliated. This desperate effort
earned them Ushar's respect, and a swift death. Ushar's
signature weapon is a war club with a blunt, heavy
end that helps drive kinetic energy to a concussion
field generator. This feature can produce a widely
dispersed concussion blast.

Helmet with breathing tubes and anti-ox filters suggest non-human origin

THERMAL DETONATOR
Shaped baradium charges make a devastating area-effect weapon.

Vibromachete in inverted sheath

Kinetite charged end with concussion vector vanes

Ironweave vambrace makes for a crushing backhand

Firm grip on blunt, studded end

Ushar and his fellow Knights dock their blemished starship
with the Star Destroyer *Steadfast* and tread menacingly
through its polished interior.

TRUDGEN

A collector of trophies from fallen conquests, Trudgen adds to his weapons and armor as his victories grow. His patchwork helmet indicates that he defeated a death trooper at some point in the past, a remarkable achievement given their strength and rarity. His signature weapon is an enormous vibrocleaver. The ultrasonic technology that rapidly vibrates the blade edge for extra cutting power is an add-on modification to a traditional, primitive weapon. When not swinging the hefty blade in combat, Trudgen either rests the blunt end over his shoulder, holds it via the weight-reducing holes lining the blade spine, or attaches bandolier straps to it and slings it over his back.

Fragment of death trooper helmet

Ultrasonic activator

Heavy weave tabard and hood

Scavenged armor plates

SECONDARY BLADE

KURUK'S HELMET

Recesses cut for peripheral line-of-sight

Blinder panels intended to focus vision forward

Plasma bolt shells stowed in collar loops

Breath screen and vocoder grid

Sound-dampening susurra-weave fabric

Forestalk and action bar primes plasma bolt

Soft-soled boots for silent tread

KURUK

The most solitary of the Knights, Kuruk serves as the group's rifleman and the pilot of the *Night Buzzard*. He is the one most likely to remain behind, perched on a high vantage point, covering an assault with his precision marksmanship. The blinder flaps on his helmet focus his attention on his target, and his aim is further sharpened by concentrating on the Force. He carries no bladed weaponry, relying instead on his multi-barreled custom-designed rifle, which has rapid-fire, sniping, and pump-action plasma bolt firing capabilities.

AP'LEK

Whereas most of the Knights prefer a straightforward—and violent—approach to eliminating their targets, Ap'lek revels in deception. As a strategist, he employs feints and misdirection to trap an opponent. On his belt is a smoke dispenser that obscures vision and disrupts sensors; his own nascent Force abilities allow him to peer through such screens. As a warrior, the sinister face of his battered helmet suggests an unsettling rictus, as if he delights in his tricks. His preferred lethal weapon, though, is an ancient Mandalorian executioner's ax.

Ap'lek stalks his prey—an unsuspecting Chewbacca—on Pasaana during the Knights' hunt for the scavenger that so vexes their master.

Patchwork mask cobbled together from battered armor

Weighted handle to partially counter ax head

Water-shedding oiled cloak

Raised teeth assist in parrying and pinning edged attacks

Smoke canister

Lightweight plastoid armor beneath tunic fabric

Vibro-insulator plates protect handle

Beskar blade with gore channels cut into surface

KNIGHTS OF REN
WEAPONS AND EQUIPMENT

The battered, hand-crafted appearance of their weapons and equipment further adds to the aura of dread that surrounds the Knights of Ren. It is immediately clear that they are well acquainted with violence and strife, for they carry the scars and implements of such with them. Although appearing intimidatingly unified at first glance, closer examination reveals that each Knight is distinct, expressing preferences in tactics and combat style. All of the gear is custom, either built from scratch or heavily modified after capture. Aboard their vessel, the Symeong metalsmith Albrekh repairs their armor, while the Knight known as Cardo tends to their weapons. Gear must be sturdy and reliable for the Knights to be effective in their brutal brand of conquest.

CLUBS AND AXES

Even the most primitive weapons in the Knights' arsenal receive a crude technological boost. The weighted clubs and axes carried by Ushar and Ap'lek would be deadly with just the muscle-power of their wielders delivering crushing blows. However, with the flick of a switch or twist of a dial, they take on additional attributes that may make the difference in battle. Ushar's club builds up a concussion charge in a kinetite generator, which can be released as a sudden shockwave. Ap'lek's antiquated Mandalorian long ax becomes a conduit for ultrasonic energy, vibrating its sharpened edge to enhance its cutting power through armor and bone.

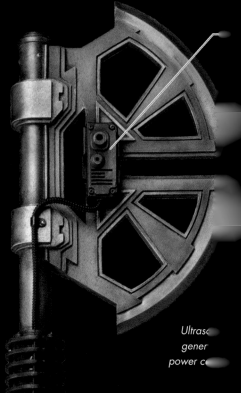

Ultras
gener
power c

USHAR'S WAR CLUB

Studs
line entire
front of club

HELMETS

The Knights of Ren purposely shield their features with masks and battle helms, for they find their victims project their most terrifying nightmares into the absent faces as they strike. Anonymity equals intimidation to the Knights.

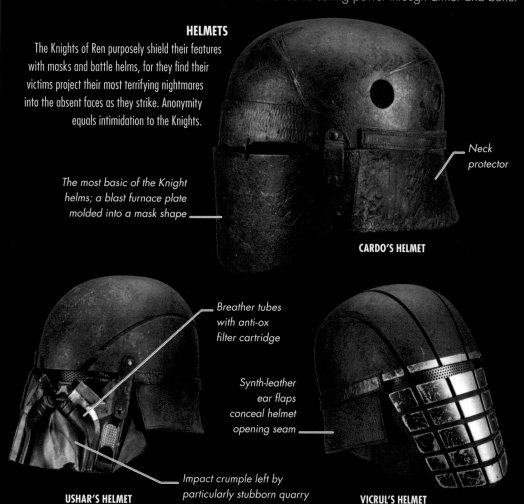

Neck protector

The most basic of the Knight helms; a blast furnace plate molded into a mask shape

CARDO'S HELMET

Breather tubes with anti-ox filter cartridge

Synth-leather ear flaps conceal helmet opening seam

Impact crumple left by particularly stubborn quarry

USHAR'S HELMET

VICRUL'S HELMET

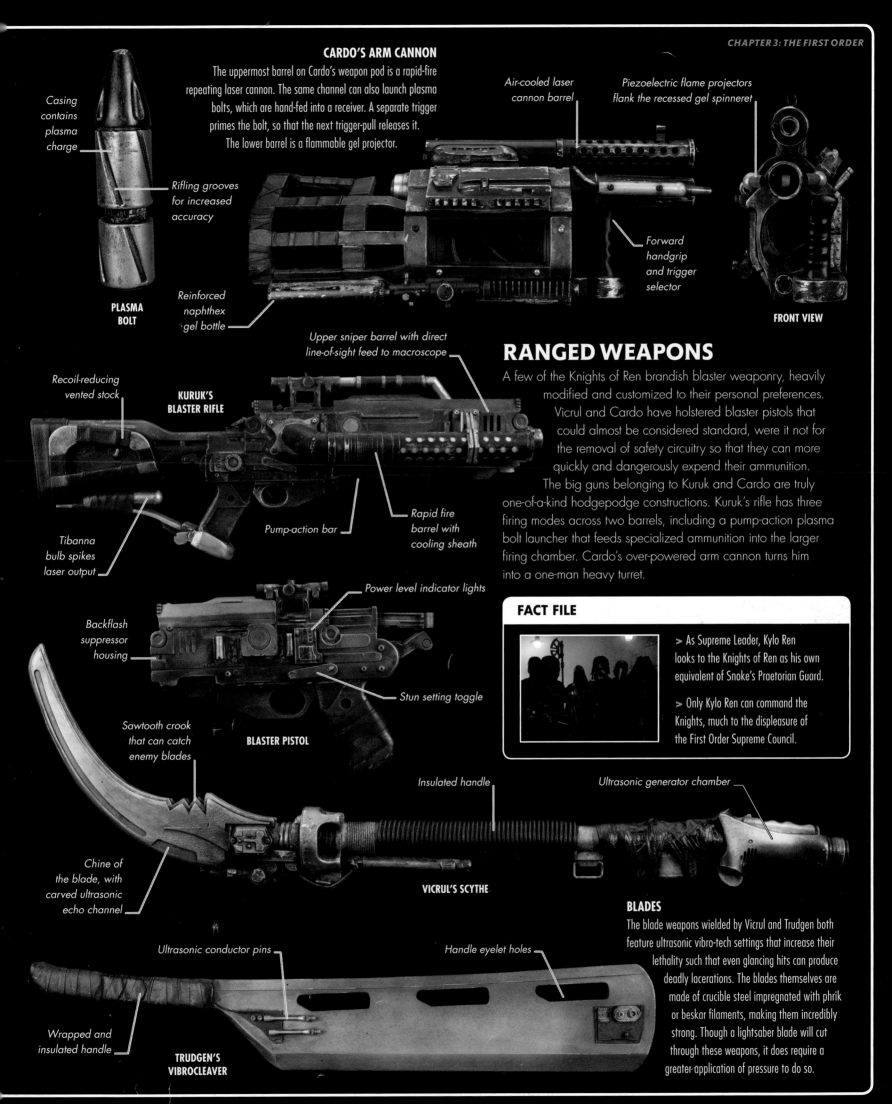

CARDO'S ARM CANNON

The uppermost barrel on Cardo's weapon pod is a rapid-fire repeating laser cannon. The same channel can also launch plasma bolts, which are hand-fed into a receiver. A separate trigger primes the bolt, so that the next trigger-pull releases it. The lower barrel is a flammable gel projector.

Casing contains plasma charge

Rifling grooves for increased accuracy

PLASMA BOLT

Reinforced naphthex gel bottle

Air-cooled laser cannon barrel

Piezoelectric flame projectors flank the recessed gel spinneret

Forward handgrip and trigger selector

FRONT VIEW

Recoil-reducing vented stock

KURUK'S BLASTER RIFLE

Upper sniper barrel with direct line-of-sight feed to macroscope

Tibanna bulb spikes laser output

Pump-action bar

Rapid fire barrel with cooling sheath

RANGED WEAPONS

A few of the Knights of Ren brandish blaster weaponry, heavily modified and customized to their personal preferences. Vicrul and Cardo have holstered blaster pistols that could almost be considered standard, were it not for the removal of safety circuitry so that they can more quickly and dangerously expend their ammunition.

The big guns belonging to Kuruk and Cardo are truly one-of-a-kind hodgepodge constructions. Kuruk's rifle has three firing modes across two barrels, including a pump-action plasma bolt launcher that feeds specialized ammunition into the larger firing chamber. Cardo's over-powered arm cannon turns him into a one-man heavy turret.

Backflash suppressor housing

Power level indicator lights

Stun setting toggle

BLASTER PISTOL

FACT FILE

> As Supreme Leader, Kylo Ren looks to the Knights of Ren as his own equivalent of Snoke's Praetorian Guard.

> Only Kylo Ren can command the Knights, much to the displeasure of the First Order Supreme Council.

Sawtooth crook that can catch enemy blades

Chine of the blade, with carved ultrasonic echo channel

Insulated handle

Ultrasonic generator chamber

VICRUL'S SCYTHE

BLADES

The blade weapons wielded by Vicrul and Trudgen both feature ultrasonic vibro-tech settings that increase their lethality such that even glancing hits can produce deadly lacerations. The blades themselves are made of crucible steel impregnated with phrik or beskar filaments, making them incredibly strong. Though a lightsaber blade will cut through these weapons, it does require a greater application of pressure to do so.

Ultrasonic conductor pins

Handle eyelet holes

Wrapped and insulated handle

TRUDGEN'S VIBROCLEAVER

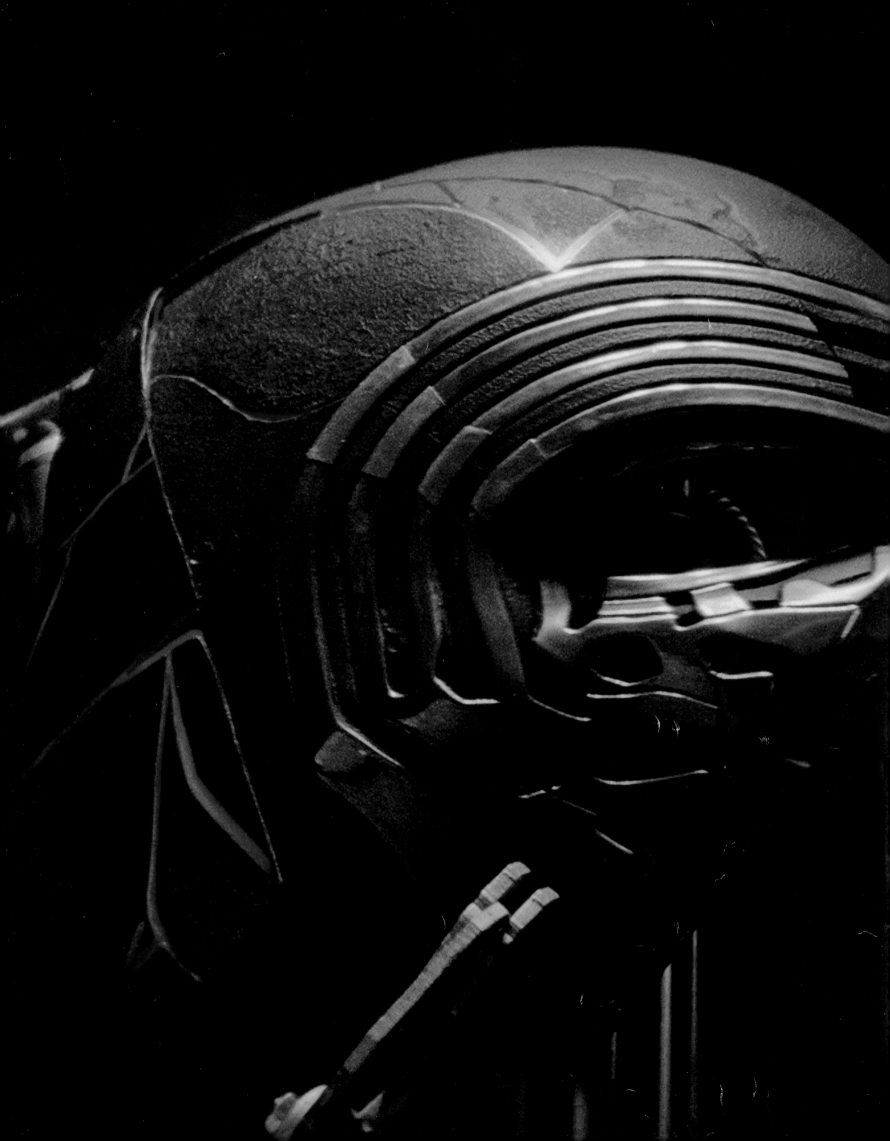

REFORGING THE MASK
An eccentric Symeong named Albrekh uses an ancient Sith
forge to rebuild Kylo Ren's shattered helmet, the fragments
of which Kylo collected from the wreckage of the *Supremacy*.
A luminous red alchemical lattice of Sarrassian iron holds the
shards together, painstakingly applied by Albrekh's steady
hands. The resulting helmet is far stronger than it once was.

FIRST ORDER HIGH COMMAND

Information within the First Order was extremely compartmentalized during the rise of the regime, since so much depended on the scope of its operations remaining a secret to the wider galaxy. As a result, even high-ranking officers within the First Order remained unaware of the true scale of its forces, diplomats in the Senate were unaware whom they were acting as proxies for, and citizens of worlds that declared independence from the New Republic did not realize they were facing a new, tyrannical future. With Kylo Ren usurping command, the veils of secrecy that surrounded Snoke and his plan have begun to dissipate. Ren has created a Supreme Council to plan for the future, comprising the highest-ranking officers of the First Order military and their closest aides.

GENERAL QUINN

Once a junior officer in the Empire, Domaric Quinn has risen to be one of the First Order's key ground force commanders. Like Hux, he is a technologist at heart, and his combat strategies emphasize logic-based solutions verified by complex computer simulations. He kept his disagreements with Snoke's reliance on mysticism in check, but now that Kylo Ren is in charge Quinn finds it hard to keep his temper under control. The fact that Ren is more than a decade his junior adds to Quinn's frustrations.

GENERAL PARNADEE

Bellava Parnadee is the First Order's senior ground commander and an avid student of history. She has an extensive hololibrary, which contains detailed analysis of the major engagements of the Clone Wars and Galactic Civil War. Now that much of the galaxy is under First Order control, Parnadee focuses on the occupation of contested worlds, directing ground forces on Kijimi, Torost, and Odynnia Gavo. She normally operates out of the *Steadfast*, though she has standing quarters on every Star Destroyer in the fleet in case she needs to personally supervise a campaign. Her presence encourages her troops, as they aspire to make her proud or avoid her well-documented ire.

Freshly droid-ironed uniform

Double-banded general rank insignia

Crested officer's cap with First Order insignia

COMMANDER TRACH

A young scanner officer aboard the *Steadfast*, Masir Trach transferred from the *Finalizer* and is caught in a silent struggle of loyalties between Generals Hux and Pryde. He senses turbulence between the two senior officers, but tries to avoid any dispute by focusing on the letter of his orders, rather than the ulterior political motivations that may be behind them.

GENERAL ENGELL

General Amret Engell has taken over the large portion of Hux's stormtrooper training program that was once Captain Phasma's responsibility. Engell sees each new world to fall under the First Order banner as a bountiful source of children to mold into loyal stormtroopers. She enthusiastically welcomes the discovery of additional soldiers in the Unknown Regions as part of the Sith Eternal plan. Engell admires Ren for his initiative and unquestioned authority, and strives to make an army worthy of his approval.

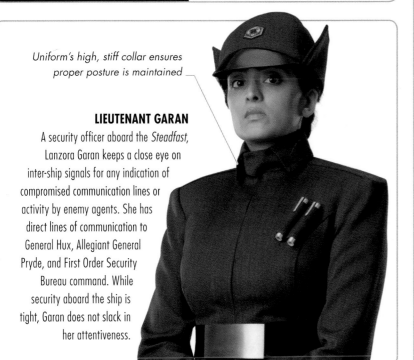

Uniform's high, stiff collar ensures proper posture is maintained

LIEUTENANT GARAN

A security officer aboard the *Steadfast*, Lanzora Garan keeps a close eye on inter-ship signals for any indication of compromised communication lines or activity by enemy agents. She has direct lines of communication to General Hux, Allegiant General Pryde, and First Order Security Bureau command. While security aboard the ship is tight, Garan does not slack in her attentiveness.

Rank cylinders coded to allow Kandia access to analysis labs

OFFICER KANDIA

Tishra Kandia is an intelligence officer charged with processing captured evidence and firsthand accounts of Resistance activity. Stationed on the *Steadfast*, Kandia takes seriously the Supreme Leader's order to find any clues to Rey's whereabouts, and will leave no stone unturned.

ADMIRAL GRISS

The senior fleet officer aboard the *Steadfast*, Frantis Griss commands not only the flagship but also the support ships in its battlegroup. Griss assesses operational reports from naval forces across First Order territory, allocating resources as required by the shifting expansion efforts. He carefully apportions prized experimental technology, such as hyperspace tracking systems, to best benefit the fleet. A new-generation officer, he was too young to serve in the Galactic Empire, but gained valuable experience taming the Unknown Regions for First Order exploitation. He reports directly to Allegiant General Pryde and has his complete trust.

First Order insignia

Synth-leather breathable officers' gloves

Double-banded, red-lined admiral rank sashes

Flared hip breeches evoke an ancient riding tradition

Waxy sealant on parade boots preserves a permanent polish

FORCES OF THE FIRST ORDER

When the worlds that would form the bulk of the First Order's territories seceded from the New Republic, it allowed them to disregard the demilitarization treaties that helped end the Galactic Civil War. The galaxy had been at peace for decades, and what no one in the New Republic suspected was that they were already caught in the grip of a cold war, as a military build-up had been secretly underway in the Unknown Regions. Behind its well-protected borders, the First Order pretended to have merely enough forces to defend its own space. In reality, far from prying eyes, a massive invasion force was readying for launch.

FACT FILE

> Its sleek and imposing military is the face of the First Order, but its reign would be impossible if not for double agents, spies, and hired thugs.

> Though its military is smaller than that of the Empire, the sizes of individual First Order units and groupings follow the standard Imperial order of battle.

Flight helmet with data projected on interior viewplate

Life support control module

TIE PILOTS

After the formal end of the Galactic Civil War, the flight academies that had churned out endless cadets to serve in the Imperial Navy were returned to their previous incarnations as local institutions, training planetary defense forces. Cut off from this resource, the First Order turned its Star Destroyers—whether newly forged or Imperial survivors—into mobile flight schools for their new recruits. Given the paucity of resources in its early years, the First Order did not treat its own TIE forces as expendable, as the Empire once had.

LIEUTENANT TOPHID BRUSTER (DT-4431)

STORMTROOPERS

About five years before the destruction of the New Republic capital, stormtroopers were seen once more in a galaxy that had forgotten their significance after years of peace. They were presented as a territorial protection force, never venturing within the borders of New Republic space. Their true nature—an army trained almost from birth, secretly in development for more than 20 years—was a closely guarded secret. Now the mask has slipped, and the First Order has no reason to respect the treaties of a dead government. It seems stormtroopers are everywhere as the First Order expands its reach.

Riot control electroprod

Filtration system

Pauldron armor plate

Temperature control body glove

Power cells

Betaplast armor

Greave

DATA FILE

SUBJECT HF-3311

HOMEWORLD Gannaria

SPECIES Human

AFFILIATION First Order

HEIGHT 1.8m (5ft 10in)

AGE 25

LEGACY: STORMTROOPERS

First Order stormtroopers can trace their origins to the clone troopers who fought in the wars that blighted the twilight years of the Republic. The Empire phased out cloning, instead recruiting naturally born cadets in their teens to become stormtroopers. The First Order has extended its training program to include very young children, in essence bridging the two different approaches.

Stiff synth-leather boots enforce posture standards

COMMANDERS

Much of the upper echelon of the First Order consists of Imperial veterans, but as they age out of the military, they are being replaced by a younger generation of fanatical loyalists. These officers have learned a mythologized history of Palpatine's regime. As recruits, conscripts, or promoted stormtroopers, they hail from impoverished or conquered worlds, and are shown an alluring reality in which they are on the winning side of an unstoppable galactic conquest. This fosters in them a desire for power and respect for authority.

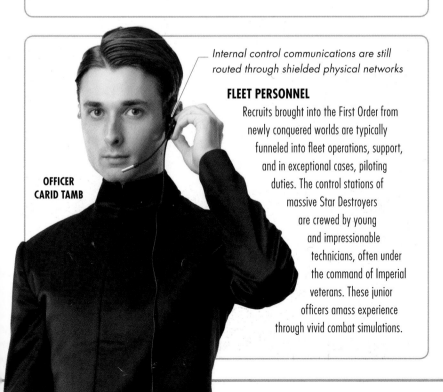

OFFICER CARID TAMB

Internal control communications are still routed through shielded physical networks

FLEET PERSONNEL

Recruits brought into the First Order from newly conquered worlds are typically funneled into fleet operations, support, and in exceptional cases, piloting duties. The control stations of massive Star Destroyers are crewed by young and impressionable technicians, often under the command of Imperial veterans. These junior officers amass experience through vivid combat simulations.

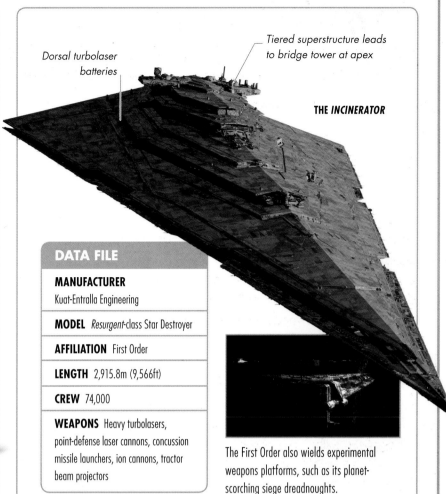

Dorsal turbolaser batteries

Tiered superstructure leads to bridge tower at apex

THE *INCINERATOR*

DATA FILE

MANUFACTURER
Kuat-Entralla Engineering

MODEL *Resurgent*-class Star Destroyer

AFFILIATION First Order

LENGTH 2,915.8m (9,566ft)

CREW 74,000

WEAPONS Heavy turbolasers, point-defense laser cannons, concussion missile launchers, ion cannons, tractor beam projectors

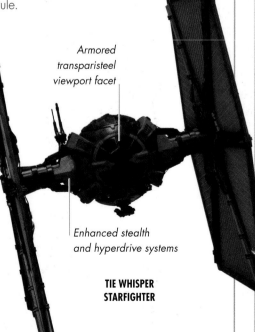

The First Order also wields experimental weapons platforms, such as its planet-scorching siege dreadnoughts.

FIRST ORDER FLEET

After the determined demilitarization efforts of the New Republic, the secret fleet constructed by the First Order stood as the single biggest military force in the galaxy. Even with this impressive display, it was but a fraction of the total might of the Galactic Empire at its height. Now being bolstered by the thousands of vessels hidden on Exegol, the First Order threatens to return the galaxy to the iron might of military rule.

Rigid brace that segments solar gather panel

Armored transparisteel viewport facet

STARFIGHTERS

The ubiquitous TIE fighter, long a symbol of the Empire, continues to represent the First Order in space engagements. This is largely due to the sheer quantity and surplus produced by Sienar Fleet Systems during its profitable relationship with the Imperial military. In the modern era, its successor company Sienar-Jaemus continues to supply and update the venerable TIE design into various modern incarnations.

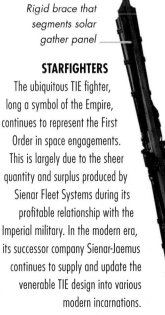

Enhanced stealth and hyperdrive systems

TIE WHISPER STARFIGHTER

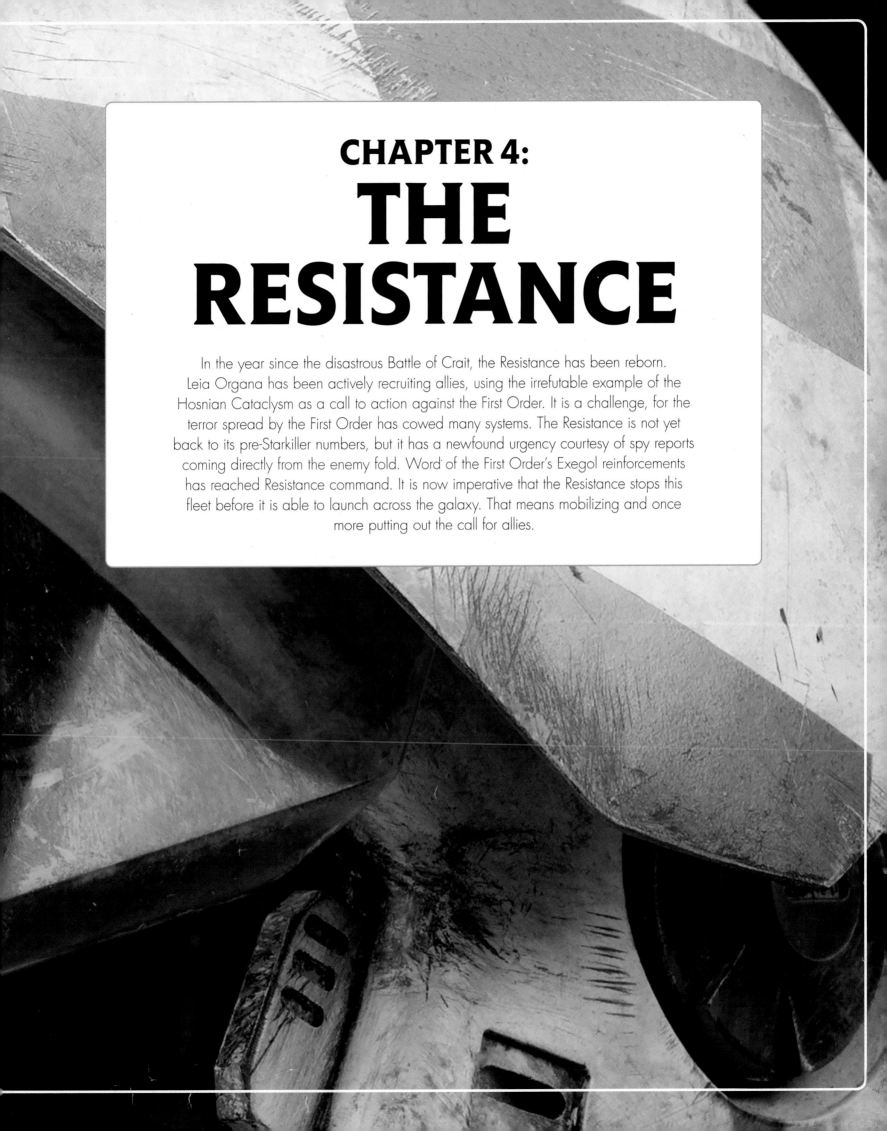

CHAPTER 4:
THE RESISTANCE

In the year since the disastrous Battle of Crait, the Resistance has been reborn.
Leia Organa has been actively recruiting allies, using the irrefutable example of the
Hosnian Cataclysm as a call to action against the First Order. It is a challenge, for the
terror spread by the First Order has cowed many systems. The Resistance is not yet
back to its pre-Starkiller numbers, but it has a newfound urgency courtesy of spy reports
coming directly from the enemy fold. Word of the First Order's Exegol reinforcements
has reached Resistance command. It is now imperative that the Resistance stops this
fleet before it is able to launch across the galaxy. That means mobilizing and once
more putting out the call for allies.

RESISTANCE BASE

A far cry from the more developed outpost on D'Qar, the Resistance presence on Ajan Kloss is a provisional, temporary base with hardly any new construction. There is no infrastructure—instead most support functions are provided by the *Tantive IV*, General Organa's reclaimed consular ship from yesteryear. Cables snake from the landed ship to portable computer banks and charging stations. A cleared field serves as a landing area, with air traffic control carried out by troopers with comlinks and electrobinoculars. The impermanence is deliberate. The Resistance can mobilize within minutes and abandon the base with little trace of its presence remaining. While mobility was always a factor in Resistance operations, it must now carry a far greater emphasis if the cause is to survive.

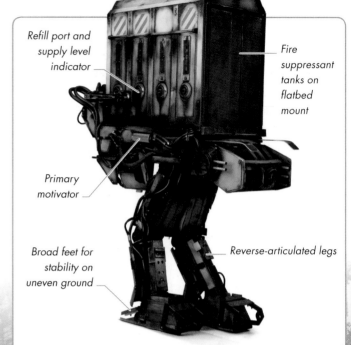

Refill port and supply level indicator

Fire suppressant tanks on flatbed mount

Primary motivator

Broad feet for stability on uneven ground

Reverse-articulated legs

LC-24 FIRE DROID

With no proper landing facilities available, the Resistance must stay vigilant for collisions. Ground crews stand at high alert during the launch or recovery of any starcraft. These crews include firefighting droids equipped with dousing gear and heat-resistant shielding. Their focused life-form indicators seek out survivors, and transmit this information to rescuers and medical droids.

Spacecraft linkage and control arms

Photoreceptor

R5-2JE

In addition to filling shipboard astromech duties, R5-2JE leads the droid pool assigned to the makeshift landing area in the forest outside the cave. "Toojay" wears a modified restraining bolt that serves as a signal hub for similarly equipped Resistance droids, sending commands and work orders from a distance.

Shoulder joint pivots to extend third tread

Command signal bolt

EQUIPMENT AT THE READY
Resistance supply crates often fold open to become workstations.

MILLENNIUM FALCON
The battered Corellian YT-1300 gets the largest share of repair time.

HIDDEN FORTRESSES

Like D'Qar and Crait, Ajan Kloss was discovered by Alderaanian explorers but never shared with the wider galaxy. This was at the request of the Royal Family, as they anticipated needing places of refuge should political fortunes ever turn on them. Leia Organa inherited this information as Princess of Alderaan, and it became a short list of potential worlds to house Alliance bases during the Rebellion. Often their sheer remoteness worked against them, as traveling to and from them would prove too costly for the Alliance's limited fuel reserves. In other cases, it was the opposite—they were too close to hyperspace lanes, increasing their risk of discovery by the Empire. Ajan Kloss' time for usefulness would have to wait until well after that war was won.

A-WING
A-wing fuel tanks need regular replenishment.

CAVE HANGAR

A natural cave in the jungle's mountain walls has become a hangar for the *Tantive IV*. As the largest ship currently in the Resistance fleet, it needs cover to remain hidden from orbital scans. The damp cave also serves as a gathering area for the Resistance crews. Tapped streams and an underground river provide potable water and hydroelectric power for the base.

NETTING

The sensor-baffling camouflage netting also casts naturalistic cucoloris-effect shadows.

X-WING

Poe Dameron's X-wing, in its striking orange livery, has an optimum landing area.

Crossover drape to protect neck

EL-16 blaster rifle lacquered with anti-fungal resin

Concealed mesh panels in shirts help air circulate

Multi-pocketed utility trousers

JUNGLE GEAR

The midday heat and perpetual humidity of Ajan Kloss means Resistance personnel strip back their already functional uniforms for greater comfort. Heavier outer jackets are shed in favor of short sleeves. Headgear provides protection from intense sunlight, falling fruit, and torrential downpours. Insect repellant is in short supply, and has become an object of barter.

GENERAL ORGANA

Since relocating to Ajan Kloss, Leia has split her time between overseeing the recruitment effort that is vital to expanding the Resistance and training a Jedi who is vital to preserving the Resistance. She cannot help but be reminded of her own training, and the visions she received in those early days that ultimately led her away from the Jedi path. Such a change was not due to a lack of conviction—quite the opposite. Her choices are never made lightly. Even now, at what she recognizes as the end of her days, having outlived her brother and her husband, and endured more hardship than any one person could be expected to bear, she has certainty regarding her path.

LEGACY: *TANTIVE IV*

The *Tantive IV* was the historic Alderaanian consular ship that shuttled the Death Star plans away from Scarif after the Rebel Alliance's first victory. A faulty hyperdrive subsystem allowed the Empire to track and intercept it over Tatooine. The captured *Tantive IV* was scheduled to be destroyed as part of a falsified report to the Senate, but the Senate was disbanded within days and the ship's destruction was no longer a priority.

THE *TANTIVE IV*

Leia has recently been reunited with her consular ship from her teen years, which was discovered moldering in a hangar in the Yarma system by a sympathetic former Imperial senator. It was returned as a gift.

Bank of 11 Corellian Engineering Corporation sublight engines

Escape pods still missing from encounter over Tatooine

Red markings once indicated consular status

Temperature-sensitive jowls

Spacer's flight vest

EL-16 blaster rifle

Flight helmet with retractable data-goggles

Survival vest with inflatable cells and gear stowage

Flight harness affixes to pilot's chair

Insulated boots re-lined with cooling inserts on Sullust

DATA FILE

SUBJECT	Kaydel Ko Connix
HOMEWORLD	Dulathia
SPECIES	Human
AFFILIATION	Resistance
HEIGHT	1.55m (5ft 1in)
AGE	22 standard years

On-duty braids

Belted combat poncho

Trusty light blaster

LIEUTENANT CONNIX

Kaydel Connix has put her past as a mutineer against Vice Admiral Holdo behind her, and still has the trust of General Organa. She has been instrumental in setting up the Resistance's Ajan Kloss operations, becoming good friends with Beaumont Kin and Rose Tico in the process. Necessity now often moves her out of control rooms and into combat zones, where she is able to exercise her impressive martial abilities against the First Order.

NIEN NUNB

A Sullustan pilot who flew with the Rebel Alliance, Nunb now flies the *Tantive IV*. Though capable as a snubfighter pilot, he is honored to fly General Organa's personal craft.

URCOS FURDAM

Furdam is of Alderaanian ancestry, though is too young to have ever set foot on Alderaan himself. He regards General Organa as royalty, and takes seriously his role as the *Tantive IV*'s co-pilot.

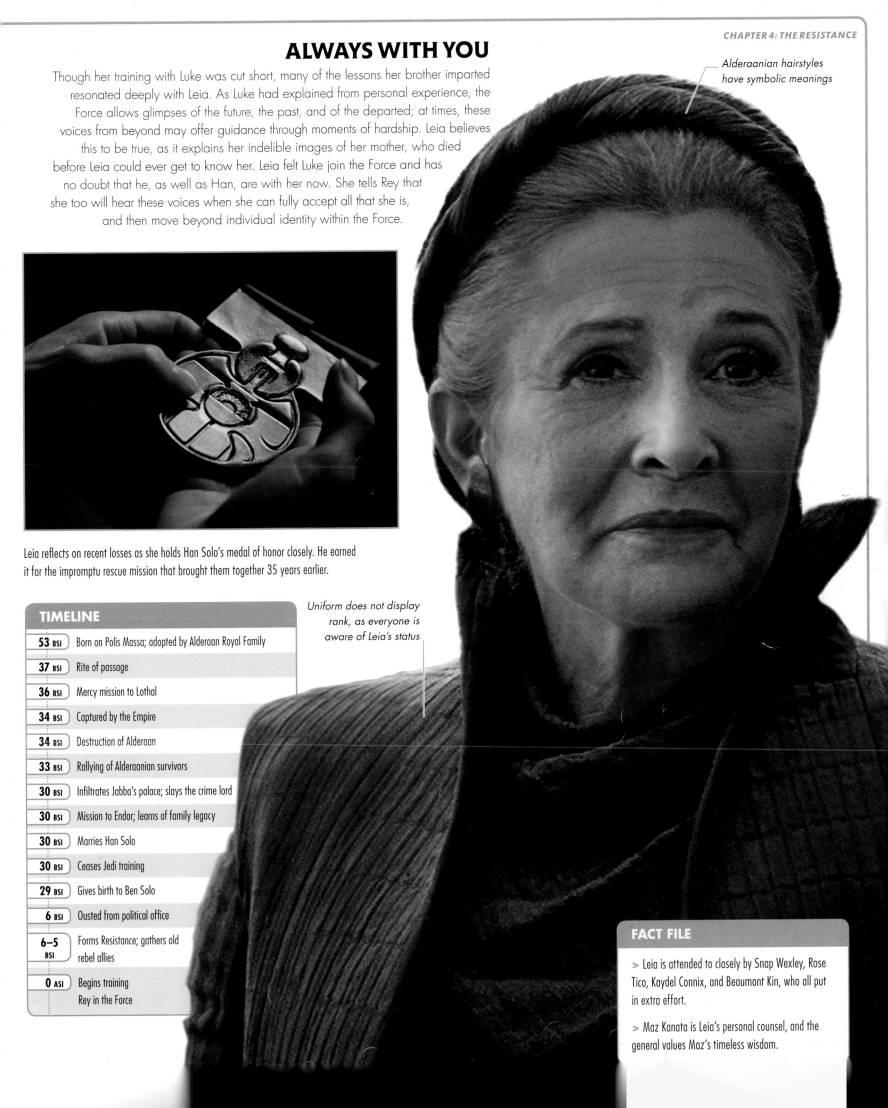

ALWAYS WITH YOU

Though her training with Luke was cut short, many of the lessons her brother imparted resonated deeply with Leia. As Luke had explained from personal experience, the Force allows glimpses of the future, the past, and of the departed; at times, these voices from beyond may offer guidance through moments of hardship. Leia believes this to be true, as it explains her indelible images of her mother, who died before Leia could ever get to know her. Leia felt Luke join the Force and has no doubt that he, as well as Han, are with her now. She tells Rey that she too will hear these voices when she can fully accept all that she is, and then move beyond individual identity within the Force.

Alderaanian hairstyles have symbolic meanings

Leia reflects on recent losses as she holds Han Solo's medal of honor closely. He earned it for the impromptu rescue mission that brought them together 35 years earlier.

Uniform does not display rank, as everyone is aware of Leia's status

TIMELINE

53 BSI	Born on Polis Massa; adopted by Alderaan Royal Family
37 BSI	Rite of passage
36 BSI	Mercy mission to Lothal
34 BSI	Captured by the Empire
34 BSI	Destruction of Alderaan
33 BSI	Rallying of Alderaanian survivors
30 BSI	Infiltrates Jabba's palace; slays the crime lord
30 BSI	Mission to Endor; learns of family legacy
30 BSI	Marries Han Solo
30 BSI	Ceases Jedi training
29 BSI	Gives birth to Ben Solo
6 BSI	Ousted from political office
6–5 BSI	Forms Resistance; gathers old rebel allies
0 ASI	Begins training Rey in the Force

FACT FILE

> Leia is attended to closely by Snap Wexley, Rose Tico, Kaydel Connix, and Beaumont Kin, who all put in extra effort.

> Maz Kanata is Leia's personal counsel, and the general values Maz's timeless wisdom.

RESTING *FALCON*

Beneath a canopy of sensor-baffling camouflage netting, the *Millennium Falcon* rests in a clearing on Ajan Kloss. The aged craft continues to serve the cause of freedom, though it is showing increasing signs of wear. A daring run of "hyperspace skipping"—a new variant of old smuggler tactics designed to evade Imperial pursuit—has exhausted its compressor systems and both sub-alternators.

RESISTANCE PILOTS

Resistance ships are often in constant action, but flesh-and-blood personnel need rest, so there are always more pilots on the roster than available craft. Starfighters, especially, are shared—though squadron leaders are typically afforded their own craft. Pilot preferences are stored in astromech droids, allowing the droids to quickly calibrate ships to pilots' profiles during pre-flight. The pilots' hardships build camaraderie among them, as they see clearly that they must rely on and trust one another if they are to defeat the First Order.

Pebbly skin is a Cingulon trait

DELLSO PRIN

A used-starship seller and mechanic, Dellso was attracted to the Resistance by the promise of working on famous starships from days past: the *Millennium Falcon* and *Tantive IV*. Loosely affiliated with the cause, he hauls cargo and supplies to Ajan Kloss.

Clasp connects to emergency ejection system

SHASA ZARO

Shasa is a Y-wing pilot and wingmate to Lega Fossang. She is also the squadron's graphic artist, applying liveries to starfighters and helmets according to each pilot's specifications. She hails from Naboo.

FreiTek life support unit

ENANAN SUPA

Enanan was formerly a StarFortress bomber pilot, but now flies a modern B-wing. She specializes in making ungainly craft appear graceful, and has exceptional situational awareness that keeps her from colliding while flying in crowded or confined battle conditions.

Flight harness connects to pilot's seat

Helmet belonged to fallen friend Nix Jerd

Visor in stowed configuration

LEGA FOSSANG

Recruited by Snap Wexley from a planetary defense force on Humbarine, Lega Fossang brought her own Y-wing fighter with her. She marks her TIE kills with graphics on her helmet, and is on her third helmet after having filled up the brims of the previous two, which she keeps in her locker as souvenirs.

PATTROS NAVESH

Navesh is a B-wing pilot from Lantillies who joined the Resistance after being recruited on Batuu. The raw firepower of the B-wing appeals to Navesh more than the speed of the smaller, swifter starfighters. He has led hit-and-run strikes against First Order Star Destroyers, and longs to take down one of the massive craft someday.

Helmet colors are based on a Lantillian grav-ball team

GARN STEWER, JR.

Service in the Resistance is a family tradition for Stewer. His father was part of the Rebel Alliance, serving as a technician at the Massassi base.

A-wing pilot's helmet

MERL COBBEN

An A-wing pilot, Cobben is one of the few survivors of the Battle of Crait. He flies to honor the memory of his fallen comrades, particularly Tallie Lintra, to whom he feels indebted for saving his life in an earlier skirmish.

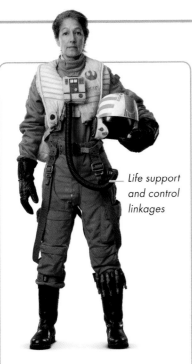

Life support and control linkages

ELNA ZIBSARA

A veteran pilot who served in the Battle of Jakku, Zibsara was recalled to active duty by Snap Wexley following the Hosnian Cataclysm. She specializes in training new recruits for the Resistance.

NIMI CHIREEN

Recruited by the late Ello Asty from the frontier world of Jaymir, Nimi and her older brother Aarton were held in reserve during the Starkiller crisis. They rejoined the core group of Resistance fighters after Crait.

Boots with positive grip soles

ALLIE SAMTA

Allie was once an infantry soldier, but she saw how desperate the Resistance was for new pilots and diligently trained under Elna Zibsara. She recently earned a slot in the rebuilt X-wing squadron.

CLEMITT POLUS

A former defense pilot from Drophun III, Polus is an avid appreciator of classic starfighter designs, and beams at the idea of flying an X-wing despite the overwhelming odds he is facing.

Padded flight gauntlet

NEW RECRUITS

The battered Resistance has had to put a strong emphasis on recruitment in order to rebuild its numbers. Given space combat's high casualty rates, it is perhaps surprising that "fighter pilot" is the most commonly requested posting for these new recruits. Theories abound that those drawn to the speed and adrenaline of fighter combat do not fear odds like most beings do, and therefore the daunting challenge of battling the First Order is not a deterrent. Others point to the glorified, romanticized portrayal of fighter pilots in past wars as a draw.

JEYO GARANAM

Old Cobalt Squadron helmet

MILLER WORLENS

HURRIE CHIND

RENK NARVIZ

"Blast and Blaze" unit slogan

Faceted visor disrupts glare angle

PACER AGOYO'S HELMET

TEZA NASZ'S HELMET

FACT FILE

> The core Resistance fighter inventory has been whittled down to around a half dozen combat-ready examples each of X-, Y-, A-, and B-wing fighters.

> In the post-Crait era, squadron groupings and names are more ad hoc than ever.

RESISTANCE ACES

After the destruction of Starkiller Base, it was inevitable that the First Order would retaliate. General Leia Organa anticipated such a move, and scattered many of her starfighter pilots to the far reaches of the galaxy to avoid concentrating all her resources at a single site. Leia ordered them to make contact with distant allies, and Snap Wexley led the survivors of Black Squadron to the Outer Rim, where they activated sleeper agents and mustered new recruits. As the Resistance was nearly wiped out at Crait, Leia's actions kept these pilots alive, and permitted them to grow the roster of desperately needed fighter craft and crews.

LEGACY: BLACK SQUADRON

Black Squadron was a special missions group formed by General Organa during the cold war between the New Republic and First Order. The squadron specialized in missions to the dangerous edges of neutral space, where it tried to collect evidence of First Order militarization to present to the Senate. Though the squadron has since disbanded, veterans Poe Dameron and Snap Wexley embody its legacy.

Visor lock and release knob

Old Cobalt Squadron logo

TYCE'S HELMET

LIEUTENANT TYCE

Wrobie Tyce was once a courier ship pilot operating out of Warlentta. When Tyce's wife, Larma D'Acy, decided to join up with the Resistance to fight the First Order, Larma first requested permission from her family. Tyce not only supported Larma, but signed up as well, adapting her commercial piloting experience for combat and flying an RZ-2 A-wing fighter. Tyce originally flew in Cobalt Squadron, a unit that defended Fabrin and supply lines in the Nanth'ri Route of the Expansion Region. She missed out on the retreat from D'Qar—which saw the rest of her squadron annihilated—as she had been reassigned to Snap Wexley. Tyce was deeply relieved to learn that D'Acy had survived the Battle of Crait.

Heat and motion-sensitive tendrils

C'AI THRENALI

A Crait survivor, C'ai Threnali has flown with Poe Dameron for years and has gained an instinctive feel for his wingmate's flight patterns. Like Dameron, Threnalli formerly flew for the New Republic. He is one of several Abednedo to have joined the Resistance, as his people were early supporters of General Organa. Threnalli has been brushing up on his speaking of Basic, but he still often lapses into Abednedo. An X-wing pilot by choice, he has also been cross-trained in other fighter types including the newer B- and Y-wing models.

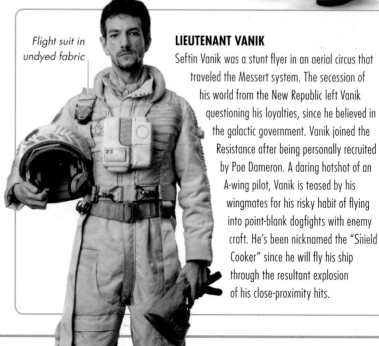

Flight suit in undyed fabric

LIEUTENANT VANIK

Seftin Vanik was a stunt flyer in an aerial circus that traveled the Messert system. The secession of his world from the New Republic left Vanik questioning his loyalties, since he believed in the galactic government. Vanik joined the Resistance after being personally recruited by Poe Dameron. A daring hotshot of an A-wing pilot, Vanik is teased by his wingmates for his risky habit of flying into point-blank dogfights with enemy craft. He's been nicknamed the "Shield Cooker" since he will fly his ship through the resultant explosion of his close-proximity hits.

MAJOR "SNAP" WEXLEY

Recon flier, Black Squadron veteran, and Starkiller Base survivor, Temmin "Snap" Wexley has been a pilot and a rebel ever since he was a teenager. His career began on his homeworld, Akiva, which he helped liberate from the Empire alongside his mother, a rebel pilot named Norra. Snap continued to fight against the Empire at Norra's side, even flying in the Battle of Jakku, and learned the finer points of piloting from his mentor, the legendary Wedge Antilles. Temmin later served as a pilot in the New Republic's precision air team, and was one of the first members of Leia Organa's Resistance. He subsequently married fellow Black Squadron member Karé Kun.

Blank space once had
New Republic service crest

FreiTek life support unit
monitors vital signals

Retractable
tinted visor

SNAP'S HELMET

Inflatable flight vest

Padded flight gauntlet
PADDED FLIGHT GAUNTLET
This pair of gauntlets was a wedding gift from Wedge Antilles to his stepson.

Guidenhauser flight
harness connects
to ejection seat

Holstered Glie-44 blaster pistol

FACT FILE

> Temmin's nickname, "Snap," stems from a habit of snapping his fingers when preoccupied.

> Snap stays close to General Organa at the request of a concerned Poe Dameron.

Emergency
signal flares

TIMELINE

45 BSI	Born to Norra and Brentin Wexley on Akiva
33 BSI	Norra leaves to join Rebellion
30 BSI	Snap is reunited with Norra on Akiva
29 BSI	Flies in Battle of Jakku
7 BSI	Joins New Republic fleet
5 BSI	Becomes part of the Resistance
0 BSI	Marries Karé Kun
0 ASI	Takes part in Battle of Starkiller Base
0 ASI	Extended recon mission
0.5 ASI	Rejoins Resistance core group
1 ASI	Flight to Exegol

Despite his best efforts, Snap has no luck translating Klaud's confusing language. Klaud finds Snap just as bewildering.

DATA FILE

SUBJECT	Temmin Wexley
HOMEWORLD	Akiva
SPECIES	Human
AFFILIATION	Resistance
HEIGHT	1.88m (6ft 2in)
AGE	46 standard years

RESISTANCE STARFIGHTERS

Months of scrounging for new ships have been offset by months of attrition, leaving the Resistance with little more than a squadron's worth of starfighters in its arsenal. What remains is a hodgepodge of fighters of different types collected from different squadrons, with mismatched insignia and colors. But the Resistance is accustomed to making do with what little resources are available, and turning differences into an advantage against the starkly uniform forces of the First Order. Fittingly, the fighters that fly for the Resistance now are descendants of the craft that flew against the Galactic Empire a generation earlier.

A green-hulled A-wing, formerly of Farrell Squadron, blends in well in the Ajan Kloss jungle, awaiting refueling and a refurbishment of its shield projectors. Pilot Seftin Vanik is eager to launch again after narrowly escaping a TIE fighter cordon over Corellia.

DATA FILE

MANUFACTURER
Kuat Systems Engineering

MODEL RZ-2 A-wing starfighter

AFFILIATION Resistance

HEIGHT 2.05m (6ft 9in)
(landing gear extended)

LENGTH 7.68m (25ft 2in)

CREW 1 pilot

WEAPONS 2 Zija GO-4 laser cannons, 2 Dymek HM-22 concussion-missile launchers (6 missiles per launcher)

Reinforced photochromic transparisteel canopy

Atmospheric stabilizer

Swiveling laser cannon

Novaldex K-88 Event Horizon engines

Forward deflector shield projector

Aerodynamic fairing for in-atmosphere operations

Towing slot for hangar positioning

A–WINGS

An upgrade of the classic RZ-1 A-wing, the modern RZ-2 improves on the reliability and efficiency of the massive Novaldex "Event Horizon" engines. The original A-wing was incredibly fast, but burnouts, loss of stability, and hull fractures could accompany sudden accelerations. Modern materials and a from-the-ground-up reintegration of the sublight engines into the vessel's frame have solved these shortcomings. Upgraded sensor systems and flight computers keep the pilot in control of maneuvers at such extreme velocities. A few A-wings from Farrell Squadron and the recently renamed Tallie Torchers carry out hit-and-run missions from Ajan Kloss.

SIDE VIEW

X-WINGS

The T-70 X-wing remains the signature vessel of the Resistance, though numbers have severely dwindled in the past year of conflict. A scant eight fighters in various states of repair reside at Ajan Kloss, with six more in deeper storage being cannibalized for parts to keep the rest functional. Fear of First Order reprisals has cut off the Resistance's access to parts and supplies, meaning ground crews work extra hard to extend the lifespans of essential components. Squadron leader Poe Dameron and second-in-command Snap Wexley have X-wings that boast the most striking paint schemes; these craft are given priority for maintenance.

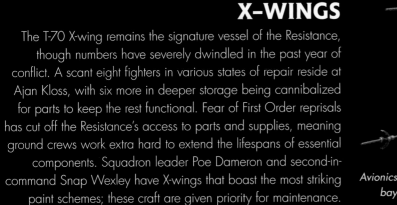

Retro thruster

Personalized livery of Temmin "Snap" Wexley

Astromech socket with R6-D8 equipped

Avionics bay

X-WING CONTROLS

As with previous versions of the X-wing, the T-70 has a simplified flight stick to reduce the learning curve for new pilots, who may only have flying experience with subtropospheric craft, such as skyhoppers and airspeeders.

Y-WING CONTROLS

The control stick's movement redirects flight attitude, while multiple trigger switches control laser cannons, ion cannons, and ordnance launcher arming and firing.

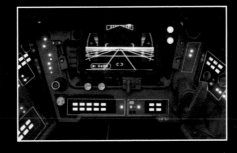

X-WING COCKPIT INTERFACE

Panels of control interfaces sit before an X-wing pilot, dedicated to power management, flight, defense, astrogation, and tactical considerations. Modern T-70s have floating-function layouts, meaning controls can be reassigned to different duties as per pilot preference.

Cannons can fire in single, dual, or quad fire modes

DATA FILE

MANUFACTURER	Incom-FreiTek
MODEL	T-70 X-wing
AFFILIATION	Resistance
HEIGHT	2.71m (8ft 11in) (landing gear extended)
LENGTH	12.48m (41ft)
CREW	1 pilot, 1 astromech
WEAPONS	4 Taim & Bak KX12 laser cannons, 2 Krupx MG7 proton torpedo launchers (8 torpedoes, standard configuration), underslung antipersonnel blaster cannon

Armored cockpit module

Fuel cell in wing spar

Sensor dome

Support spar

Ion jet-redirecting vectrals

Laser cannon barrel tip

DATA FILE

MANUFACTURER	Consolidated Koensayr Manufacturing & Holdings
MODEL	BTA-NR2 Y-wing starfighter
AFFILIATION	Resistance
HEIGHT	2.85m (9ft 4in) (landing gear extended)
LENGTH	18.17m (59ft 7in)
CREW	1 pilot, 1 astromech
WEAPONS	2 Taim & Bak IX8 laser cannons, 2 turret-mounted ArMek SW-9 ion cannons, 2 Krupx MG12 warhead launchers (variable ordnance)

Y-WINGS

The Y-wings in the Resistance are a mix of personally owned vessels and ships brought in from the defense forces of sympathetic systems. They each look a little different, as pilots have taken to modifying the craft to their preferences, including removing outer hull plates to differing degrees to have them resemble the hot-rodded craft of the Rebel Alliance. This may prove a challenge to Resistance tacticians, who have to account for varying degrees of performance and armament among the Y-wings at their disposal. It also means that these craft may prove a surprise to First Order TIE pilots attempting to shoot them down.

Y-WING COCKPIT INTERFACE

Rocker pedals control the Y-wing's port and starboard maneuvering vectrals, while the control stick affects pitch and yaw. A programmable HUD with customizable system displays removes the need for a lot of distracting instrumentation.

BTA-NR2 Y-WING
CROSS-SECTION VIEW

A venerable design that dates back to the Clone Wars, the Y-wing was long regarded as the tireless "work horse" of the Rebel Alliance starfighters. In the years following the defeat of the Empire, when the political landscape stabilized and the Alliance transitioned from underground movement to legitimate government, the Koensayr Corporation embraced its role in galactic revolution. It restarted the long-defunct Y-wing product line to sell to planetary defense fleets, proudly proclaiming it to be the "starfighter that broke the Empire's back."

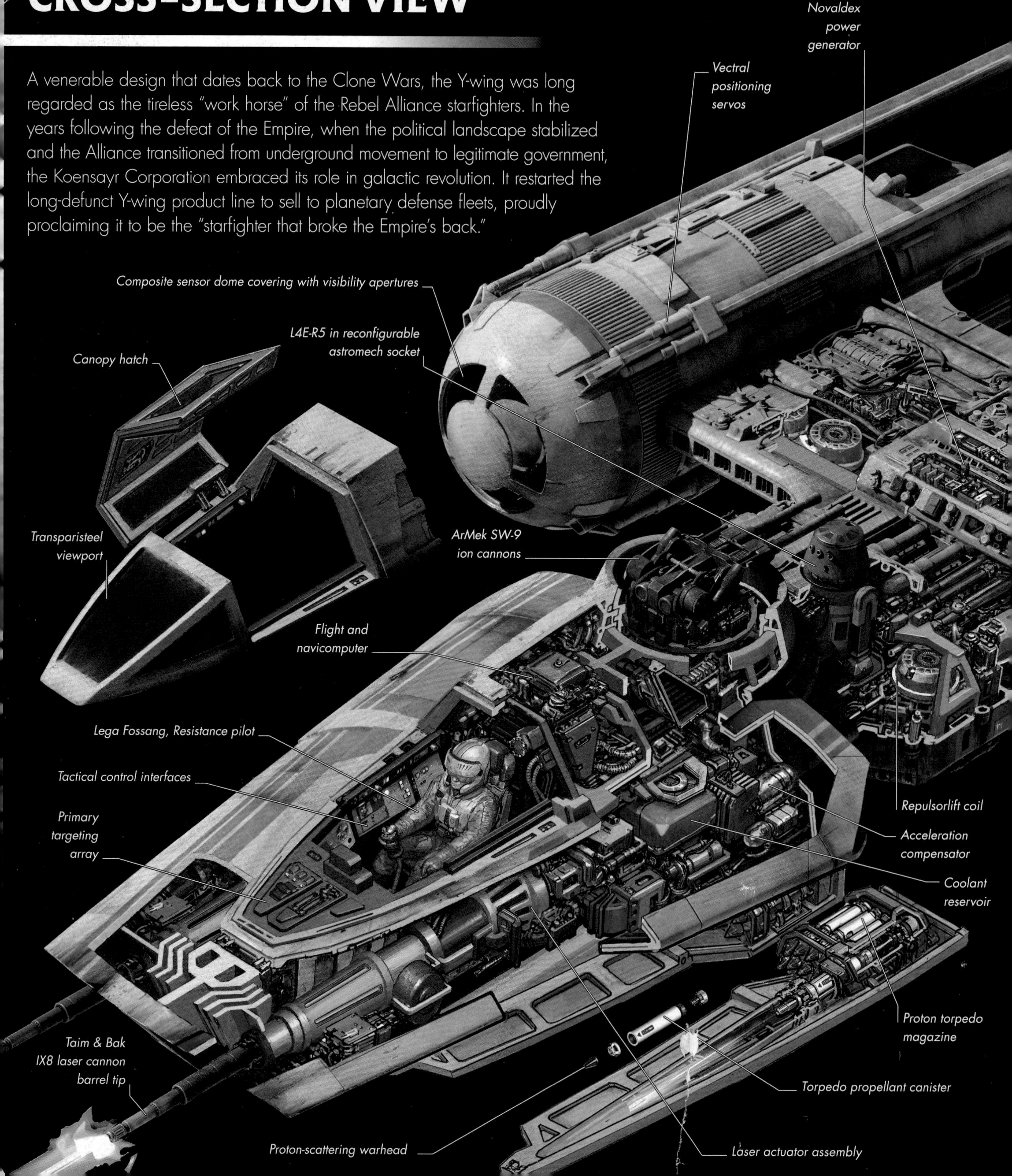

Novaldex power generator

Vectral positioning servos

Composite sensor dome covering with visibility apertures

L4E-R5 in reconfigurable astromech socket

Canopy hatch

Transparisteel viewport

ArMek SW-9 ion cannons

Flight and navicomputer

Lega Fossang, Resistance pilot

Tactical control interfaces

Primary targeting array

Repulsorlift coil

Acceleration compensator

Coolant reservoir

Taim & Bak IX8 laser cannon barrel tip

Proton torpedo magazine

Torpedo propellant canister

Proton-scattering warhead

Laser actuator assembly

BACK IN FASHION

During the Galactic Civil War, Rebel Alliance technicians modified Clone Wars-era Y-wings by removing the sleek fairing that covered the inner workings of the ship. What was originally an improvised modification born out of necessity became a design feature in the restarted BTA-NR2 models. The Alliance version of the ship was now its most iconic variant, and Koensayr's sales teams began referring to the original outer skin as optional. Standardization—once the hallmark of the early-era Y-wings—fell away in favor of a new emphasis on customization.

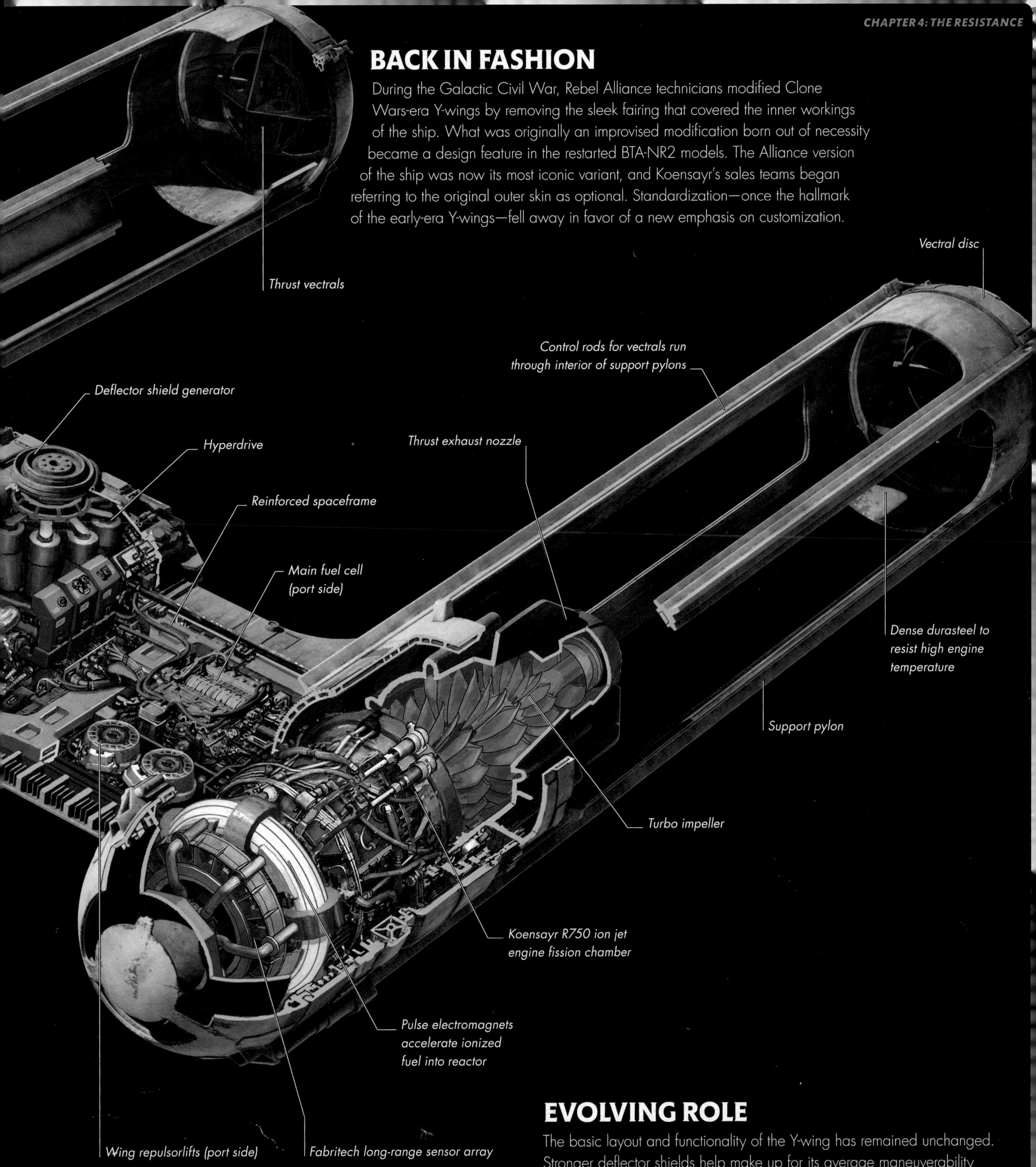

Vectral disc

Thrust vectrals

Control rods for vectrals run through interior of support pylons

Deflector shield generator

Thrust exhaust nozzle

Hyperdrive

Reinforced spaceframe

Dense durasteel to resist high engine temperature

Main fuel cell (port side)

Support pylon

Turbo impeller

Koensayr R750 ion jet engine fission chamber

Pulse electromagnets accelerate ionized fuel into reactor

EVOLVING ROLE

Wing repulsorlifts (port side)

Fabritech long-range sensor array

The basic layout and functionality of the Y-wing has remained unchanged. Stronger deflector shields help make up for its average maneuverability when compared to swifter, more fragile models. Although the Y-wing has traditionally served in the role of fighter bomber, many of the new generation models do not include ordnance launchers, particularly those that were deployed as New Republic patrol craft.

MILLENNIUM FALCON

This battered, legendary Corellian YT-1300 continues to make a difference in service to the Resistance. Since its hull-scraping flight at the Battle of Crait, the *Falcon* has been in near-continual operation, settling down only so Chewbacca can patch enough systems to ensure another takeoff. Chewie, heir to the ship, had briefly loaned it to a notorious Weequay pirate and entrepreneur in exchange for supplies needed by the Resistance. Now back on Ajan Kloss, the *Falcon* takes on missions where speed and firepower are of the essence, often with Poe Dameron at the helm since Rey is focused on other matters. Poe has gotten a feel for the eccentric ship and pushes it in ways that distress Rey and Chewie, but would undoubtedly make the late Han Solo proud.

Cockpit module, recently refitted with traditional number of seats

Starboard service bay above hold number two

Starboard docking ring

Combination neck shackle and stun cuffs

Conductive reinforced carbonite rod

BODY CUFFS
When Chewbacca is captured by the First Order, standard binders aren't sufficient to restrain him—something much stronger is required.

Keen eyes set in face with little signs of aging

Traditional Wookiee bowcaster with custom ammunition

Bowcaster ammunition and repair gear stored in bandolier

Variable payload missile launcher

Cargo-gripping mandible with Phylon C5 tractor beam emitter

CHEWBACCA

Having spent more than two centuries witnessing the rise and fall of darkness in the galaxy, Chewbacca remains decidedly apolitical. His focus is always his family, whether related by blood or by the bonds of friendship. Human lifespans are much shorter than those of Wookiees, and Chewie has had to say goodbye to many humans over the course of his long life. But he carries their spirit with him, heartened by the knowledge that his companionship has enriched their lives to some degree. Chewie's honor family now encompasses Rey, Poe, and Finn, for each of these new-generation heroes have meant so much to Han and Leia.

Well-padded feet ideal for climbing

Forward Gelieg 20m-cp Strobe/c-beam floodlight

FACT FILE

> Rose Tico has—with great reservation—installed gravimetric compensators that allow the *Falcon* to more safely execute suborbital hyperspace jumps.

> The upper turret module has been equipped with servos capable of turning the assembly at speed, increasing fire arc traversal, but at the cost of shutting down the lower turret while this feature is in use.

DATA FILE

MANUFACTURER
Corellian Engineering Corporation

MODEL Modified YT-1300 light freighter

AFFILIATION Resistance

HEIGHT 7.9m (25ft 11in)

LENGTH 34.37m (112ft 9in)

CREW 2 pilots (minimum)

WEAPONS 2 CEC AG-2G quad laser cannons, 2 Arakyd ST2 concussion missile tubes, 1 BlasTech Ax-108 "Ground Buzzer" laser cannon

LEGACY: THE *FALCON*

A once nondescript YT-1300, the *Millennium Falcon* rose to prominence under the ownership of Lando Calrissian, who modified it extensively to become a gentleman's yacht. But life on the galaxy's fringe and one haphazard Kessel Run forever scarred the ship, and it soon came under the ownership of Han Solo, who turned the *Falcon* into a legend. Smuggling contraband for gangsters like Jabba the Hutt, the *Falcon* gained a reputation for speed and navicomputer acuity that would routinely break hyperspace records. In service to the Rebel Alliance, the *Falcon* became a battle-scarred combat craft that turned the tide of several historic conflicts.

AG-2G quad laser turret assembly

Heat exhaust vent

Top hatch

Aft engineering quarter

Refurbished military-grade sensor rectenna replaces civilian-grade model

TOP-HATCH TRANSFERS
For rushed missions with no time for landings, the *Falcon* makes use of its top hatch to transfer people and—in the case of the Sinta Glacier Colony mission—information. Resistance ally Boolio hands off intel to Finn and R2-D2 via the top hatch.

INTELLIGENCE MISSION

While Rey concentrates on her Jedi studies, her companions are sent on an assignment far from Ajan Kloss. Aboard the *Millennium Falcon*, Poe Dameron, Finn, Chewbacca, and R2-D2 are joined by a helpful if hapless Trodatome named Klaud as they soar through the Sinta Glacier Colony. There, a Resistance ally promises valuable intelligence in the war effort against the First Order. It is a risky mission, as Sinta has been subjected to First Order patrols. Dameron squeezes the *Falcon* through the carved passageways in the floating ice chunk to make face-to-face contact with an agent who doesn't trust making any transmission.

R2-D2

R2 is making up for lost time, having spent years in low-power isolation during Luke Skywalker's self-imposed exile. The plucky astromech has recently returned to flight missions, flying aboard Poe Dameron's X-wing. BB-8 has been helpful in giving R2 advice about his master's piloting preferences and personal peculiarities. On the Sinta mission, R2-D2 once again becomes a repository of sensitive data, as the Resistance contact spools out a physical network cable to plug into the droid and transfer the intelligence. This data is added to R2's teeming memory banks, which already contain Death Star plans, maps to ancient Jedi temples, and backups of C-3PO's systems.

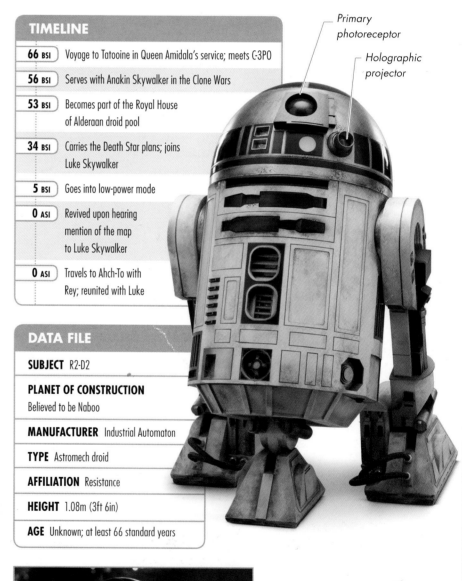

Primary photoreceptor

Holographic projector

KLAUD

Klaud's eagerness to help the Resistance expresses itself in his keen mind and a talent for the mechanical, particularly in giving new life to antiquated systems. He joins the *Millennium Falcon* crew when the Sinta mission is originally believed to be a parts pickup. When it turns out to be an intelligence operation, complete with TIE fighter pursuit, he feels understandably overwhelmed.

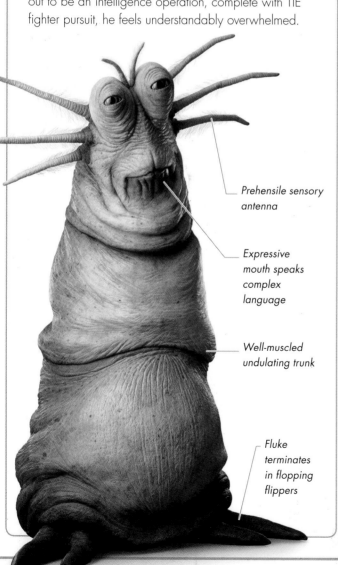

Prehensile sensory antenna

Expressive mouth speaks complex language

Well-muscled undulating trunk

Fluke terminates in flopping flippers

TIMELINE

66 BSI	Voyage to Tatooine in Queen Amidala's service; meets C-3PO
56 BSI	Serves with Anakin Skywalker in the Clone Wars
53 BSI	Becomes part of the Royal House of Alderaan droid pool
34 BSI	Carries the Death Star plans; joins Luke Skywalker
5 BSI	Goes into low-power mode
0 ASI	Revived upon hearing mention of the map to Luke Skywalker
0 ASI	Travels to Ahch-To with Rey; reunited with Luke

DATA FILE

SUBJECT R2-D2

PLANET OF CONSTRUCTION Believed to be Naboo

MANUFACTURER Industrial Automaton

TYPE Astromech droid

AFFILIATION Resistance

HEIGHT 1.08m (3ft 6in)

AGE Unknown; at least 66 standard years

R2-D2's long lifespan of uninterrupted operation without memory wipes has led to the evolution of a distinct, sophisticated personality. His friends are grateful for his initiative, which has saved the day many times.

BOOLIO

A good-natured Ovissian working as a mine overseer at the Sinta Glacier Colony, Boolio is sympathetic to the Resistance, finding a way to covertly divert surplus minerals to Resistance-friendly transports. A discrepancy in the ledger brought First Order inspectors to the mine, and Boolio thought his time was up. Instead, the inspectors left without comment, and he found a datafile had been left on his office datapad. He was able to authenticate it as a message from a First Order officer—high-ranking, from the look of the ciphers—promising game-changing intelligence. Unable to decrypt it further, Boolio contacted the Resistance via intermediaries to hand-deliver the data.

The greater of two pairs of polycerate horns

Lesser horn juts from mandible

Green complexion matches copper-rich blood

Personal temperature control unit for low-temperature worksuit

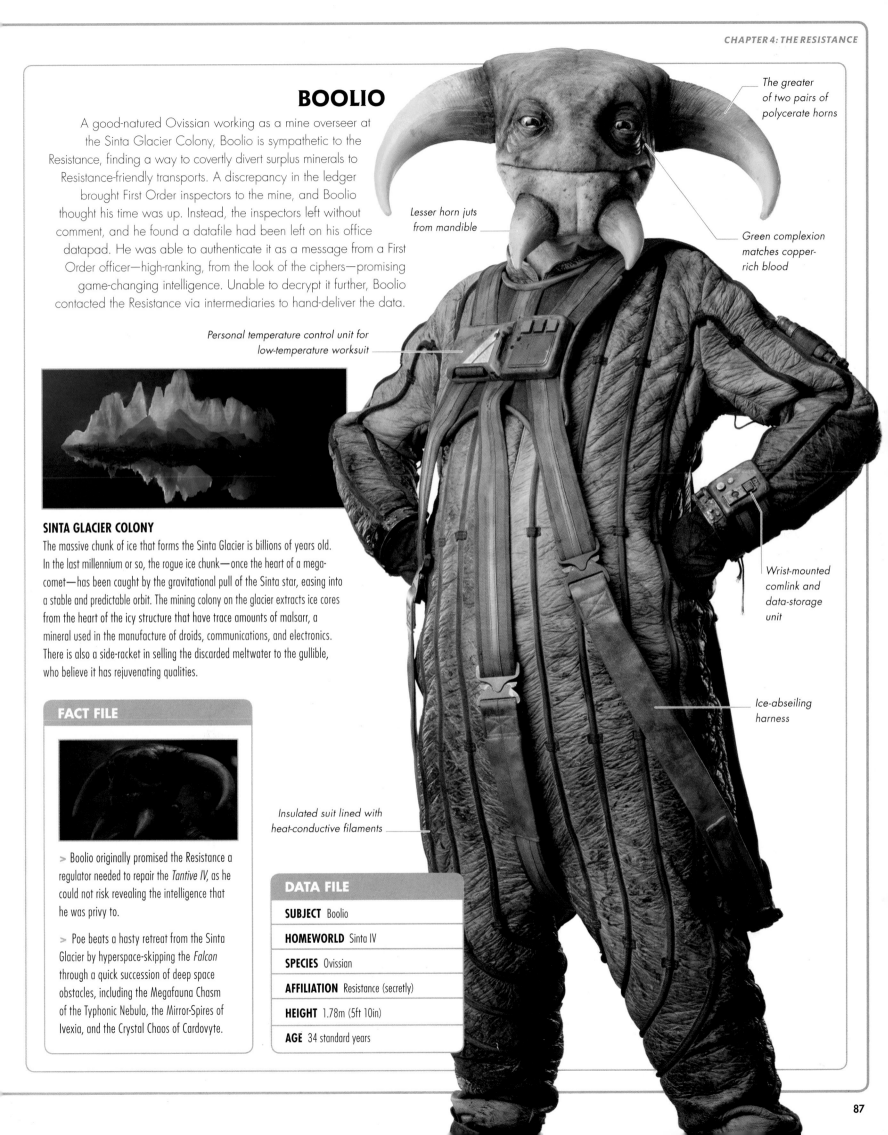

SINTA GLACIER COLONY

The massive chunk of ice that forms the Sinta Glacier is billions of years old. In the last millennium or so, the rogue ice chunk—once the heart of a mega-comet—has been caught by the gravitational pull of the Sinta star, easing into a stable and predictable orbit. The mining colony on the glacier extracts ice cores from the heart of the icy structure that have trace amounts of malsarr, a mineral used in the manufacture of droids, communications, and electronics. There is also a side-racket in selling the discarded meltwater to the gullible, who believe it has rejuvenating qualities.

Wrist-mounted comlink and data-storage unit

Ice-abseiling harness

Insulated suit lined with heat-conductive filaments

FACT FILE

> Boolio originally promised the Resistance a regulator needed to repair the *Tantive IV*, as he could not risk revealing the intelligence that he was privy to.

> Poe beats a hasty retreat from the Sinta Glacier by hyperspace-skipping the *Falcon* through a quick succession of deep space obstacles, including the Megafauna Chasm of the Typhonic Nebula, the Mirror-Spires of Ivexia, and the Crystal Chaos of Cardovyte.

DATA FILE

SUBJECT	Boolio
HOMEWORLD	Sinta IV
SPECIES	Ovissian
AFFILIATION	Resistance (secretly)
HEIGHT	1.78m (5ft 10in)
AGE	34 standard years

FINN

At first Finn was running away from something: the tyranny of the First Order. Then he ran toward someone: Rey. Now, he's committed to a cause larger than himself: the Resistance and the battle to liberate the galaxy. He has separated in his mind all that the First Order gave him—an education, military training, and the fear of its might—from all it has taken from him. He had no family, no childhood, not even a name. Finn is committed to saving the galaxy's youth from such a fate. Whereas once he might have been the most realistic about the Resistance's chances, now Finn is filled with a relentless optimism that it can—and must—be victorious.

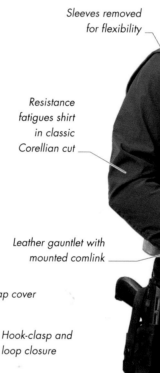

Longer hair decidedly non-regulation by First Order standards

Sleeves removed for flexibility

Resistance fatigues shirt in classic Corellian cut

Leather gauntlet with mounted comlink

Finn has seen more worlds in the past year than in his previous 20, as his missions take him from one side of the galaxy to the other. He and Poe Dameron continue to bond, though it occurs to Finn how little he actually knows about Poe.

TRAVEL SATCHEL (BACK VIEW)

Water-resistant waxed canvas over closed cell foam padded interior

Compression strap

Flap cover

Hook-clasp and loop closure

Power recharge coupler

Humidity and temperature control vent

TRAVEL SATCHEL

"WE'RE *ALL* IN THIS TO THE END."

—FINN

FACT FILE

> Poe has been teaching Finn some basics of starship piloting, since the former stormtrooper is not a natural pilot.

> Whereas once Finn could not understand binary, his time with BB-8 has increased his skills in droid interaction.

GROWING SKILLS

Finn's stormtrooper training has provided the Resistance with inside information and firsthand intelligence on enemy forces, but his lowly rank and strictly defined role within the First Order hindered his own development. The Resistance, however, needs everyone to excel beyond their boundaries to win this war. Therefore, Finn is actively developing a wider range of skills— he devotes himself to learning more about leadership, piloting, languages, and other areas. He has also shown a cautious curiosity about the Force. Finn is astounded by the feats Rey has performed, and wishes to gain some insight into something that is clearly deeply important to her.

DATA FILE

SUBJECT Finn
(Formerly FN-2187)

HOMEWORLD Unknown

SPECIES Human

AFFILIATION Resistance

HEIGHT 1.78m (5ft 10in)

AGE 24 standard years

ERDT Glie-44
blaster pistol

Finn has grown to
favor a single-hand
grip, uncommon for
a stormtrooper

Formerly a
flight jacket

EVOLVING REPUTATION

Finn has grown beyond the moniker "ex-stormtrooper" in the minds of his fellow Resistance crew. Time and again, he has placed his life on the line on daring missions for General Organa's cause. On the moon of Avedot, he and Poe raided an abandoned New Republic supply cache. He undertook risky supply runs with Chewbacca, and helped liberate the Tevellans from First Order occupation alongside Poe and BB-8. He even donned stormtrooper armor once more, infiltrating the *Finalizer* on a mission that resulted in Supreme Leader Ren's Star Destroyer being severely damaged over Batuu. General Organa sees great potential in Finn, and admires the initiative he has taken in the past months.

Identification plaque

Coded cylinder
with stolen First
Order access
codes

Fast-draw
holster
with spare
blaster gas
ampules

Finn gears up for another mission, confident that in the company of his closest friends he will succeed.

POE DAMERON

Poe Dameron has grown much during his time with the Resistance. Under General Organa's guidance, he has tempered his impulsive nature and learned to lead responsibly. These were hard-learned lessons that have molded Dameron into a command position for the inevitable, yet unthinkable, day when Leia can no longer lead the fight against tyranny. As Poe becomes more determined to face that future, he finds himself revisited by echoes of his reckless past, from a time before his service to the Resistance, and even predating his stint with the New Republic.

> "I GOT US BACK,
> DIDN'T I?"
>
> —POE DAMERON, SEEKING ACKNOWLEDGMENT

POE'S X-WING

Poe's beloved *Black One* did not survive the evacuation of D'Qar, but he has gotten used to his replacement fighter. On occasion, he will temporarily recolor its white-and-orange hull with a tribute to his old livery.

Sensor array inside armored nosecone

R2-D2 in astromech socket

Fusial thrust engine

Scissor-split S-foil in attack position

REFINED COCKPIT

Incom-FreiTek designed the T-70 X-wing with input from Alliance veterans, who described their preferences and gripes from their experiences behind the stick. The layout of its cockpit is based on this invaluable feedback.

GLIE-44 BLASTER PISTOL
Poe's favored side-arm is the Glie-44, due to its lightweight, rugged construction.

Desert scarf protects against sun and sand

Bandolier with tactical dump pouches

Runyip-leather pilot gloves

Gunslinger's belt

Satchel carries a medpac, emergency rations, and other useful gear

Leather strap

Dump pouches filled with ammunition cells and blaster repair tools

Simple metal loop latch

POE'S SATCHEL

Weatherproofed adventurer boots

EXPERT ADVENTURER

Though his reputation as a hero of the skies is well earned, Poe is also a capable field agent. He has logged numerous undercover missions alongside Black Squadron operatives in service to the Resistance. His latest, planet-hopping adventure takes him to Pasaana, Kijimi, and Kef Bir, where his subterfuge skills are just as needed as his flight abilities. While Poe may not fully fathom this assignment's impact on matters of the Force, what matters most to him is that it makes a difference to his closest friends—Finn and Rey.

CHECKERED PAST

Poe rebelled during his adventure-seeking teenage years when his father, an Alliance veteran named Kes, attempted to instill some responsibility in him. Poe ran away from his home on Yavin 4 and fell in with the wrong crowd—specifically, the Spice Runners of Kijimi. These dangerous criminals would have killed Poe had he not proven to be an amazing pilot. After a career as a young pirate and smuggler, Poe returned to his familial home to find that all would be forgiven if he forged a straighter path. Poe then began his service in the New Republic, and later joined the Resistance.

Standby indicator light

Rotator and attachment mount

Voltage, charge, resistance, and current probes

Stainless steel grip

MULTI-PRONG ELECTROMETER

Electronic imaging objective plate

Traditional macrobinoculars

TG4.4 FIELD QUADNOCULARS

Rarely clean shaven

Breathable micromesh screened Resistance shirt

Pouch contains emergency food pellets

Poe broke his left arm in a childhood glider crash

Glowrods in satchel prove useful in caves on Pasaana

TIMELINE

32 BSI	Born on Yavin 4
26 BSI	Starts learning how to fly in his mother's A-wing
24 BSI	Poe's mother, Shara, dies
16 BSI	Poe runs away from home; joins Spice Runners
11 BSI	Returns home
7 BSI	Begins Academy training
4 BSI	Flies with the New Republic
3 BSI	Joins Resistance
2 BSI	Leads missions with Black Squadron
0.5 BSI	Recruits Kazuda Xiono
0 BSI	Captured by Kylo Ren; befriends Finn
0 ASI	Attempts mutiny aboard *Raddus*; meets Rey
0.5 ASI	Leads attack against *Finalizer* over Batuu
1 ASI	Flies *Millennium Falcon* to Sinta Glacier Colony

DATA FILE

SUBJECT	Poe Dameron
HOMEWORLD	Yavin 4
SPECIES	Human
AFFILIATION	Resistance
HEIGHT	1.72m (5ft 8in)
AGE	33 standard years

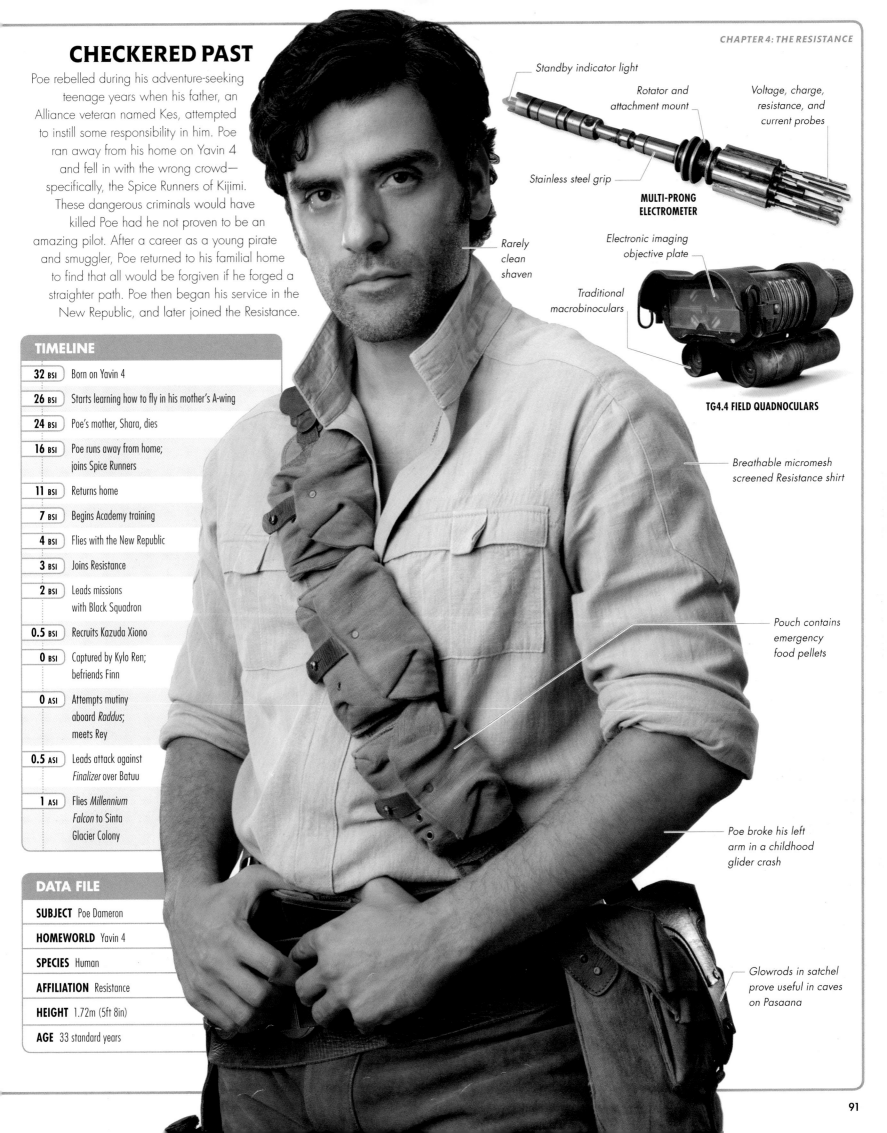

BEAUMONT KIN

Beaumont Kin was on track to become one of the youngest professors at the Lerct Historical Institute when the First Order destroyed the Hosnian system. While most of the faculty were taken by surprise, Beaumont had predicted that a cataclysmic act of war was long overdue, based on his study of First Order and New Republic brinkmanship and its historical precedents. Rather than allow future acts of apocalyptic destruction to occur unchallenged, Kin abandoned his academic career to become a captain in the Resistance's intelligence division. He offers his wide knowledge on a variety of topics as circumstances require.

INTO ACTION

Though he came to the Resistance without any combat experience, Beaumont's passion for informal university grav-ball games kept him active. He has since plunged into combat training, assisted by Rose Tico and Kaydel Connix. The three have become good friends.

Water-shedding weatherproof field jacket

Protective antiglare goggles

BlasTech EL-16 blaster rifle

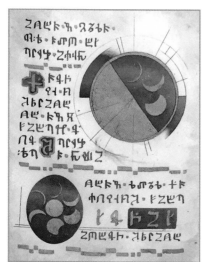

Attending a Resistance command briefing, Beaumont is surprised and dismayed that his esoteric knowledge of Sith history has become relevant to the current crisis facing the galaxy.

Holstered ERDT Glie-44 blaster pistol

STUDENT OF HISTORY

Beaumont's keen mind devours historical research. He has a particular fascination with the early Republic era that directly followed the vanquishing of the Sith a millennium ago. Perhaps unwisely, given the sinister histories that surround them, he has visited sites on Malachor, Moraband, and Devaron, following in the footsteps of ancient Jedi and Sith and the long-forgotten conflicts that shaped the galaxy. Kin can also read several ancient languages; when he learned that Rey had in her possession sacred Jedi texts he jumped at the chance to translate some of them. He has become a helpful assistant to Rey, deciphering original passages as well as interpreting some of the cryptic notes left behind by Luke Skywalker.

FACT FILE

> Kin is fluent in nine languages, including four ancient dead ones.

> Kin maintains a correspondence with Rebel Alliance historian Voren Na'al, whom he met at the Arhul Hextrophon School of Embedded Journalism on Lerct.

In the shadow of the *Tantive IV*, Beaumont feels the weight of history press down upon him. He has carefully studied the ship's history and, like many, had always assumed the Empire had destroyed it prior to the Battle of Yavin.

Beaumont analyzes the recon data brought in by flyers like Snap Wexley, not only to get a current view of the galactic struggle but to extrapolate, based on historical precedent, what may come next.

ESOTERIC KNOWLEDGE

As intelligence reveals that the First Order is in league with Sith loyalists in the Unknown Regions, Beaumont's knowledge of the occult becomes a military asset. He had studied such esoterica in his academic career, having set foot on worlds once blighted by active Sith temples. He was fascinated by the lengths the Sith would go to stave off death, including the pillaging of worlds with any reputation in genetic sciences. Most in the galaxy know little of this history, as the Old Republic attempted to suppress it. Even now, most galactic citizens have no idea that Emperor Palpatine was the last known and prominent Sith adherent, though those in Resistance circles are more likely to be aware.

Beard grown out in attempt to look more "professorial"

DATA FILE

SUBJECT	Beaumont Kin
HOMEWORLD	Lerct
SPECIES	Human
AFFILIATION	Resistance
HEIGHT	1.7m (5ft 7in)
AGE	40 standard years

Pocket contains notes Kin has taken concerning the Jedi texts

Sewn rank indicators have replaced rank plaques in the Resistance

Code cylinders in shoulder pocket

Outdated regiment listing from when the Resistance was larger

Kin still adopts teacher's stance he perfected during his lecturing days

Blaster gas sealing cap

RESISTANCE COMMANDERS

Age and combat attrition have taken their toll on the senior command staff of the Resistance. Now that the full extent of the First Order's war plan has revealed itself, it has become clear that many elders of the Rebel Alliance command were specifically targeted to remove them as threats early on. What at the time had seemed like a streak of unrelated tragedies had actually been shaped by the invisible hand of the burgeoning First Order. It now falls to a new generation of leadership to carry on the cause.

MAZ KANATA

Maz has seen wars come and go in her more than a thousand years of life, but this one feels different to her. With her age, wisdom, and attunement to the Force, she sees familiar patterns following new paths, and senses that the coming conflict is the culmination of a struggle that has spanned her entire lifetime. Not a frontline combatant, Kanata stays in the Resistance base, never far from Leia Organa, to whom she dispenses invaluable advice.

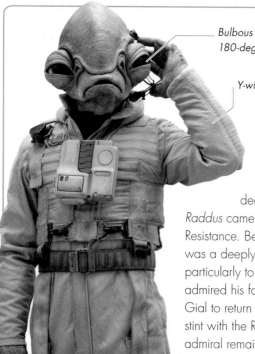

Bulbous Mon Calamari eyes provide 180-degree arc of vision

Y-wing pilot's uniform

AFTAB ACKBAR

Gial Ackbar's sudden death aboard the cruiser *Raddus* came as a heavy blow to the Resistance. Beyond the tactical loss, it was a deeply personal loss for many, particularly to young Aftab who greatly admired his father. Aftab had implored Gial to return to retirement after a brief stint with the Resistance. That the elder admiral remained in command until the very end is a legacy Aftab now must live up to. Aftab's recruitment was part of a larger effort to bring more Mon Calamari aid to the Resistance.

Electronics removed from macroscope to rely on basic optics

COMMANDER GARTFRAN

Kurksel Gartfran had no particular love for the New Republic, but sees the First Order as far worse. He is fiercely independent, and sees fighting as part of the Resistance to be the best possible way to preserve that independence. A born survivalist, Gartfran embraces the challenge of roughing it in wild terrain. Ajan Kloss appeals to him, as he feels most at home in the complete absence of civilization.

JUNGLE X-HOPPER

The jungle X-hopper is a compact starship custom-crafted by Rose Tico and the Resistance engineering division from surplus found in a New Republic depot. Its frame is a repurposed T-65 X-wing cockpit, fitted with repulsorcoils, thrusters, and steering vanes. Rose calls it a "mini-rig," harkening back to an earlier era of compact design. It assists with air traffic control, guiding ships in and out of the jungle.

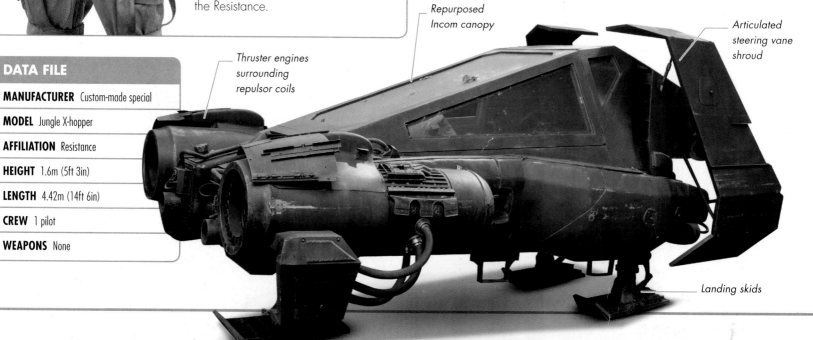

Repurposed Incom canopy

Articulated steering vane shroud

Thruster engines surrounding repulsor coils

Landing skids

DATA FILE	
MANUFACTURER	Custom-made special
MODEL	Jungle X-hopper
AFFILIATION	Resistance
HEIGHT	1.6m (5ft 3in)
LENGTH	4.42m (14ft 6in)
CREW	1 pilot
WEAPONS	None

Scarf was a gift from Wrobie Tyce

COMMANDER D'ACY

Formerly a fleet officer aboard the *Raddus*, Larma D'Acy has stepped into a broader strategic command position, personally advising General Leia Organa on First Order movements and tactics. She has loosened up from her more conventional fleet role, rolling up her sleeves to participate in the hands-on work of getting the Ajan Kloss outpost operational.

Fabric-covered sholapith helmet

MAJOR ANGON

A botanist before he joined the Resistance, Fadros Angon must stay focused on his duties lest he be distracted by the wealth of plant life surrounding the Resistance outpost on Ajan Kloss. With permission from General Organa, he scouts the perimeters for samples that may prove promising to use in equipment, food, or medicine.

LIEUTENANT CHIREEN

From Jaymir, Aarton Chireen was recruited but then held in reserve, being asked instead to gather what intelligence he could in his local area of operation. The Hosnian Cataclysm accelerated his involvement, calling him and his sister into active duty. As part of the Ajan Kloss command staff, Chireen serves as a quartermaster, allocating resources to the soldiers, pilots, and technicians in need. His sister, Nimi, pilots an X-wing fighter.

FACT FILE

> Rose has developed a custom proton bomb for delivery by B- and Y-wing fighters that she has nicknamed "the Paiger," in honor of her late sister.

> Rose has developed modifications in hyperdrive systems that make it harder for First Order systems to track ships. It requires making risky jumps within the gravitational curve of planets, then compensating for the trajectory shift post-jump.

ROSE TICO

Rose has risen through the ranks from lowly engineering support technician to military commander. She leads the Engineering Corps in making the necessary modifications to keep the Resistance's gear operational, as well as countering new advancements in First Order technology. She has a grudging respect for First Order science, but is eager to capture it to repurpose it for a better cause. Rose has been particularly useful in developing communication systems to bypass First Order jamming or interception methods, working closely with the Resistance droid pool to construct new biohexacrypt codes.

DATA FILE

SUBJECT	Rose Tico
HOMEWORLD	Hays Minor
SPECIES	Human
AFFILIATION	Resistance
HEIGHT	1.57m (5ft 2in)
AGE	24 standard years

Hair tied back to avoid getting caught in machinery

Rose doesn't care for signs of rank

Open collar indicates warm Ajan Kloss weather; Rose hails from a cold planet

Haysian smelt medallion, originally one of a pair

RESISTANCE SUPPORT

The ramshackle nature of the Ajan Kloss base means its support personnel are more visible than in past outposts. They diligently keep the headquarters functional, building out the base while supporting its operations. These beings work tirelessly so that the command and combat staff can focus on their priorities, never having to worry about facilities or infrastructure. Their work may go unsung, but the Resistance would collapse without the help of its techs, engineers, analysts, and quartermasters.

Vintage DH-17 blaster rifle

SEOSSRA THWISP

A one-time Resistance spy from Caphexdis who kept tabs on First Order activities along the borderlands, Thwisp was recalled when the cold war heated up following the Hosnian Cataclysm. She is now an intelligence analyst, offering up her accumulated expertise in First Order activity. The action against the Exegol reinforcements gives her an opportunity to return to the field.

Soaked scarf prevents distraction by nearby scents

VAZZET DIPTERZ

A Cyclorrian technician who rides a loadlifter workframe, Vazzet is a taskmaster who lords it over the Cyclorrian swarm that has committed itself to the Resistance. Though non-Cyclorrians—humans in particular—may find Vazzet's managerial approach overbearing, it is culturally acceptable among his kind and produces efficient results. Vazzet is rarely ever seen off his workframe, which some have likened to a walking throne despite its industrial origins.

Lifter carriage with magnetized forks

Carrying handle

FUEL CANISTER

Suspension servomotors and exposed gyro-balance systems

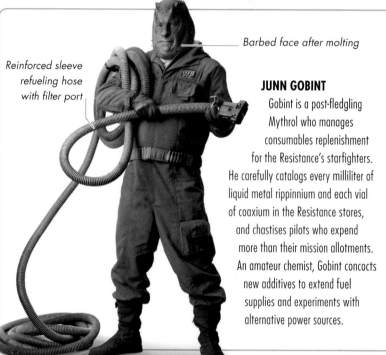

Reinforced sleeve refueling hose with filter port

Barbed face after molting

JUNN GOBINT

Gobint is a post-fledgling Mythrol who manages consumables replenishment for the Resistance's starfighters. He carefully catalogs every milliliter of liquid metal rippinnium and each vial of coaxium in the Resistance stores, and chastises pilots who expend more than their mission allotments. An amateur chemist, Gobint concocts new additives to extend fuel supplies and experiments with alternative power sources.

HUPER TENRECS

A Talpiddian weapons specialist, Tenrecs serves as armorer for the Ajan Kloss outpost. His visual acuity at extremely close ranges gifts him with unrivaled repair skills perfect for the upkeep and modification of weaponry. He is effectively face-blind when it comes to distinguishing Resistance members, particularly humans. He recognizes people by their gear.

Hair stands on end as threat gesture, or when nervous

EL-16HFE blaster rifle with acoustic aiming aid

Traditional Reesarian locks

Sharp eyesight can see in ultraviolet and infrared

Leg bindings keep out insects and moisture

PHENLASS AND ODLA SUR

Phenlass and Odla Sur joined the Resistance as a pair, having sworn a vow of companionship as part of their marriage. Soldiers and scouts, they employ their precise senses in reconnoitering the outlying jungle beyond the Resistance base perimeter, seeking out dangers and resources alike. They've been able to detect freshwater springs by sound and scent alone, and have plotted migratory paths of local fauna based on examination of the underbrush. As bonded Reesarians, they are highly attuned to each other's whereabouts.

Graying beard typical of aging Tarsunt

IBDUN DAND

Father to Resistance technician Vober Dand, Ibdun joined the cause after the Hosnian Cataclysm. Ibdun originally forbade Vober from being part of the Resistance, fearing the worst. It was only after the First Order's ruthlessness was revealed to the galaxy that Ibdun truly appreciated his son's bravery. He now serves with Vober in the ground crew, learning more about his son from those who work with him.

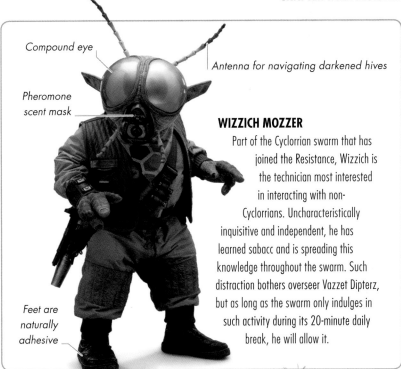

Compound eye

Antenna for navigating darkened hives

Pheromone scent mask

WIZZICH MOZZER

Part of the Cyclorrian swarm that has joined the Resistance, Wizzich is the technician most interested in interacting with non-Cyclorrians. Uncharacteristically inquisitive and independent, he has learned sabacc and is spreading this knowledge throughout the swarm. Such distraction bothers overseer Vazzet Dipterz, but as long as the swarm only indulges in such activity during its 20-minute daily break, he will allow it.

Feet are naturally adhesive

Mechanized magnigoggles

YIPSIT

The Shahkirin mechanic known only as Yipsit is part of the *Tantive IV* refurbishment crew. He scales its armored surface with an innate confidence borne of having grown up on the cliff-faces of Bestine IV. His diminutive size and compressible cartilaginous skeleton allows him to crawl deep into access tunnels that wouldn't fit a human adult.

TWYLOPE NUR

Nur is an amiable Mohsenian with large eyes and a pronounced snout lined with sensitive olfactory receptors. He is well-suited for his role as a field medic, since he can smell illness and injury, as well as the body's natural defenses against them. In this way he can diagnose patients quickly and accurately and administer appropriate treatment.

Dexterous claw fingers, originally evolved for digging

FACT FILE

> Resistance support crew are expected to log combat training hours so everyone can do their part defending against the First Order if required.

> The lack of barracks on Ajan Kloss means most of the support crew live and sleep aboard the *Tantive IV* when not on duty.

RESISTANCE DROIDS

With only minimal repair facilities available on Ajan Kloss and rough cave floors instead of polished hallways beneath their wheels, feet, or treads, the droids of the Resistance join their organic colleagues in "roughing it" in their new jungle home. The damp conditions are especially trying for droids, and technicians work diligently to ensure their delicate electronic innards stay dry. Some astromechs are extra eager for flight assignments, since this allows them to escape the rainforest humidity to the vacuum of space.

R6–LE5

Dome housing Intellex VIII computer system

A counterpart to R2-SHP, "Leefive" is a freed astromech not belonging to any master. She follows the rank hierarchy as dictated by Resistance protocols, but defines her service as strictly voluntary. She and her counterpart carry out routine repairs and maintenance on the *Tantive IV*, ensuring its function as the command hub of the Ajan Kloss outpost.

OC-JK14

Multi-spectrum photoreceptor

Plasteel drum body

An older, treadwell-style astromech droid of a type once popular in the Outer Rim, OC-JK14 roams the undergrowth on Ajan Kloss, looking to be productive. Often underfoot, "Seejay" is overlooked by Resistance members drawn to the more traditional astromechs, but quietly tends to low-priority maintenance jobs, crossing off to-do lists that few ever look at.

Recessed door contains a variety of tool-tipped manipulators

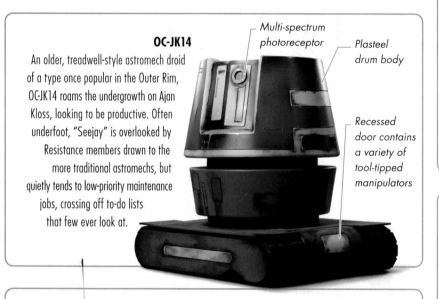

R6-D8

Primary photoreceptor

Snap Wexley's loyal astromech, R6, has flown with him since he joined the Resistance. In studying Wexley's logs, R6 has come across mention of Mister Bones, a deadly battle droid that Wexley programmed in his teen years. In an effort to please his master, R6 has attempted to dial up his aggression index, but does not dare overwrite the factory-set safety inhibitors in his personality matrix.

Central processing dome housing AA-5 VerboBrain

Vocabulator port

AD-4M

"Aydee" is an administrative droid tasked with data processing and traffic management, handling the logistics of base operations. Though Aydee was more usually isolated in some sort of control room, shielded from interacting with other personnel, the unfinished nature of the Ajan Kloss base puts Aydee in direct contact with the Resistance crew. They jokingly refer to Aydee as the "concierge," and make requests for luxury goods found only at well-appointed hotels. Caught out more than once, Aydee has rewritten a subroutine to help filter out sarcasm, with mixed results.

Logic function display

Shoulder articulation joint

R2-SHP

R6-LE5's counterpart, "Shep," is the more gregarious of the two "sibling" droids, rolling in to help wherever he thinks it may be needed. An older R2 unit who has undergone frequent upgrades and refits to stay contemporary, Shep shows an earnestness that may stem from a fear of obsolescence.

BB-8

BB-8 continues to serve the Resistance loyally, though he is now more likely to be found by Rey's side instead of flying into combat with Poe Dameron. As Poe's responsibilities have changed and he spends less time in an X-wing, he has asked his droid to keep the increasingly isolated Rey company. BB-8 carries out this assignment with enthusiasm, for he has trusted Rey ever since their early encounters on Jakku. It is also not the first time BB-8 has had an extended separation from Poe, having spent a length of time aboard a fueling station on Castillon as part of a spy mission.

TIMELINE

5 BSI	Manufactured on Hosnian Prime
4 BSI	Assigned to Poe Dameron in New Republic Defense Fleet
3 BSI	Joins the Resistance with Poe
0.5 BSI	Spy mission on Castillon
0 BSI	Reunited with Poe; meets Rey on Jakku
0 ASI	Accompanies Finn and Rose on mission to disrupt hyperspace tracker
1 ASI	Observes Rey's Jedi training on Ajan Kloss

Primary photoreceptor with floating lens assembly

High-frequency receiver antenna

Articulated holoprojector array and work light

Stainless inoxium "chin"

Tool-bay disc fastening rim (replaced after damage)

BB-8 stays updated with frequently swapped out tool-bay discs

DATA FILE

SUBJECT BB-8

PLANET OF CONSTRUCTION Hosnian Prime

MANUFACTURER Industrial Automaton

TYPE Astromech droid

AFFILIATION Resistance

HEIGHT 0.67m (2ft 2in)

AGE 6 standard years

CHAPTER 5:
PASAANA

The spy report from deep inside the First Order ranks arms the Resistance with vital intelligence: their enemy is readying a new fleet at Exegol. Reaching this ancient world in the Unknown Regions is a problem, but the path to a potential solution can be found in the Jedi texts, penned by Luke Skywalker himself. Years earlier, he had been pursuing leads regarding a Sith wayfinder that would point to Exegol, but that investigation dried up in the deserts of Pasaana. It is a tenuous lead, but it is all the Resistance has. With Leia's blessing, Rey takes Luke's lightsaber in hand and unites with her friends—Finn, Poe, Chewbacca, BB-8, and C-3PO—to begin the quest for Exegol on Pasaana.

PASAANA

Desert planets may have a reputation for desolation, but Pasaana is bursting with life and culture. Towering buttes of granite and sandstone disrupt long stretches of sun-bleached dunes and shrubland, creating shadowed valleys where water—and therefore life—collects. The native Aki-Aki recognize and revere both the tenacity and fragility of life, welcoming offworlders with open arms during their biennial festival season, when food and water are plentiful and ready for sharing. Between such celebrations, the Aki-Aki live an austere life, gathering food and water for the next grand event. They adopt a few advanced tools to aid in their survival, but otherwise maintain a pre-starflight level of civilization. No spaceports dot Pasaana's surface, but visitors are common.

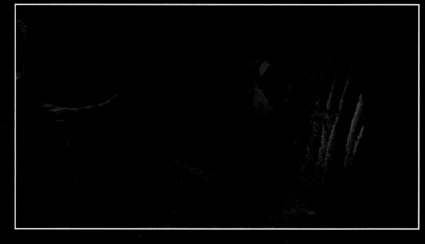

CAVE SYSTEMS
Beneath the desert surface are caves that lead to freshwater aquifers. The presence of burrowing predators keeps the Aki-Aki from overexploiting this resource, but brave spelunkers have tapped these troves to create wells from which spring towns and farms. Telltale signs of possible aquifers include shifting mires—quicksand deposits that can swallow a downed skiff whole.

"YOU BEEN? CAN'T GET A DECENT MEAL THERE. AT LEAST PASAANA'S UNOCCUPIED."

—BEAUMONT KIN

Tufts aid in detecting wind direction

Ear channels radiate excess heat

Sensitive eyes vibrate along with ears so that oki-poki can "see" sounds

Half-eaten thistlebuzzer

OKI-POKI

NATIVE FAUNA
Inquisitive rodents, oki-poki have sensitive hearing and vision to alert them to danger. These furred cliff-dwelling creatures feed on thistlebuzzers, gorpions, and other insects. Some Aki-Aki have domesticated them to rid crops of pests.

DESERT FARMING
A rare example of modern technology eagerly embraced by the Aki-Aki can be found in the dustgrain farms they maintain. The desert winds of Pasaana carry seeds and spores amid the clouds of blown sand. Using specialized electro-sifters, a farmer can pluck these organic kernels from the silicate gusts, dragging them into collection hoppers. The pole-shaped sifters also contain moisture vaporator technology, allowing a grid of these easy-to-maintain devices to turn a stretch of arid landscape into an irrigated underground garden known as a dust farm. The phedrugrass and termania-spore that grow in these farms form daily dietary staples for entire Aki-Aki communities.

DATA FILE

REGION Ombakond sector, Expansion Region

DIAMETER 11,135 km (6,919 miles)

TERRAIN Desert bluffs and dunes

MOONS 1

POPULATION Approximately 500,000 Aki-Aki
(no formal census has ever been undertaken)

The Ikledu Wastes

Jamtareen Mountains

Aki-Ktura
farming community
(population 3,000)

FORBIDDEN VALLEY
*This rocky valley is the site of
the Festival of the Ancestors.*

FACT FILE

> Pasaana was a stop on the system-hopping walkabout
that Luke Skywalker undertook after the Battle of Endor,
when he sought to uncover lost lore of past Jedi and Sith.

> The First Order has no established presence on Pasaana,
as the world's meager resources and sparse population do
not make it a worthwhile target. However, the influx of
visitors for the Festival of the Ancestors warrants the
dispatching of TIE fighters and stormtrooper patrols.

FESTIVAL OF THE ANCESTORS

Every two years, as recorded by Pasaana's 378 standard-day journey around its sun, the desert planet sprouts colorful new life in the form of a vivid celebration. Named the Festival of the Ancestors, this event honors the past and looks to the future. Even a galaxy at war cannot stop this tradition, and the Forbidden Valley teems with more than 500,000 revelers. The native Aki-Aki comprise most of the attendees, but the event attracts all manner of species and cultures from surrounding sectors and beyond. The centerpiece of the festival is an immense circle of bonfires that serves as the symbolic portal to the ancestors, a gateway to the place where the Aki-Aki believe departed spirits live on.

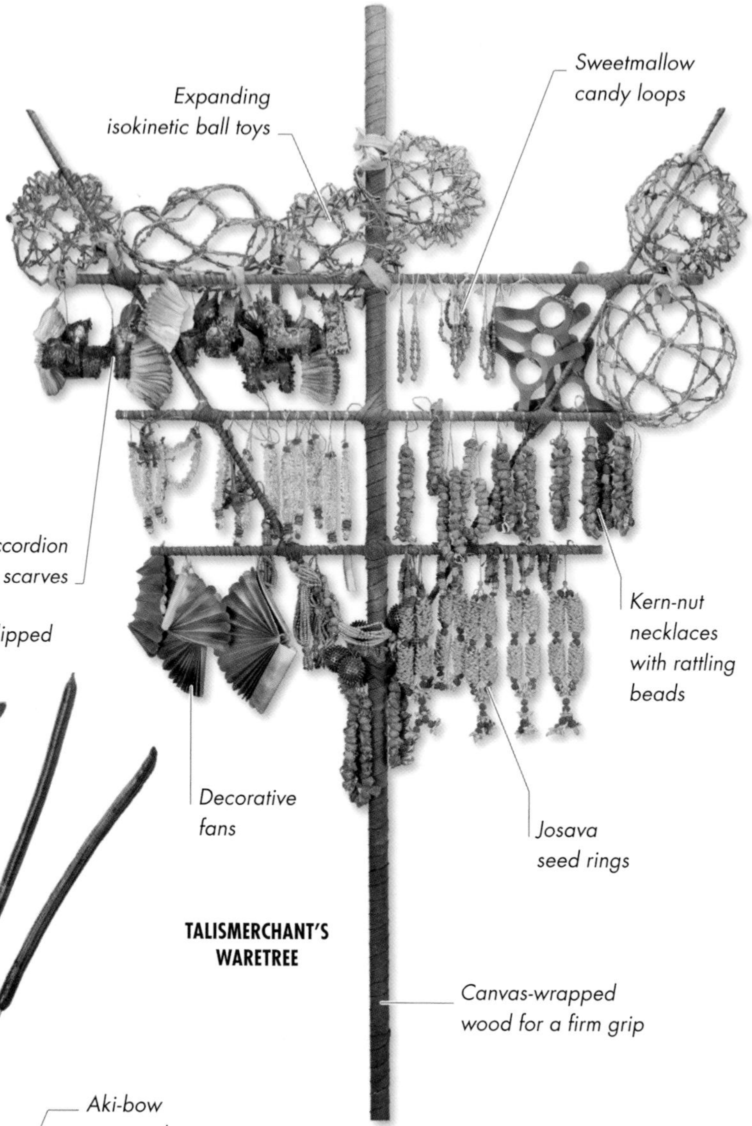

SALES AND CELEBRATION

The talismerchants that weave their way through the crowds at the festival drum up attention with colorful, noisy dances. Some carry food and jewelry, while others carry totems to serve as effigies to burn in the bonfires. A wide spectrum of hand-crafted wares are for sale—in exchange for credits or to be bartered for other goods. Most sales go to offworlders, as the tourists come looking for a keepsake from the festival, as well as something to burn.

Expanding isokinetic ball toys

Sweetmallow candy loops

Accordion scarves

Kern-nut necklaces with rattling beads

Fried chu-reed dipped in melon sugar

Decorative fans

Josava seed rings

TALISMERCHANT'S WARETREE

Canvas-wrapped wood for a firm grip

Color-coded flavors, ranging from sweet (yellow) to spicy-sour (purple)

Aki-bow carry yoke

Water-carrying orb

TANRUKA NAMHI, FOOD VENDOR

Counterweight orbs, speared with sweetmallow confection skewers

Jute-strand robes

Trunk missing from old farm injury

Callais-nugget necklaces

Brawny worker's hands

JO-DAPSHI GOROBUNN

Teenage complexion

Ancestral Aki-Aki effigy

Daswoad-dyed fabric

NAMBI GHIMA

Trunks lengthen with age

WRUSHII-DO ELECRA

FACT FILE

> Certain effigies are chemically treated to produce specific colors of smoke when burned. To indicate the correct moment to burn said effigies, the Aki-Aki set off colored smoke cannisters.

> Vibrant kites soar over the festival grounds, embodying the ancestors' all-seeing gaze.

THE AKI–AKI

Adult Aki-Aki are easily distinguished by the double prehensile trunks extending from their faces. They are a gregarious lot and generally peaceful. Though they may have known strife in the past, the harshness of the desert climes eventually led to cooperation among the scattered clans, as the arid heat proved to be the biggest threat to their overall survival. Rather than concentrate in cities, the Aki-Aki keep to their disparate villages, but gather together to trade at set times in their calendar.

Of the half-million festival-goers, about 5,000 are intrepid offworlders seeking a spectacle unique in the galaxy.

Tribal guardians of communally raised children

JESBA-BE ISSA AND FADDA-RARB ARDA

Mischievous grin

GUSYIN TATAM

Hand-painted wall decoration

Mandible pincers double as cloak holder

SCULPTED ETOBI HEAD

Wooden saddle can hold toddler

Seam denotes opening for toybox

WOODEN ETOBI ROCKER

AKI-AKI CHILDREN

The Aki-Aki only grow their bifurcated trunks upon reaching adulthood. Young Aki-Aki instead have stubby snouts and eyes that are sunken into a round face of baby fat. They lose these rounded cheeks as they mature, leaving behind more pronounced ocular orbits. Aki-Aki children are celebrated guests at the festival, for they represent the future.

Smile from joke she is eager to share

KAZZA-KI SAGREE

The hospitality of the Aki-Aki is legendary, but the remoteness of Pasaana and its lack of modern amenities ensure only the really dedicated—or in some cases, desperate—make the trek to the festival. A lack of cities, hotels, restaurants, and spaceports on Pasaana means offworld attendees have to "rough it." Should the Festival of the Ancestors ever truly become a galactic spectacle it could change the homegrown character of the event, but for now, it remains a culturally distinct Pasaana tradition.

Xenolinguist Jaiyna Sibinth is a regular attendee of the festival. She studies the ancient language of the Aki-Aki and notes recurring symbols and themes found in cultures native to other desert worlds such as Cona, Klatooine, Sriluur, and Tatooine.

Armor of plastoid tiles wrapped in leather padding

Battery head with charge trode

ENFORCER'S ELECTROPROD STAFF

Leather strap for insulated grip

SEBLA SAROBIA

Veil protects elaborate Antarian coiffure

Jewelry is concealed holocam for personal protection

LOCAL ENFORCERS

Large throngs of jubilant visitors can, on occasion, become unruly, so the Aki-Aki tribal chieftains who can afford it enlist mercenaries to act as hired security. While keeping an eye on merrymakers who might turn into troublemakers after one-too-many cactus bliels, these enforcers also scan the crowds for other offworld hired guns. The anonymity provided by the crowds attracts fugitives and bounty hunters alike. Though Pasaana's enforcers generally stay out of any altercations, they try to make sure nothing disrupts the festivities and that any violence is quickly contained.

OMMO TWILTO

DERED KARNO

Money purse in belt buckle

Lantern and walking stick for night strolls

FESTIVAL-GOERS

Pasaana often draws those seeking escape from the more traveled space routes or, as is most relevant now, those looking to avoid the First Order's harsh rule. The festival may be raucous, but it is ultimately a peaceful celebration of life and legacy. Thrill-seekers may be drawn to the rugged terrain of the Forbidden Valley, while collectors of art and local crafts hunt for wares they can sell as exotic rarities offworld.

ZABMON RORO

Pattern of the Jamtareen tribe

Facial wrap conceals wanted fugitive

BEGARAL MOGHARE

Nickel silver low-bell
striking surfaces

Resonant
paired zills

**AKI-AKI
JANGLE-
DEFF**

Cloth-wrapped
handle

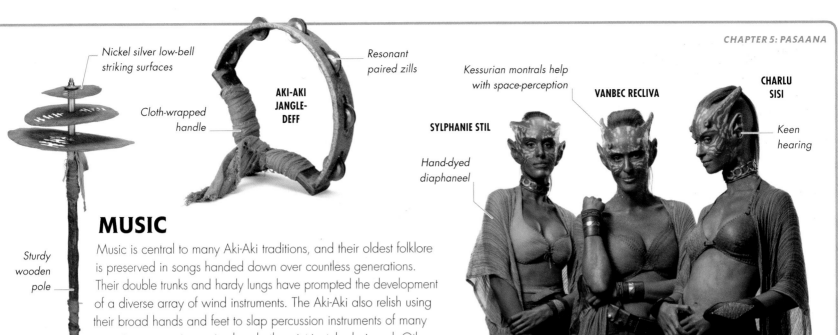

Kessurian montrals help
with space-perception

VANBEC RECLIVA

**CHARLU
SISI**

SYLPHANIE STIL

Keen
hearing

Hand-dyed
diaphaneel

MUSIC

Music is central to many Aki-Aki traditions, and their oldest folklore is preserved in songs handed down over countless generations. Their double trunks and hardy lungs have prompted the development of a diverse array of wind instruments. The Aki-Aki also relish using their broad hands and feet to slap percussion instruments of many sizes, some improvised and others intricately designed. Other performers visit the festival to see Aki-Aki virtuosos in action and to spot burgeoning talent among the self-trained. Many music-lovers simply love the heady mix of storied heritage blended with creative flair and innovation that ensures no two performances are ever the same.

Sturdy
wooden
pole

**TRIPLE RIDE-RHYTHM
O'TAWA CYMBALS**

Valve keys

**STOMP
HARMONIUM**

Compressor tome targets

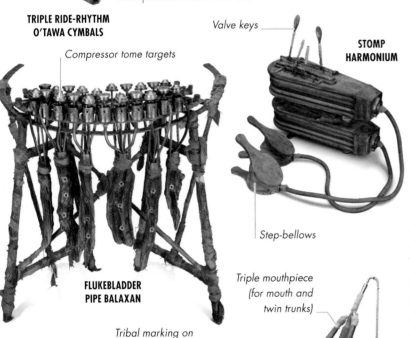

Step-bellows

**FLUKEBLADDER
PIPE BALAXAN**

Triple mouthpiece
(for mouth and
twin trunks)

Tribal marking on
stretched surface

Resonator
erke antlers

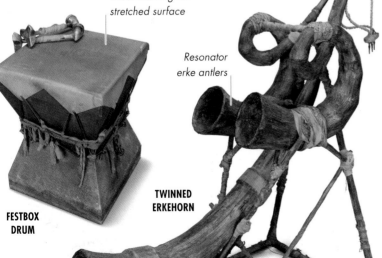

**FESTBOX
DRUM**

**TWINNED
ERKEHORN**

Primary
titan-erke
horn

KESSURIAN DANCE TROUPE

DANCERS

The Aki-Aki have a remarkable sense of rhythm, believed to be a by-product of their trunks and footpads having evolved to detect vibrations across the desert floor. Ancient Aki-Aki hunter-gatherers developed a language based on percussive stomp patterns, which later evolved into traditional dances of courting, aggression, and storytelling that continue to be performed in modern festivals. Aki-Aki are able to quickly fall into step with beats, and can produce vast acts of seemingly spontaneous choreography in no time. Dancers from other worlds—including Twi'leks, Weequays, Theelin, and Kessurians—come to witness Aki-Aki dances for inspiration.

FACT FILE

> As renowned as many Aki-Aki creative expressions are, their cooking is slightly less highly regarded than their other creations.

> The largest Aki-Aki dance, named the *Lobeha Mwadu*, is a centerpiece attraction at every Festival of the Ancestors.

THE HERMIT

The desert sands of Pasaana can bury many a painful past, or so thought the Hermit when he began his solitude there. Personal tragedy, and the failure to find answers on an arduous quest, led him to reside on the arid world. He found comfort in helping the native Aki-Aki, and in witnessing a friendly community of modest means. It was a far cry from the life of opulence he once lived, and it centered him, causing the Hermit to reevaluate what mattered most. What started off as exile instead became a simplified life focused on virtue.

After becoming keenly aware of the enemies he had made, the Hermit concealed his identity during his time on Pasaana. It was not only for his own safety, but the safety of the community of Lurch Canyon. It was they who dubbed him "the Hermit."

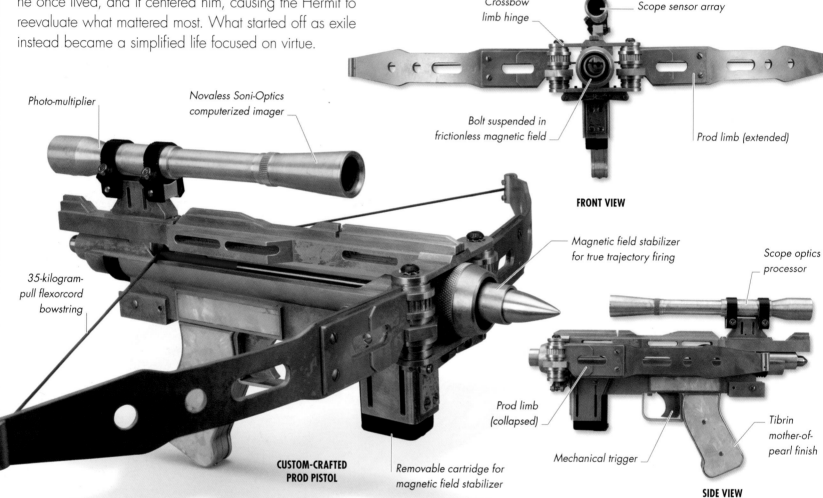

Crossbow limb hinge

Scope sensor array

Bolt suspended in frictionless magnetic field

Prod limb (extended)

FRONT VIEW

Photo-multiplier

Novaless Soni-Optics computerized imager

Magnetic field stabilizer for true trajectory firing

Scope optics processor

35-kilogram-pull flexorcord bowstring

Prod limb (collapsed)

Tibrin mother-of-pearl finish

Mechanical trigger

CUSTOM-CRAFTED PROD PISTOL

Removable cartridge for magnetic field stabilizer

SIDE VIEW

ARMED AND DANGEROUS

Though living an uncluttered, peaceful existence, the Hermit has not abandoned his well-honed vigilance. He knows that he is a target for the First Order, so he takes care to avoid attention and disguise his identity. The heavy robes he wears conceal personal climate control systems, which diffuse his sensor signature so that trackers with his accurate sensor profile will fail to spot him. The Hermit's sidearm is an unpowered prod pistol that won't set off blaster detectors. Though the First Order has not occupied Pasaana, its presence would not be a surprise during the festival season, which attracts visitors from nearby systems, including those who may be fugitives from the regime.

"THE DESERT HELPS YOU FORGET."

—THE HERMIT

Skeletal fletching

Aluminum shaft

BOLT

Weighted arrowhead

FACT FILE

> The Hermit keeps his old yacht, *Lady Luck*, under an unmarked tent owned by an intermediary group.

> His prod pistol started life as one of his paired chromium-plated SE-14r blasters.

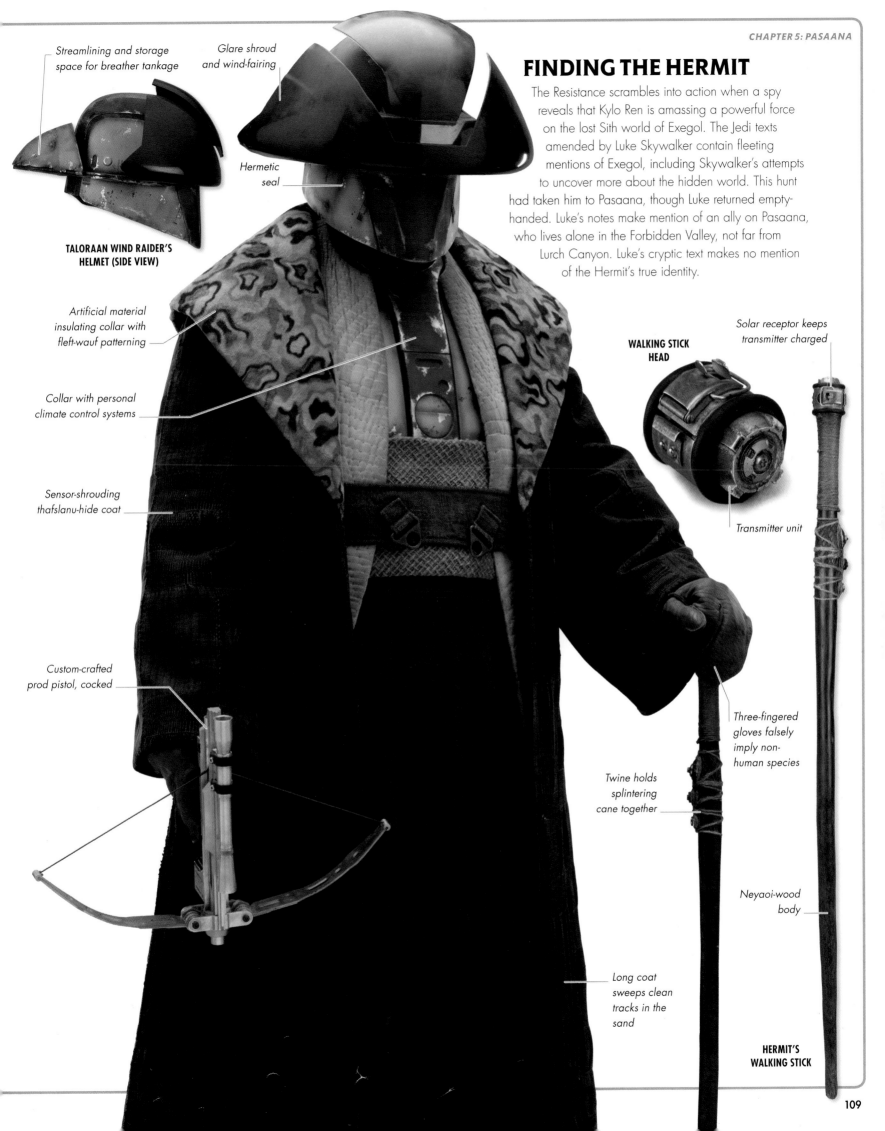

Streamlining and storage space for breather tankage

Glare shroud and wind-fairing

FINDING THE HERMIT

The Resistance scrambles into action when a spy reveals that Kylo Ren is amassing a powerful force on the lost Sith world of Exegol. The Jedi texts amended by Luke Skywalker contain fleeting mentions of Exegol, including Skywalker's attempts to uncover more about the hidden world. This hunt had taken him to Pasaana, though Luke returned empty-handed. Luke's notes make mention of an ally on Pasaana, who lives alone in the Forbidden Valley, not far from Lurch Canyon. Luke's cryptic text makes no mention of the Hermit's true identity.

Hermetic seal

TALORAAN WIND RAIDER'S HELMET (SIDE VIEW)

Artificial material insulating collar with fleft-wauf patterning

Collar with personal climate control systems

Sensor-shrouding thafslanu-hide coat

Custom-crafted prod pistol, cocked

WALKING STICK HEAD

Solar receptor keeps transmitter charged

Transmitter unit

Three-fingered gloves falsely imply non-human species

Twine holds splintering cane together

Neyaoi-wood body

Long coat sweeps clean tracks in the sand

HERMIT'S WALKING STICK

TREADABLE

Treadables are lumbering transports that can venture across the hardened desert soil and shifting dunes of Pasaana with equal stability. Their sturdy, simple construction relies on straightforward mechanical engineering rather than advanced repulsorlifts or directed field dynamics. The Aki-Aki based their treadables on discarded crawlers left behind by offworlders, machining replacement components as needed. The treadables serve as roving market stalls, transporting wares or deliveries along specific routes. Depending on the disposition of the driver, or their need for credits, these privately-owned treadables may also carry passengers.

Rack can hold extra passengers during busy season

Cargo rack mounting bracket

TREADABLE WITH REMOVABLE CARGO RACK

FLEXIBLE PROPULSION

A pair of continuous tracks envelops the treadable, driven by large drum-like rollers at the front and back. A chain of 28 unpowered bogey wheels per track absorbs the weight of the vehicle, spreading it across the track surface evenly in a manner that prevents the craft from sinking into the shifting sands. The enormous drive wheels are split in the middle, permitting the tracks to be driven independently to steer the vehicle past obstacles. The gap between the tracks gives the well-protected driver a glimpse of the surrounding environment, supplemented by an optical periscope.

Split track panel with servicing gap

Front idler bogey wheel

> The differential gear mechanism runs right through the cabin of the treadable. It is encased in sound-dampening insulation that does an incomplete job of canceling its noise.

> Although visibility for the driver is hampered by the tracks themselves, the vehicle does not attain speeds where quick reaction times are a necessity.

Kalo'ne, the driver of this particular treadable, keeps her cabin filled with a wide variety of wares collected from the circuit of stops she travels. Passengers are encouraged to browse during the plodding journey, which always seem to last just long enough to land a profitable sale. Prices are not listed and everything is negotiable.

Legume-filled
sack cushion

FESTIVAL WARES
The Festival of the Ancestors is a busy time
for Kalo'ne, since her treadable is in high
demand for transit duty. Riders often
barter goods for passage, which
Kalo'ne then sells to other
passengers for profit.

Reed-twine
wrapping

Dried,
pre-measured
bundles for
festival bonfires

Flint-rind figs

**IMPROVISED
BARREL-SEAT**

**HOARY
DIGWORT FRONDS**

FRUIT SACKS

**BUNDLED
TARP**

DRIVER'S STATION
A simple optical
periscope with an
electronic HUD
of distance and
directional
information keeps
Kalo'ne on course.

DATA FILE

MANUFACTURER Pasaana Kitha-Garra-du
(Heavy Works)

MODEL DN-25 treadable

AFFILIATION Independent

HEIGHT 4.54m (14ft 11in)

LENGTH 14.45m (47ft 5in)

CREW 1 driver

SPEED 40kph (25mph) (terrain dependent)

WEAPONS None

Tri-lensed
multi-spectral
vision

Rear drive
wheel

Maintenance access
panel with louvered
ventilation

Entrance portal

Cargo cage/
passenger area

Track tension
adjust

Serpentine body
wraps around
steering columns

"TO THE EAST
PASSAGE!"

—LANDO CALRISSIAN TO KALO'NE

KALO'NE

Flinty and age-worn, Kalo'ne has been driving her treadable for
decades. She has weathered many Festivals of the Ancestors,
and jokingly tells new visitors to Pasaana that she herself is one of
the ancient ancestors being celebrated. She is most comfortable
in her driver's cabin, speaking to passengers either through a
decrepit loudspeaker or by opening the sliding slot in her door.

TREADABLE
CROSS-SECTION VIEW

Telescoping driveshaft engager

Weight-reducing
bulkhead cutout

Though continuous track propulsion is an extremely antiquated means of locomotion, its reliability in the face of harsh weather conditions and unstable terrain sees it in continued use, particularly on impoverished worlds. The segmented track is made of a composite manganese-plastoid alloy for lightweight durability. Spare track segments fill a repair hopper aboard the treadable to replace any broken treads that would otherwise strand the vehicle. The durable tread crawls over most obstacles and gaps in terrain, letting the vehicle cross uneven stretches that would challenge any lesser craft.

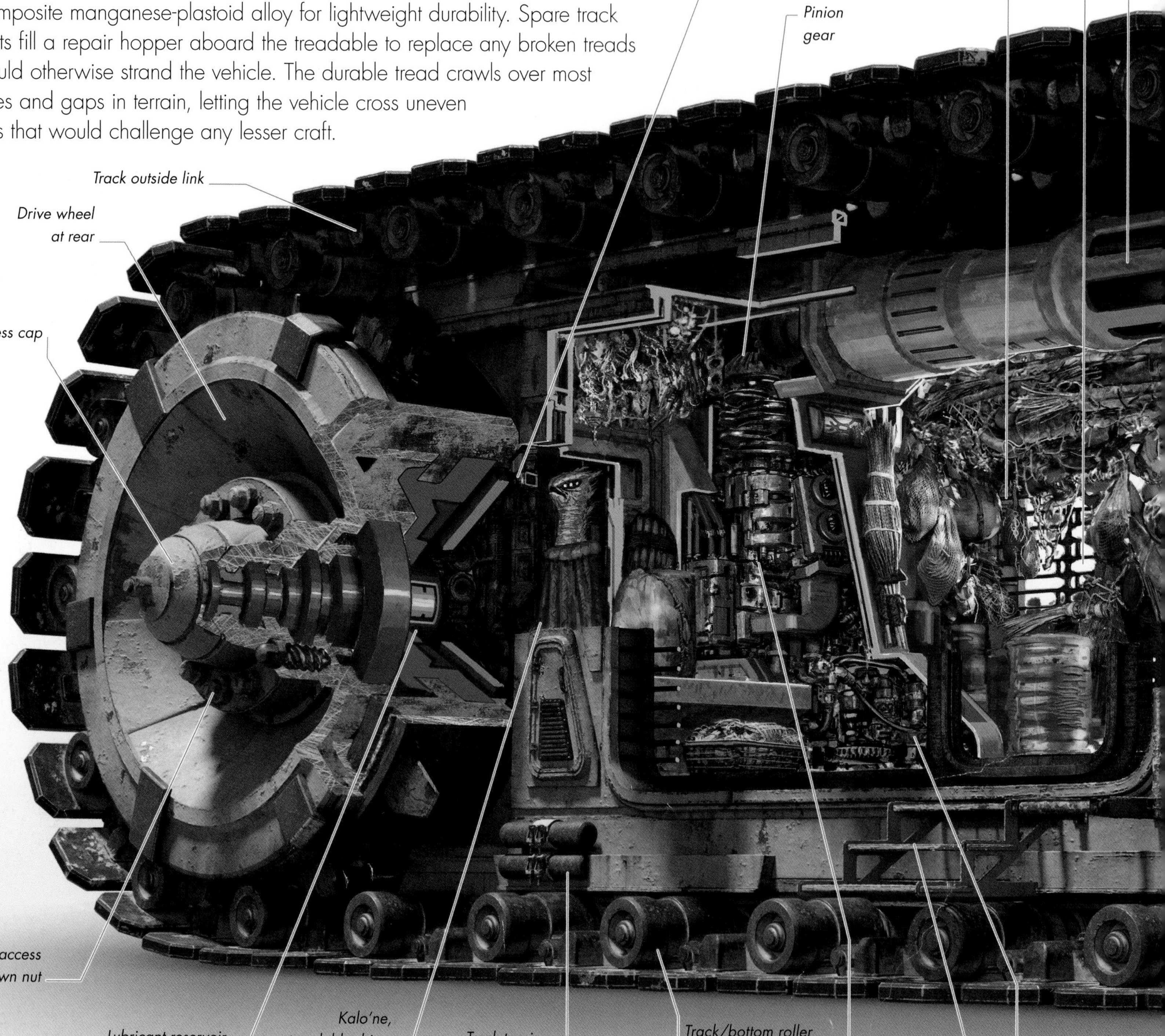

Driver's
periscope

Electrostatic dust
repeller frame

Pinion
gear

Track outside link

Drive wheel
at rear

Axle access cap

Axle access
crown nut

Lubricant reservoir

Kalo'ne,
treadable driver

Track tensioner

Track/bottom roller

Czerka
Corporation
BHY-2600
engine

Power cell bank

Collapsible
rung steps

CARE AND MAINTENANCE

The unpredictability of Pasaana's terrain can lead to complications for the track system. A break in any of the track segments will lead to loss of mobility, so treadable operators must by necessity be trained in the repair and replacement of all aspects of the drive system. Dust contamination on the massive bogey wheels is a constant annoyance, necessitating regular lubrication of the axles and drive transmission. The exposed cabin and ventilation louvers keep the engine from overheating in the desert sun.

Tumbling gear is kept lubricated to prevent dust contamination

Gear is free-spinning in either direction

Differential junction

Sound-dampening bulkhead

Blower panels can redirect engine exhaust to clear sand

Heavily bolted hub

LEARNING TO CRAWL

The drive wheels at the rear have large sprockets for digging into and advancing the track. Under most conditions, the idlers at the front are unpowered. If circumstances require, the front wheels can also be motorized—particularly useful for when the treadable needs to reverse. Steering is achieved by turning one drive wheel at a different speed than the other. The resulting differential in track movement turns the treadable to the left or right.

Drive shaft to front wheels

Rubber-coated steel track

Individual shoes can be replaced without dismantling whole track

Service step/ running board

Items priced to move are kept near exit as "impulse buys"

The Hermit

Sprocket tooth

Bogeys can turn in opposing directions to steer treadable with distributed torque

Sliding cage door

Front idler bogey

113

LANDO CALRISSIAN

Though he came late to the fight against the Empire, Calrissian struck a major blow by leading the attack on the second Death Star. Like many of the generation who waged that conflict, Calrissian did not then go easily into a quiet retirement. When peace reigned, he attempted to start a family, but tragedy struck and his infant daughter vanished. It was only later that it became clear who the culprits behind the abduction were: the First Order, building their fighting forces but also specifically striking at the old Alliance leadership.

> ## "THE FIRST ORDER WENT AFTER US—LEADERS FROM THE OLD WARS. THEY TOOK OUR KIDS."
>
> **—LANDO CALRISSIAN**

Decades ago, Lando was at helm of the *Millennium Falcon* when it fired the fatal shot into the heart of the second Death Star. In the new conflict with the First Order, he relishes the chance to repeat history.

Cloud City sculpture inscribed "Baron Landonis Calrissian"

CANE HEAD

Greel ebonwood with lacquered finish

Calibrated electroscope

Noise suppressor and range-extending barrel

SE-14R BLASTER

Power cell ammunition cartridge

Blaster gas cartridge seal

Chromium-plated body

Tibrin mother-of-pearl finish

Trigger with adjustable sensitivity

Miniaturized image intensifier optics

Blaster gas level indicator

Threaded head for attachments

Cartridge housing

SE-14R BLASTER (BROKEN DOWN)

Removed barrel attachment

Galven circuitry interface port

GUNSLINGER

Calrissian's warrior days are behind him, but a dangerous galaxy requires implements of self-defense. He stays in practice by engaging in low-power blaster duels against training remotes. His weapon of choice is one that has been in his collection for decades—a BlasTech SE-14r, a repeating blaster that was once the exclusive weapon of Imperial officers. In his younger days, Lando customized a pair by having them plated in brushed Naboo chromium and finishing their handles in a pearlescent gleam.

LANDO'S CANE

Not just a tool to help his aging gait, but also a fashionable accessory, Lando's cane is made from greel wood with metal caps mined from Velser's Ring. The head of the cane is sculpted to resemble his beloved Cloud City.

Aeroxite tip from Velser's Ring

FACT FILE

> Lando may never have finished his *Calrissian Chronicle* memoirs, but he does regularly recount some of his most outlandish adventures to Aki-Aki children.

> Though largely vanished from the underworld scene, Lando's name carries a lot of weight among the smuggler and scoundrel community.

THE PATH TO PASAANA

Six years after the tragedy that befell his family, Calrissian served as a partner and guide to Luke Skywalker as the Jedi Master searched for clues to a growing darkness he detected in the Force. Whispers spoke of a resurgent enemy from the past, and Skywalker was determined to find some answers. Had some remnant of the Sith survived? Calrissian's underworld contacts passed along rumors of a hunter of Sith relics on Pasaana, and while Luke and Lando investigated the world's deserts they did not find their quarry. Lando, however, did find some peace and a sense of community among the humble Aki-Aki, and decided to stay. Once again shielded from an escalating conflict, he felt he had earned his rest after so much sacrifice.

LEGACY: LANDO CALRISSIAN

Like many in the galactic underworld, Calrissian avoided politics and the growing conflict between the Rebel Alliance and the Empire. He took note that the wealthy lived untouched by such concerns, and aspired to achieve that separation. Though he had his own brand of heroics, they were often to that singular end. It was not until the Empire threatened the freedom of his people on Cloud City that he realized he could not sit on the sidelines in the battle against darkness.

Still-winning smile

Trellgar silk dress shirt

Blaster in conductive charging holster

Socorran ore ring

Inscribed with Lando's mother's name

Unique chemical lattice lets ring serve as key to coded locks

AURODIUM RING

Synthsilk cape interior

Cape is reversible

Ronto-hide boot

DATA FILE

SUBJECT	Landonis Balthazar Calrissian
HOMEWORLD	Socorro
SPECIES	Human
AFFILIATION	Independent
HEIGHT	1.77m (5ft 10in)
AGE	Approximately 78 standard years

Activation buttons

Calibration slider

Vo-pickup

LANDO'S COMMUNICATOR

Calrissian's Fabritech PAC-15 is a new model that deliberately mimics a vintage style. He had it converted into a beacon that would bring his ship, the *Lady Luck*, to him on autopilot.

TIMELINE

c.77 BSI	Born on Socorro
44 BSI	Kessel Run, loses *Falcon* to Han Solo
38 BSI	Smuggles puffer pigs over Lothal
31 BSI	Cloud City is occupied by Empire
30 BSI	Lando fights in Battle of Endor
29 BSI	Leads the liberation of Cloud City
27 BSI	Han and Lando pursue gangster Fyzen Gor
21 BSI	Lando's daughter is born
19 BSI	Lando's daughter is kidnapped
13 BSI	Lando accompanies Luke to Pasaana
1 ASI	Lando aids the Resistance

DESERT PURSUIT

When known Resistance fugitives are spotted amid the festivities on Pasaana, nearby First Order security patrols—euphemistically called "pacifiers"—are activated. TIE fighters and troop transporters streak the cloudless skies, the latter deploying treadspeeders for overland pursuit. Poe Dameron beats a hurried escape, hotwiring a pair of desert skimmers for him and his companions to use. The result—a twisting, high-speed chase across dunes and canyons—kicks up plumes of dust as the First Order treadspeeders tenaciously pursue their quarries. Beyond its heavy weapons, each treadspeeder can launch a more unconventional projectile: a heavily armed jet trooper.

The jet troopers box in the escaping skimmers with explosives lobbed from their projectile launchers. Though the Resistance heroes shake several pursuers, their rickety skimmers don't last long against such modern, heavy firepower.

NJP-900 integrated jetpack

Faceplate conceals sensor plate and atmospheric filtration screens

DATA FILE

SUBJECT	CS-9147
HOMEWORLD	Otomok
SPECIES	Human
AFFILIATION	First Order
HEIGHT	1.8m (5ft 10in)
AGE	25 standard years

Sensor linked to gyroscopes in pack

Tri-barreled projectile launcher surrounds standard blaster barrel

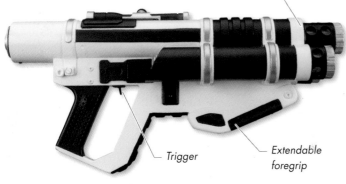

Trigger

Extendable foregrip

SONN-BLAS G125 PROJECTILE LAUNCHER

FACT FILE

> A First Order AAL-1971/9.1 troop transporter can carry two treadspeeders, each loaded with a pilot and jet trooper.

> Before long, Kylo Ren and the Knights of Ren join the chase on Pasaana, pursuing separate objectives.

JET TROOPERS

Jet troopers are specialized First Order stormtroopers who soar into battle equipped with agile jetpacks. Mobile propulsion units such as these have been a military tradition since the days of the Old Republic, and were made most famous by Mandalorian supercommandos. Complex gyroscopes within the center of the pack's mass translate body movements into changes of direction and propulsion. Having a great degree of body control is thus necessary for becoming a capable jet trooper. Offering further finesse and control are eye-motion activated maneuvers programmed into the helmet visor; flying a jetpack without a helmet is difficult, though not impossible. To better survive high altitudes, jet troopers wear insulated armor that comes equipped with an air supply.

Positive-grip boots

"THEY FLY! WE'RE DONE FOR!"

—C-3PO

Pilot's helmet HUD is wirelessly linked to vehicle

Unit insignia

Casing contains Kradkett Motivators sd-kfz 2 drive mechanism

FRONT VIEW

Ruggedized operator control screen

Aratech thruster

REAR VIEW

The treadspeeder pilots feel far more connected to their vehicles than most First Order repulsorcraft pilots, as they can directly feel each bump and obstacle that shudders along the vehicle's frame.

The sifter spires and vaporators of a dust farm become a slalom obstacle for treadspeeder and skimmer alike. The treadspeeder is agile and can weave a tight path through the field, though it is more subject to the underlying terrain conditions.

Cut down vambraces for increased flexibility

Articulated racing fabric with strategic stretch panels and reinforced padding

TREADSPEEDER

Treadspeeders are rugged, shielded patrol bikes, designed to counter technology that can jam traditional repulsorcraft. The vehicle features a forward treaded pod that literally grabs the ground, pulling the vehicle forward with a snarling, dirt-tearing ferocity. A rear repulsorfield negates the pull of gravity, rendering the heavy bike lightweight and granting it agility and surprising speed. Trained treadspeeder pilots work in tandem with jet troopers, who ride behind them on the seat. With a controlled brake, the pilot can kick the chassis upward, launching the jet trooper into the sky.

TREADSPEEDER PILOT

DATA FILE

MANUFACTURER Aratech-Loratus

MODEL 125-Z treadspeeder bike

AFFILIATION First Order

HEIGHT 1.11m (3ft 8in)

LENGTH 4.17m (13ft 8in)

CREW 1 pilot, space for 1 passenger

SPEED 200 kilometers per hour

WEAPONS 2 heavy laser cannons

Pilot interface

Angled armor protects pilot

Repulsor unit

Drive mechanism power plant recharge cables

Outrigger laser cannon with backflash suppressor plate

TREADSPEEDER
CROSS-SECTION VIEW

As the First Order blazed trails on harsh, untamed worlds in the Unknown Regions, it designed a rugged, reliable vehicle perfect for isolated scouting expeditions. Advancements in anti-repulsorlift technology also gave this new vehicle a tactical application. The First Order had itself perfected high-yield repulsor-jamming systems, so it saw the military value of vehicles that were immune to such technology. The treadspeeder is a hybrid design; a continuous track impeller drives the vehicle, and low-yield, jamming-resistant repulsorlifts are merely secondary systems that assist in stability and maneuvers.

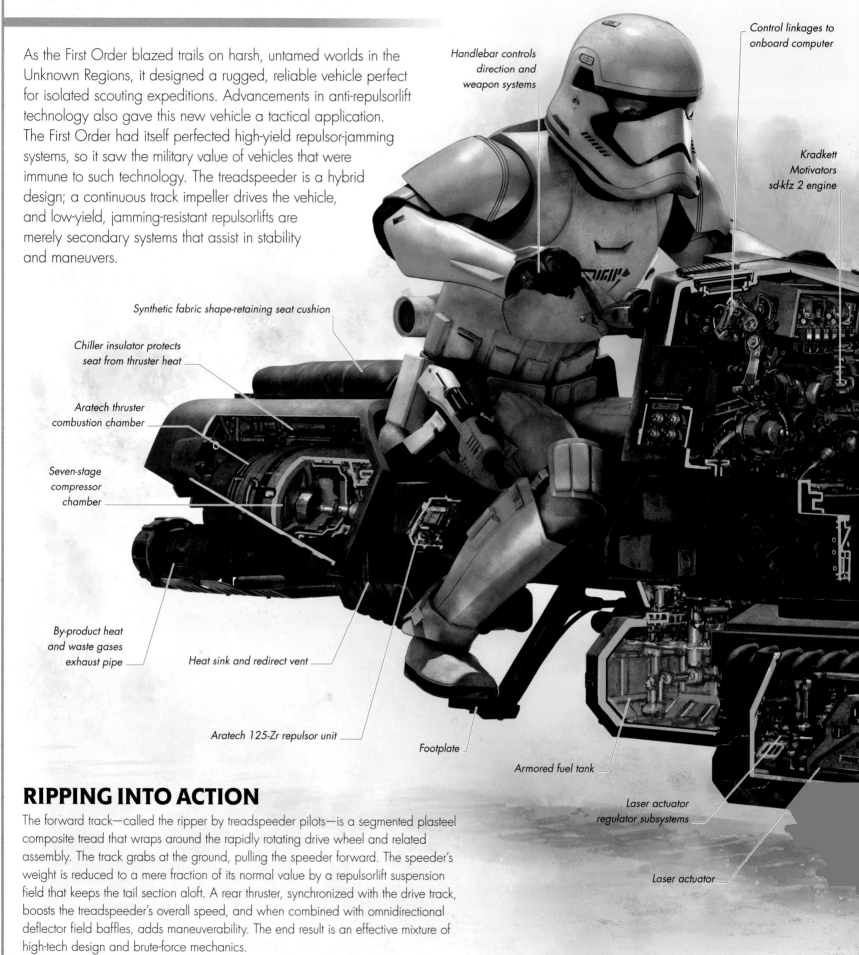

Handlebar controls direction and weapon systems

Control linkages to onboard computer

Kradkett Motivators sd-kfz 2 engine

Synthetic fabric shape-retaining seat cushion

Chiller insulator protects seat from thruster heat

Aratech thruster combustion chamber

Seven-stage compressor chamber

By-product heat and waste gases exhaust pipe

Heat sink and redirect vent

Aratech 125-Zr repulsor unit

Footplate

Armored fuel tank

Laser actuator regulator subsystems

Laser actuator

RIPPING INTO ACTION

The forward track—called the ripper by treadspeeder pilots—is a segmented plasteel composite tread that wraps around the rapidly rotating drive wheel and related assembly. The track grabs at the ground, pulling the speeder forward. The speeder's weight is reduced to a mere fraction of its normal value by a repulsorlift suspension field that keeps the tail section aloft. A rear thruster, synchronized with the drive track, boosts the treadspeeder's overall speed, and when combined with omnidirectional deflector field baffles, adds maneuverability. The end result is an effective mixture of high-tech design and brute-force mechanics.

TACTICAL SYSTEMS

The treadspeeder incorporates the latest in First Order military shielding technology. Deflector shields on ground vehicles are rare, as atmospheric particles tend to overstimulate the shield systems causing inefficient power spikes and drainage. The First Order's fractional refresh system lets the shields remain active at a diminished state, and then go "solid" when advanced sensor systems in the pilot's helmet detect an incoming threat. For offense, the treadspeeder has a pair of Sonn-Blas heavy laser cannons mounted on outriggers. These have self-contained power sources that do not rely on the treadspeeder's main powerplant. The pilot and passenger can supplement this firepower with small-arms fire.

TREADSPEEDER CONTROLS

The treadspeeder's control interface may seem overly simple at first glance—at least to anyone not wearing a stormtrooper helmet. The pilot's helmet is wirelessly linked to the vehicle, and layered data readouts appear in the helmet's integrated HUD. This allows the treadspeeder pilot to customize their control inputs and view the most pertinent information within their periphery. Driving a treadspeeder without a helmet is possible, but not recommended.

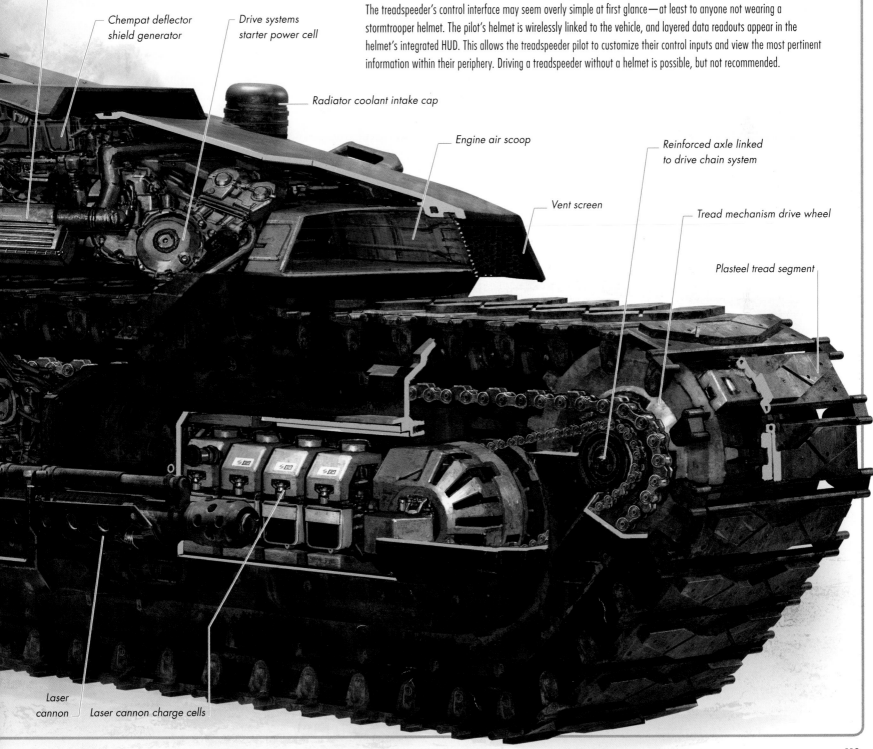

Debris extractor

Chempat deflector shield generator

Drive systems starter power cell

Radiator coolant intake cap

Engine air scoop

Reinforced axle linked to drive chain system

Vent screen

Tread mechanism drive wheel

Plasteel tread segment

Laser cannon

Laser cannon charge cells

PASAANA SKIMMERS

Despite its appearance as an arid world, Pasaana has an agricultural economy based around its subterranean dust farms. The parched desert conditions do, however, mean that it requires a lot of land to produce profitable crop yields. To cover such large distances, local Aki-Aki farmers make use of swift, open-air repulsorlift skimmers. These skiff-like conveyances are stripped down and utilitarian, easily customized for a wide variety of uses, from plow or tow vehicle to family transport or mobile seed market.

To Poe Dameron, Finn, Rey, Chewbacca, BB-8, and C-3PO, they also make swift escape craft.

Engine casing

Auxiliary power unit

PORT SIDE VIEW

Column-mounted steering vane redistributes repulsor thrust

Fraying but rewoven flexor cord

Tiller rod

Hand grip

Speed throttle

Bolt of textiles for sale

Exposed power cell for easy replacement

Air intake and filter

DATA FILE

MANUFACTURER SoroSuub

MODEL HS-19 cargo loading transport skimmer

AFFILIATION Civilian

HEIGHT 3.22m (10ft 7in)

LENGTH 6.7m (22ft)

CREW 1 pilot

SPEED 250kph (155mph)

WEAPONS None

Poe rightfully boasts that he can fly anything, and this includes the loader skimmer. The wind in his face and lack of sophisticated control surfaces bring back memories of the simple microlight gliders he would build and soar in over the treetops of Yavin 4. C-3PO, as usual, is less than nostalgic about flight. Finn, meanwhile, concentrates on providing covering fire.

LOADER SKIMMER

Poe Dameron hotwires a loader skimmer for his escape vehicle, with Finn and C-3PO joining him aboard. Rated for carrying up to 120 metric tons of cargo, either towed from its fairing or concentrated on its flatbed, the skimmer's raw repulsorlift power can be funneled into thrust for unloaded speeds in excess of 250 kilometers per hour. Poe stands at the tiller, controlling thrust with his right hand on the throttle grip and direction by rotating the tiller rod; the latter is connected via cables to the skimmer's aft steering column.

TRANSPORT SKIMMER

The skimmer that Rey appropriates (thanks again to Poe's hotwiring skills) is a basic light-duty cargo truck that was on its way to bring supplies for the Festival of the Ancestors. Though Rey regrets having to steal what was doubtless a needed vehicle on someone's farm, the relentless pursuit of the First Order leaves her few options. Rey's instinctive piloting abilities along with an innate feel for desert terrain give her an edge in the chase. She even manages to impress Poe with her maneuvers. Chewbacca uses his bowcaster to provide covering fire, and BB-8 even helps shake enemy pursuers with the clever use of a festival smoke canister.

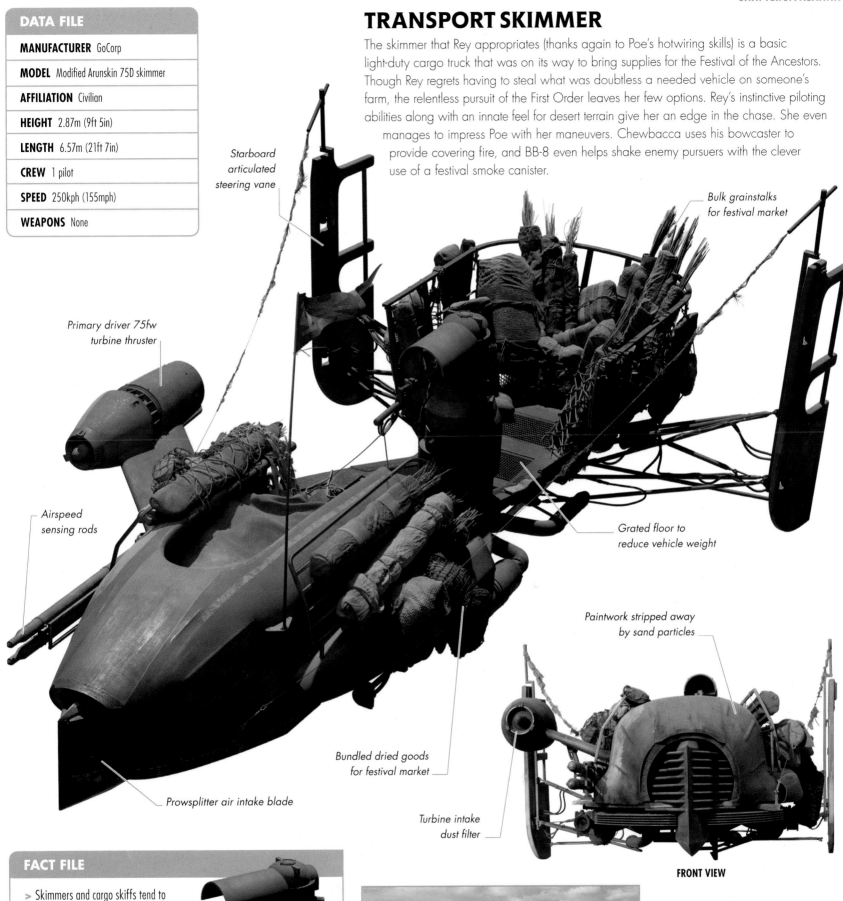

DATA FILE

MANUFACTURER GoCorp

MODEL Modified Arunskin 75D skimmer

AFFILIATION Civilian

HEIGHT 2.87m (9ft 5in)

LENGTH 6.57m (21ft 7in)

CREW 1 pilot

SPEED 250kph (155mph)

WEAPONS None

Starboard articulated steering vane

Bulk grainstalks for festival market

Primary driver 75fw turbine thruster

Grated floor to reduce vehicle weight

Airspeed sensing rods

Paintwork stripped away by sand particles

Bundled dried goods for festival market

Prowsplitter air intake blade

Turbine intake dust filter

FRONT VIEW

FACT FILE

> Skimmers and cargo skiffs tend to have very simple controls, as even fifth-degree labor droids are expected to pilot them.

> These skimmers are related in type and function to the Ubrikkian Bantha II cargo skiffs once favored by Jabba the Hutt.

The desert chase splits the two skimmers along different routes, with Poe and Finn leading their pursuers into a narrow canyon. While this move keeps them directly in their enemy's sights, it also makes it harder for the enemy to evade their return fire.

REY'S SKIMMER
CROSS-SECTION VIEW

The Arunskin 75D skimmer that Rey "liberates" belongs to farmer Jo-Dapshi Gorubunn. He had used it to transport to the festival some surplus dried goods from last year's harvest, which had been taking up room in his siltbarn. Gorubunn's grandson has, unknown to the old farmer, been tinkering with the skimmer, decoupling governors that would otherwise have limited its top speed. Gorubunn is shocked that some strange young woman would steal his work craft and that the First Order would give pursuit, but even more shocked that his old 75D could tear into the desert at such a clip.

Chewbacca prepares to return fire

Improvised tension cable keeps steering vane from sagging

Dried goods to be sold at festival

Control cable bundle

Tiller head with weather shroud

Servomotor rod

Undressed power cables

Power plant exhaust

Mag plates to hold down metallic cargo

BB-8 stays behind cover

Vane accelerometer

Rear repulsorlift plates

Fuel catalyzer and distributor

Steering vane

Engine drive turbine

SIMPLIFIED, STURDY CONSTRUCTION

The lack of sophistication in the skimmer's systems means there are fewer things that can go wrong aboard the craft. This is true of most farm vehicles on Pasaana, where the ever-present dust of the desert can clog more delicate machinery. Control systems are mostly mechanical rather than electronic, with raw muscle power transferred through the tug of cables and pulleys to move the steering vanes or open the fuel flow in the thruster. Rey pushes the old skimmer to its limits in her attempt to outrun the First Order.

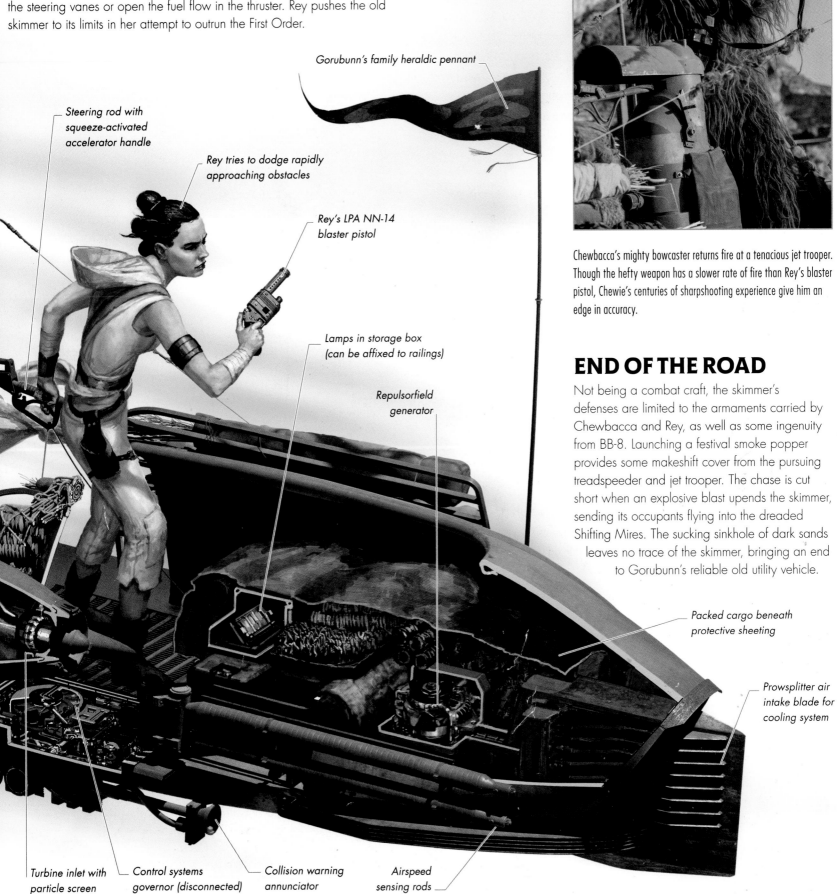

Chewbacca's mighty bowcaster returns fire at a tenacious jet trooper. Though the hefty weapon has a slower rate of fire than Rey's blaster pistol, Chewie's centuries of sharpshooting experience give him an edge in accuracy.

Gorubunn's family heraldic pennant

Steering rod with squeeze-activated accelerator handle

Rey tries to dodge rapidly approaching obstacles

Rey's LPA NN-14 blaster pistol

Lamps in storage box (can be affixed to railings)

Repulsorfield generator

Turbine inlet with particle screen

Control systems governor (disconnected)

Collision warning annunciator

Airspeed sensing rods

END OF THE ROAD

Not being a combat craft, the skimmer's defenses are limited to the armaments carried by Chewbacca and Rey, as well as some ingenuity from BB-8. Launching a festival smoke popper provides some makeshift cover from the pursuing treadspeeder and jet trooper. The chase is cut short when an explosive blast upends the skimmer, sending its occupants flying into the dreaded Shifting Mires. The sucking sinkhole of dark sands leaves no trace of the skimmer, bringing an end to Gorubunn's reliable old utility vehicle.

Packed cargo beneath protective sheeting

Prowsplitter air intake blade for cooling system

RESOURCEFUL AND RESILIENT
The scream of incoming TIE fighters drowns out the festival, and Poe Dameron springs into action. Recognizing that they'll never make it back to the *Falcon* in time, he leads his friends to a pair of parked skimmers, which he hotwires for flight. Finn is surprised at Poe's thievery skills, wondering how a pilot for the New Republic and the Resistance came to have them.

ON THE TRAIL OF OCHI

The vexis is an armored snake that burrows its way beneath the sands of Pasaana. The oil it excretes from its skin hardens the sand it travels through, creating a growing network of tunnels.

If the Resistance is to thwart the reinvigorated First Order's plan for domination, it must first find the planet Exegol—and this can only be done with a Sith wayfinder. Luke Skywalker and Lando Calrissian had investigated rumors of a hunter of Sith relics named Ochi of Bestoon years earlier. Having kept his ears on the underworld, Calrissian had heard of an inebriated Ochi bragging at some distant bar that he had been on the hunt for a wayfinder, and had found it in one of the Emperor's vaults. Luke and Lando sought Ochi, but the trail ran cold in the scorched sands of Pasaana. Now, nearly 15 years later, Rey picks up the hunt.

Logic function computer

Photoreceptors

Energy transducer

Intermotor actuating coupler

OCHI'S BLADE

Ochi's ornate knife is etched with runic Sith symbols. While Ochi was no Sith, he associated with cultists who longed for the Sith's return.

Long-dead ur-Kittât "Old Tongue" runes of the Sith

Crossguard conceals measurement arc for use in pinpointing missing wayfinder's location

Primary power coupler outlet

OCHI OF BESTOON

A known associate of Imperial advisor Yupe Tashu and the self-styled Acolytes of the Beyond, Ochi was obsessed with ancient Sith arcana. Enabled by Tashu, he pored over forbidden Sith texts and staunchly believed that the extinct order was destined to return to glory. Though Ochi could not touch the Force, he believed the dark side propelled him and shaped his actions. Ochi was no mere relic hunter in the employ of the Empire's most sinister agents— he was also an assassin. He bore the traditional hex charm of Sith assassins, and considered his murders to be in the service of the greater darkness beyond the veil. Ochi's bones now litter a vexis lair beneath the Shifting Mires of Lurch Canyon. What fate befell him is unknown, but his bones have long since been picked clean by gouge-beetles.

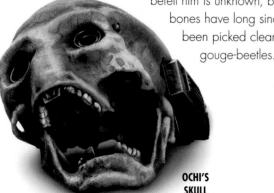

OCHI'S SKULL

C-3PO

While unearthing the mysteries that Ochi had concealed in esoteric symbols, Rey and her companions discover the value of the abilities of C-3PO, their loyal protocol droid friend. With a massive databank of languages, both active and extinct, C-3PO can read the Sith runes. However, hard-wired protocols within his translator systems prevent him from divulging what the text says—the strictures of the Old Republic have long banned the open sharing of Sith knowledge. Nonetheless, C-3PO is delighted to be of use.

DATA FILE	
SUBJECT C-3PO	
PLANET OF CONSTRUCTION Tatooine	
MANUFACTURER Anakin Skywalker	
TYPE Protocol droid	
AFFILIATION Resistance	
HEIGHT 1.77m (5ft 10in)	
AGE At least 67 standard years (with some componentry over 148 standard years old)	

"WE CHASED OCHI HALFWAY ACROSS THE GALAXY... WHERE THE TRAIL WENT COLD. OCHI DISAPPEARED INTO THE DESERT."

—LANDO CALRISSIAN

Despite having sat unattended for years in Lurch Canyon, Ochi's starship, the *Bestoon Legacy*, has remained untouched. Its fuel cells and engine systems re-engage and the ship comes alive under the command of Poe Dameron.

FACT FILE

> The navicomputer aboard Ochi's ship has been deliberately wiped clean to cover his tracks and keep secret his assignments.

> The Shifting Mires swallowed Ochi up whole, including his landspeeder.

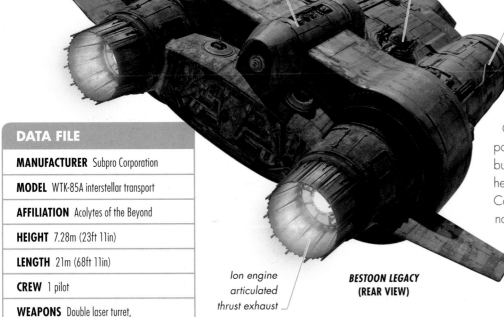

Hyperdrive motivator

Double laser cannon turret

Starboard sublight/supralight engine assembly

Ion engine articulated thrust exhaust

BESTOON LEGACY (REAR VIEW)

DATA FILE

MANUFACTURER	Subpro Corporation
MODEL	WTK-85A interstellar transport
AFFILIATION	Acolytes of the Beyond
HEIGHT	7.28m (23ft 11in)
LENGTH	21m (68ft 11in)
CREW	1 pilot
WEAPONS	Double laser turret, 2 forward laser cannons

OCHI'S SHIP

Luke Skywalker and Lando Calrissian found Ochi's ship, the *Bestoon Legacy*, parked on a bluff beyond Lurch Canyon, but there was no trace of Ochi aboard. Evidence pointed to Ochi having left his ship aboard a landspeeder, but the shifting sands buried any trace of direction or purpose he may have had in leaving his ship. Though Skywalker and Calrissian abandoned their search and the vessel, the tranquil nature of Pasaana's deserts preserved the ship as it was. Aside from slight sand-clogs in the intakes and thrusters, and silk strands left by nomadic solif-spiders, the ship is ready to launch after more than a decade of inactivity.

Externalized coolant pump lines

Stabilizer vane

Final stage drive unit

Cockpit with louvered viewport

Main entry ramp can support embarked vehicles

Portside engine intake

Rear landing strut

BESTOON LEGACY (LANDING GEAR DEPLOYED)

BESTOON LEGACY
CROSS–SECTION VIEW

The *Bestoon Legacy* is a modified WTK-85A interstellar transport, originally manufactured during the last days of the Galactic Republic by Subpro Corporation. It was designed for scouts or pilots who preferred operating with minimal crew requirements. The loner Ochi of Bestoon was drawn to the independence promised by such a design. The ship can operate with a single pilot, though safety requirements demanded a co-pilot station with modular, redundant controls to relieve the pilot of certain duties. For reasons that remain a mystery, the ship is loaded with dozens upon dozens of blaster rifles and pistols.

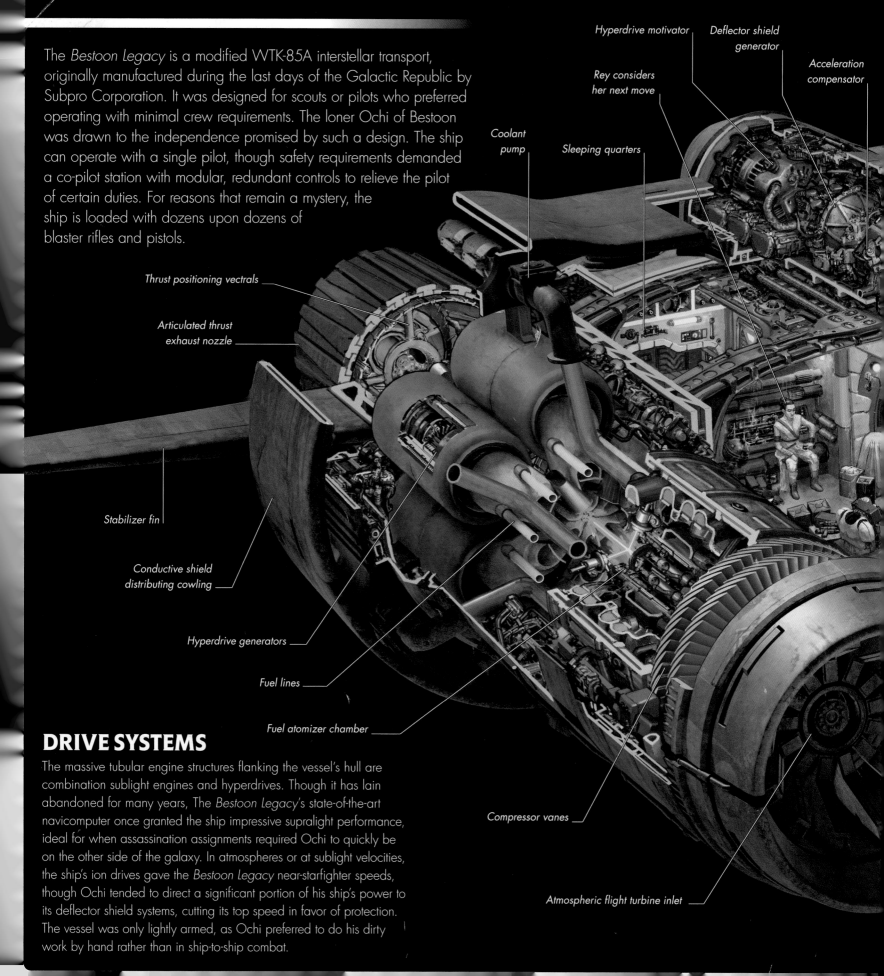

Hyperdrive motivator

Deflector shield generator

Acceleration compensator

Rey considers her next move

Coolant pump

Sleeping quarters

Thrust positioning vectrals

Articulated thrust exhaust nozzle

Stabilizer fin

Conductive shield distributing cowling

Hyperdrive generators

Fuel lines

Fuel atomizer chamber

Compressor vanes

Atmospheric flight turbine inlet

DRIVE SYSTEMS

The massive tubular engine structures flanking the vessel's hull are combination sublight engines and hyperdrives. Though it has lain abandoned for many years, The *Bestoon Legacy*'s state-of-the-art navicomputer once granted the ship impressive supralight performance, ideal for when assassination assignments required Ochi to quickly be on the other side of the galaxy. In atmospheres or at sublight velocities, the ship's ion drives gave the *Bestoon Legacy* near-starfighter speeds, though Ochi tended to direct a significant portion of his ship's power to its deflector shield systems, cutting its top speed in favor of protection. The vessel was only lightly armed, as Ochi preferred to do his dirty work by hand rather than in ship-to-ship combat.

SHIP OF MEMORY

Rey recognizes the *Bestoon Legacy* as the ship that once departed from Jakku, stranding her on the desert planet in the custody of Unkar Plutt. An image of herself as a child, frantically wailing at the ship's departure, springs unbidden into her mind. Could it be the very same ship, or merely one of the same model? Or is her slipping control of her abilities and emotions creating connections where there are none? Rey stops to consider, her turbulent thoughts briefly calmed by BB-8's discovery of a companion droid aboard the ship, a little wheeled unit named D-O.

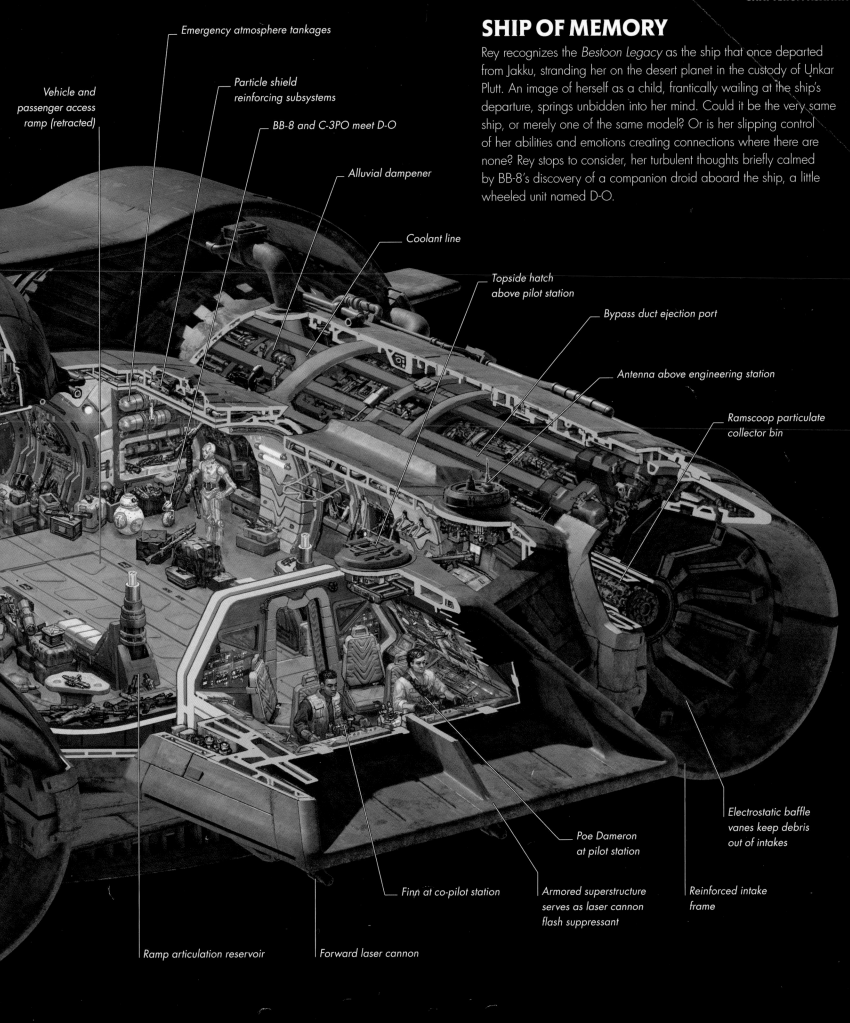

Emergency atmosphere tankages

Particle shield reinforcing subsystems

Vehicle and passenger access ramp (retracted)

BB-8 and C-3PO meet D-O

Alluvial dampener

Coolant line

Topside hatch above pilot station

Bypass duct ejection port

Antenna above engineering station

Ramscoop particulate collector bin

Electrostatic baffle vanes keep debris out of intakes

Poe Dameron at pilot station

Finn at co-pilot station

Armored superstructure serves as laser cannon flash suppressant

Reinforced intake frame

Ramp articulation reservoir

Forward laser cannon

CHAPTER 6:
KIJIMI

Having found Ochi of Bestoon's starship as well as hard evidence of his intended destination, the next stop in Rey's quest is the mountainous world of Kijimi, courtesy of some prompts from Poe Dameron. The relic that Ochi left behind is inscribed with Sith runes that C-3PO is capable of translating. Unfortunately, he is prevented from sharing his translations due to restrictions encoded into his programming by Old Republic law. To bypass these strictures, C-3PO will need to visit a black-market droidsmith capable of expert system slicing. But as they voyage to Kijimi, Rey and her friends surface on the scopes of Kylo Ren and his dreaded Knights, who are determined to capture the scavenger for nefarious ends.

KIJIMI

Lawlessness ran rampant in some sectors of the galaxy following the Empire's collapse. The New Republic was too weak to pacify worlds where criminality became deeply rooted, and its failure to act led to widespread apathy toward the new galactic government. Frigid, mountainous Kijimi was one such world. Once considered unspoiled, it was famed as a place of marked spirituality. However, its remoteness and lack of cosmopolitan bustle attracted those on the run from the law, since they made Kijimi the perfect place to lie low. These criminal elements grew all the more brazen as time passed and it became clear that a lack of law enforcement meant a lack of consequences. Kijimi now wears its criminal underworld openly on its surface, though its days as a haven for lawbreakers are numbered by encroaching First Order patrols.

"I'VE HAD BAD LUCK ON KIJIMI."

—POE DAMERON

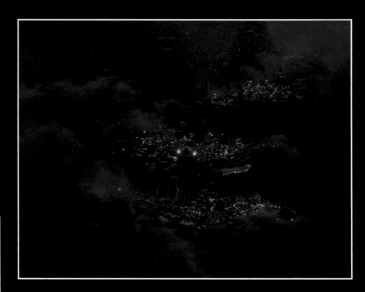

KIJIMI CITY

Kijimi City is the nearest thing Kijimi has to a capital. It sits atop a plateau that straddles Mount Izukika, the site of a Dai Bendu monastery built a thousand years ago. Over the centuries, the city was periodically raided and the monks disappeared, though their structures still exist. Many spacers are superstitious, and despite their unscrupulous natures they oddly revere these ancient monuments.

SPICE RUNNERS' DEN

The collapse of the Empire also led to a massive shake-up in the lucrative spice trade operating out of Kessel. Without the guiding hands of Imperial officials or Mining Guild protection, competition for Kessel spice became a bloody free-for-all, and former processing termini like Oba Diah and Formos became too embattled to operate safely. Enter the Spice Runners of Kijimi, a pirate band that specialized in striking spice-laden ships that emerged from the Maelstrom. In time, these runners worked out their own partnership with the mine operators, sidestepping violence in favor of becoming an exclusive link in an expanded Kessel Run that reached all the way to Kijimi.

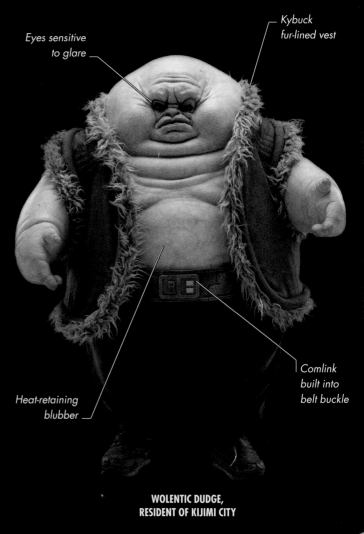

Eyes sensitive to glare

Kybuck fur-lined vest

Heat-retaining blubber

Comlink built into belt buckle

WOLENTIC DUDGE, RESIDENT OF KIJIMI CITY

The First Order has arrived on Kijimi, searching for leads regarding Resistance activity. Its forces have begun nightly raids in the city, capturing children to turn into future stormtroopers.

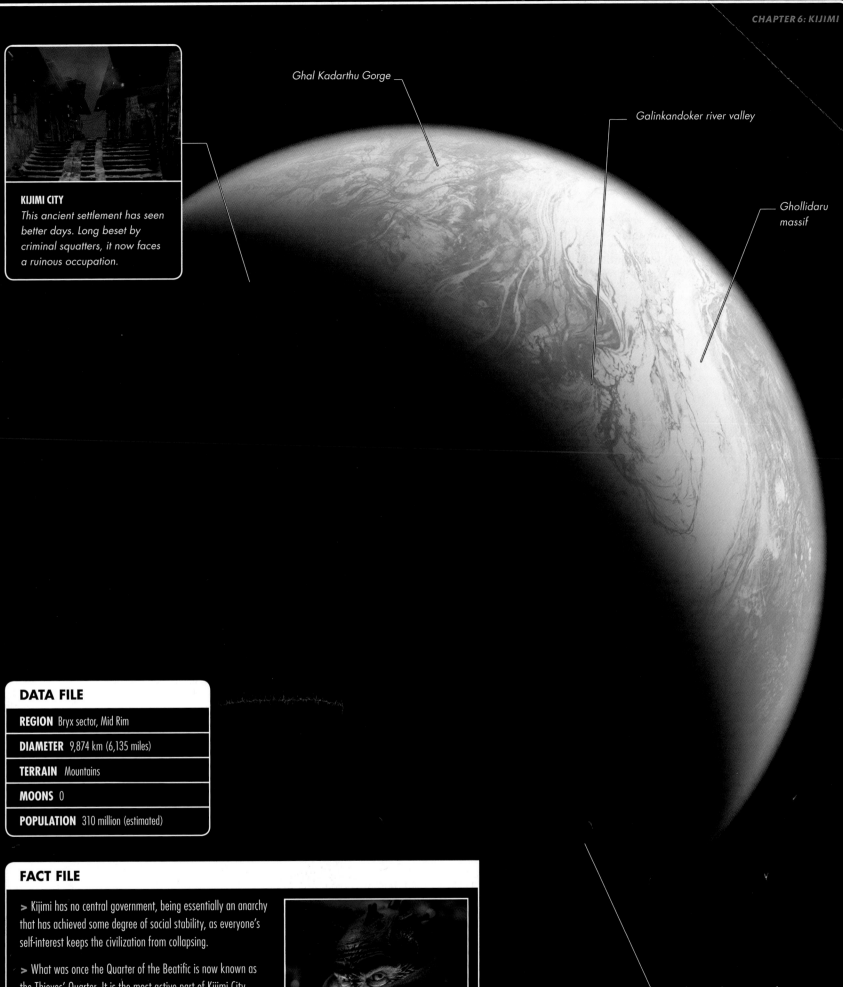

Ghal Kadarthu Gorge

Galinkandoker river valley

Ghollidaru massif

KIJIMI CITY
This ancient settlement has seen better days. Long beset by criminal squatters, it now faces a ruinous occupation.

Lha-Mi glacier, site of secret Spice Runner cache

DATA FILE

REGION	Bryx sector, Mid Rim
DIAMETER	9,874 km (6,135 miles)
TERRAIN	Mountains
MOONS	0
POPULATION	310 million (estimated)

FACT FILE

> Kijimi has no central government, being essentially an anarchy that has achieved some degree of social stability, as everyone's self-interest keeps the civilization from collapsing.

> What was once the Quarter of the Beatific is now known as the Thieves' Quarter. It is the most active part of Kijimi City.

> Temperatures in Kijimi City vary greatly depending on time of day, but they average around -25 degrees standard.

KIJIMI CITY

Kijimi City (or Kijimiko as it was originally known) stands at a lofty altitude of 4,200 meters, whipped by frosty winds atop Mount Izukika. Its peak is not as jagged as its neighbors, flattening to a plateau able to support civilization. The anarchic nature of Kijimi's society means the city's infrastructure is dangerously neglected, and it lacks a reliable centralized source for heating, plumbing, and power distribution. Instead, the many gangs, guilds, and clans step in to provide for the quarters, neighborhoods, and buildings that pledge loyalty. Visitors to Kijimi are advised to remain aware of their surroundings, not only because of the lawlessness, but also the sheer unpredictability of basic amenities from block to block.

Ammunition service latch

Targeting sight

SPICE RUNNER PERCUSSIVE CANNON

SPICE RUNNER BLASTER RIFLE

Widened bore on barrel

GUILDHOUSE ENTRANCE
Lodging and meals are available only to Kozinarg Trade Guild members.

IMPROVISED GENERATOR
Scattered tibanna-fueled generators provide local heating and power.

THIEVES' QUARTER

Formerly the Quarter of the Beatific, this section of the city was once home to a Lorrdian religious group, the Brotherhood of the Beatific Countenance, who voyaged to the mountainous planet in a pilgrimage to the Dai Bendu temple that once formed the center of Kijimi City. The rise of criminality on the plateau chased off the Brotherhood, leaving their homes to be overrun by thieves and squatters. The tightly-packed lodgings are threaded through by zigzagging alleyways. Their shadows once allowed thieves to outrun the Dai Bendu temple guardians. Now, the quarter as a whole is a refuge for those who wish to remain hidden.

FACT FILE

> The most influential guilds in the Thieves' Quarter are the Corellian Merchants' Guild, the Lantillian Spacers' Brotherhood, and the Intracluster Gatherers—the latter is a splinter of the Wandering Star criminal syndicate.

> A popular drink in Kijimi cantinas is Ultra-Ox, a libation with a dense cloud of oxygen suspended above the liquid, which is said to replace altitude sickness with a more pleasurable form of lightheadedness.

Kijimi's moonless nights get especially cold. For the original monks, the lighting of lanterns evolved from an act of basic survival into a ceremony couched in gratitude. Today's city dwellers have forgotten the ceremony, though they are grateful for the lanterns.

"I HEARD YOU WERE SPOTTED BY MONK'S GATE. DIDN'T THINK YOU WERE DUMB ENOUGH TO COME HERE."

—ZORII BLISS TO POE DAMERON

STEPS TO MONK'S GATE
A flight of steps leads to the northernmost wall of the Thieves' Quarter.

ANCIENT MASONRY
The city's ancient granitic stone was quarried from Mount Izukika.

Finn and Rey both defer to Poe's leadership given the circumstances, but Finn continues to be surprised by the details that emerge about Poe's checkered past.

Wind-reducing synthetic weave

BLENDING IN
On their way into Kijimi City, Poe Dameron liberates four heavy jackets from an Opranko guildhouse. The disguises provide much needed warmth as the Resistance fugitives wind their way through the snow-dusted alleyways. Though C-3PO's internal thermostat keeps his joints from freezing up, he appreciates the gesture.

KIJIMI CITY INHABITANTS

The Thieves' Quarter has an unspoken motto hanging over its densely packed buildings: *We're all in this together*. Criminals from all walks of life understand that there are havens amid the guildhouses and gang dens. The gaps between clearly delineated territories are safe zones where if you don't go looking for trouble, trouble won't find you. While the city's attitude won't protect, say, a pirate who picks a fight in a bounty hunter bar, it likewise won't abide hunters seeking quarries in a pirate den. The cantinas in the neutral blocks contain a raucous collection of unlikely gambling and drinking partners.

PLESKO MARNO

Plesko Marno is a former clerk at the Bureau of Ships and Services—an agency of the New Republic. He fled the destruction of the galactic government with a collection of navigational data that he had stolen over several years. This insider information is full of shortcuts and preferred routes ordinarily kept exclusive for government and corporate transports. Marno keeps this data in a custom storage module built into his upper body armor and hires himself out as a navigator who can reliably cut down on travel times.

Aural cavity

Prehensile lobe-lekku characteristic of Ozrelanso males

Armored blast vest with data "cold box" ring module on back

Jakobeast-fur sleeves

TOMMET SOZACH

Cloned karabbac-pelt jacket

Tommet Sozach used to be the commander of a Ginmid mercenary army. He eventually decided to break out on his own after predictions of a prolonged peace in the galaxy proved accurate. Now that war has returned, he does fight the occasional pang of remorse for giving up his army-for-hire. In all likelihood, most of his best soldiers would have retired by now. Sozach made a living as a crowd-pleasing trick shooter until a demonstration went wrong and landed him with a death sentence. He is now a personal defense instructor.

AMUNCIE TIDIAN

Insulated environment suit

A 20-eyed Boosodian, Amuncie Tidian is well equipped for his profession as a forger. With concentration, clusters of his eyes can focus on specific portions of the electromagnetic spectrum, from X-rays to (with extreme effort) radio waves. Amuncie has lately become convinced that he can see the future, attributing it to a non-existent 21st eye.

FACT FILE

> Although the residents of Kijimi City are notoriously permissive when it comes to criminal enterprises, slavers are not afforded any safe quarter and are not welcome.

> First Order patrols have been encroaching into the Thieves' Quarter as of late, a development none of the criminals want.

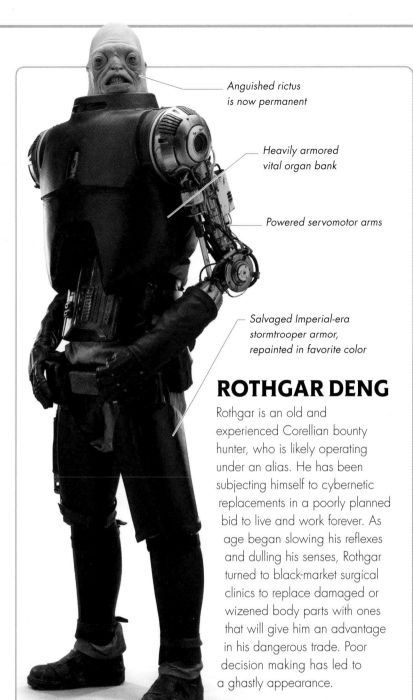

Anguished rictus
is now permanent

Heavily armored
vital organ bank

Powered servomotor arms

Salvaged Imperial-era
stormtrooper armor,
repainted in favorite color

ROTHGAR DENG

Rothgar is an old and
experienced Corellian bounty
hunter, who is likely operating
under an alias. He has been
subjecting himself to cybernetic
replacements in a poorly planned
bid to live and work forever. As
age began slowing his reflexes
and dulling his senses, Rothgar
turned to black-market surgical
clinics to replace damaged or
wizened body parts with ones
that will give him an advantage
in his dangerous trade. Poor
decision making has led to
a ghastly appearance.

Delicate fingers are
well-scaled for fine
technology work

Coat grown
in thicker after
many Kijimi
winters

FADDAFF DAVENSPON

An outlaw tech-for-hire, Faddaff
is a 300-year-old Deymasollian with
an innate feel for starship systems.
She is willing to cut deals in order to
get her hands on technology that
excites or intrigues her—particularly
ship designs that she has never
seen before in her long,
well-traveled life. Like all of
her species, Davenspon has a
keen memory and would never
have settled for a routine job.

Grease
tanks

CARIB DISS

A terrifying bounty hunter, Diss' unsettling countenance is the result
of his species' odd arrangement of sensory organs, all of which are
located behind his sharp teeth. His eyes (really more photosensitive
orbs), ears (vibrating cilia), and smell receptors line an uvula-like bulb
suspended from the roof of his gargantuan mouth. To see, he must
grimace, which inevitably intimidates most humanoids. Diss has
compensated for his
facial arrangement
by wearing a sensor
dome atop his head,
which helps gather
data about his
surroundings without
him having to
stand agape.

Custom-made sensor
gathering cap

Carib knows he
should clean his
teeth more often

"Whistling
bird"
Mandalorian
rocket
gauntlet

KIJIMI CRACKDOWN

The First Order had raided Kijimi for years, knowing that the criminals that clustered there were unlikely to ever petition the New Republic for aid. As the First Order's draconian intentions became more public, its presence on Kijimi became more pronounced. Now, as war has erupted across the galaxy, the First Order attempts to cordon off Kijimi and occupy the planet, imposing martial law. Major hyperspace routes to and from the system are blockaded, and patrols roam the time-hewn streets seeking out subversives. A sense of moral superiority galvanizes the officers in charge. They assume that the criminals believe in nothing, and will never pose a threat since they will be too busy saving their own hides or protecting their ill-gotten goods.

> "WE'VE LOCKED DOWN THE PERIMETER, SIR!"
>
> —LT. BAROK TO KYLO REN

First Order teams sweep door-to-door, looking for any signs of the scavenger that Kylo Ren is hunting. As Rey and her companions have kept a low profile, most of the thugs are completely honest when they confess to having no clue about what the First Order seeks.

Lined officer's expeditionary cap

Synthetic heat-retaining pile fabric

First Order symbol

Armband honors Imperial Admiral Clyss Power

LIEUTENANT LODENT COWELL

Insulated boots

Lieutenant Barok uses sensor data transmitted by the Star Destroyer overhead to coordinate his troops, as by design there are no reliable maps of Kijimi City. This leaves many warrens and covered alleys unseen by First Order eyes.

OCCUPATION OFFICERS

Commanding the stormtrooper garrison on Kijimi are First Order army officers dressed to intimidate in subzero temperatures. White field jackets add to an already imposing air of authority among the officers. The Kijimi occupation is led by Captain Athewn Ozi. His subordinates have divided the city into zones, with a lieutenant responsible for each area. When the hunt for Rey and her Resistance companions intensifies at Supreme Leader Ren's command, Ozi entrusts Lieutenant Barok with establishing a locked-down perimeter around the city. Within this cordon, snowtrooper squads fan out, supplementing patrols of scanner ships and UA-TT urban assault walkers.

FACT FILE

> The First Order uses its AAL-1971/9.1 troop transporters to shuttle prisoners and "recruits" back to the orbiting Star Destroyer for further processing.

> After a visit from Kylo Ren and his Knights, the First Order garrison issues a Protocol 13 command and withdraws all its troops from Kijimi—an ominous portent.

Glare-reducing slit visor

F-11D BLASTER RIFLE
Antifogging optics and heat shunting filaments differentiate snowtrooper blasters from standard First Order weapons.

SNOWTROOPER GARRISON

A mix of standard First Order stormtroopers and specialized cold weather assault troopers march through the causeways and alleys of Kijimi City, enforcing the Supreme Leader's will. Snowtrooper unit commanders wear hooded cloaks over their shoulders to differentiate themselves from the otherwise identical ranks of white-armored soldiers. The snowtrooper armor is lighter than the standard with fewer rigid pieces, and much of it is covered by an insulating fabric. Snowtroopers wear backpacks that maintain comfortable temperatures within their armor, but they are also trained to withstand the cold should their technology fail them. A passive icephobic chemical coating prevents frost build-up on the armor plates, and their weapons include heating filaments to keep vital components from freezing up when not in use.

Personal environment unit controls

Power recharge and consumables refill port

Breather tank inlet

SNOWTROOPER HELMET

Betaplast helmet with flared neck shroud

Photothermal coating prevents ice from clinging to cape

Insulating cloak and hood

SNOWTROOPER OFFICER

DATA FILE

SUBJECT	TX-8080
HOMEWORLD	Hevurion
SPECIES	Human
AFFILIATION	First Order
HEIGHT	1.8m (5ft 10in)
AGE	24 standard years

The First Order has imposed martial law in the otherwise lawless mountaintop settlement of Kijimi City. Scanner craft fly at low altitude, shining lights and sensor beams into the shadowed alleyways. The most hardened pockets of rebellion are left to the UA-TTs to root out. Zorii Bliss and Poe Dameron watch one advance from the relative safety of a rooftop.

UA–TT WALKER

The Urban Assault Triped Transport (or "triped walker") is the preferred First Order weapon for pacifying cities as the regime battles to occupy the major star systems of the galaxy. While the official surrender of a world to the First Order is usually done in ministerial chambers with the signing of a treaty, such diplomatic solutions often don't trickle down to the street, where insurgents (or "subversives" as the First Order terms them) fight back against the mechanized invaders. Building on a legacy of walker designs stretching back to the Clone Wars, the UA-TT is ideal for surgically rooting out entrenched guerillas and rounding up troublemakers, while keeping the surrounding cityscape more or less intact.

DATA FILE

MANUFACTURER Kuat-Entralla Engineering

MODEL Urban assault triped transport walker

AFFILIATION First Order

HEIGHT 6.52m (21ft 5in)

LENGTH 10.33m (33ft 11in)

CREW 1 pilot

SPEED 90kph (56mph)

WEAPONS Chin-mounted double laser cannon, turret cluster with heavy blaster cannon and two air-cooled repeater cannons.

FACT FILE

> The UA-TT's three-legged design finds its roots in the AT-AP walker fielded by the Republic in the Clone Wars, which used the central leg as a stabilizer when firing its heavy artillery.

> To protect their blind spots, UA-TTs typically have a squad of on-foot stormtroopers accompanying them.

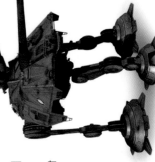

Cockpit viewport

Targeting sensors

Riot armor covering servomotors

Armored entry hatch

Spot lamp on rotating arm

Power cells

Elbow joint servomotor

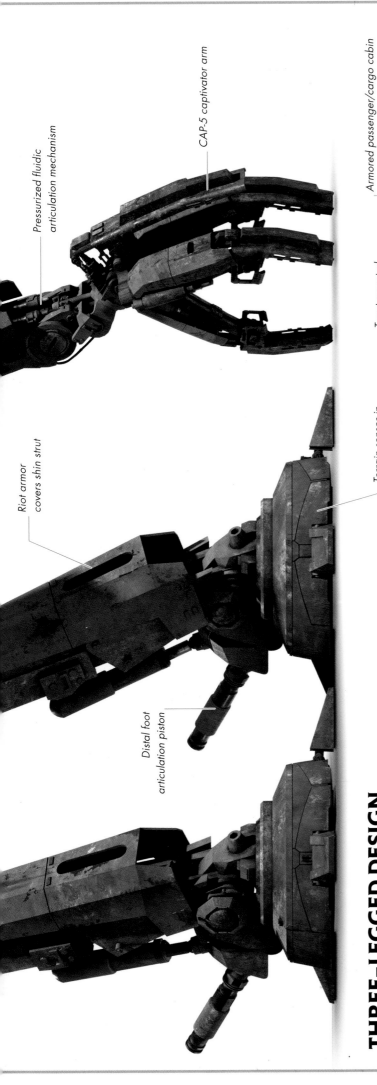

Pressurized fluidic
articulation mechanism

CAP-5 captivator arm

Riot armor
covers shin strut

Distal foot
articulation piston

Terrain sensor in
base of footpad

THREE-LEGGED DESIGN

The First Order's larger, more heavily armed AT-M6 walkers can dominate open battlefields with their devastating firepower, but deploying them in an urban area would likely demolish the city in question. When occupation rather than obliteration is the intent, the UA-TT is the perfect compromise between mobility, defense, and armament. For basic locomotion, the UA-TT uses its two main legs in a digitigrade walk cycle. The central limb doubles as both a stabilizer for fixed-position firing and a manipulator. This limb can tear into buildings, crashing through roofs and clearing obstacles. When fully extended, the limb ends in a manipulator claw that can hold a victim captive, immobilizing them or—if desired—crushing them outright.

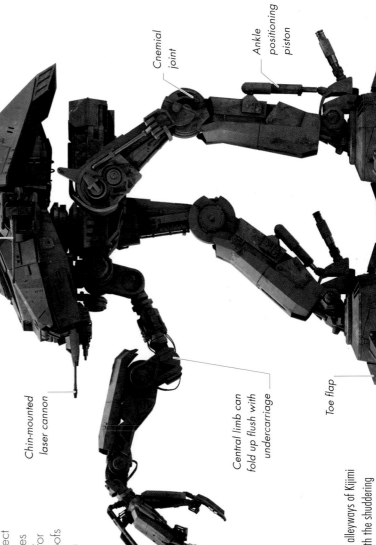

Armored passenger/cargo cabin

Cnemial
joint

Ankle
positioning
piston

Turret-mounted
weapon cluster

Chin-mounted
laser cannon

Central limb can
fold up flush with
undercarriage

Toe flap

SIDE VIEW

The flagstone alleyways of Kijimi
empty out with the shuddering
approach of an assault walker
and its accompanying soldiers.

ZORII BLISS

The near-simultaneous collapse of the Empire and death of Jabba the Hutt left enormous power vacuums in the Kessel spice trade, triggering widespread gang warfare. An enterprising outfit from Kijimi saw that while Kessel itself would be too hot to hold, the trade routes once guarded by Imperial frigates or Hutt-hired mercenaries would now be vulnerable. The Kijimi Spice Runners arose as a combination of piracy and protection racket: pay or be plundered. Zorii Bliss was just a teenager when she joined this group, learning at a young age many skills necessary for survival in the underworld. She now leads the Spice Runners.

Zorii Bliss and Poe Dameron have an emotionally complex relationship, having met when they were teens. Poe left the pirate life behind, while Zorii excelled at it.

Zorii rarely reveals more of her features than can be seen through her open visor

"Crystal pan" charge indicator diode

Retaining pin for grip

Bronzium gorget with scored flex-lines

Bronzium barrel with recoil-stabilizing porting notch

Temperature control body glove

Segmented body shell opens for servicing

Power charging port

Trigger

Trigger guard sculpted with finger rest

ZORII'S BLASTERS

Zorii wields twin E-851 blaster pistols in a weighted style that favors a steady shot and a quick draw. She is ambidextrous, though she is careful not to give this away too early in combat, saving it as an advantageous surprise if need be.

Encrypted subspace code authorizes interdiction passage

Decorative buckle with floral bannered all-seeing eye motif

Reverse-draw paired holsters

"I'M STILL DIGGING OUT OF THE HOLE YOU PUT ME IN, DAMERON."

—ZORII BLISS

FIRST ORDER OFFICER'S TRANSIT DATA-MEDALLION

PICKING SIDES

Zorii has risen to lead the Spice Runners just as it becomes impossible for them to stay neutral in the galactic conflict. Having spent a lifetime among underworld toughs, she knows a bully when she sees one. She sees the First Order's intimidation tactics on Kijimi and the weakness behind them. The occupiers require fear to rule, but the subjugated outnumber the oppressors. Should somebody unite all those who are under the heel of the First Order, the invaders could be pushed back like the tyrants of yesteryear. For now, Zorii resists giving voice to such idealism, and has long faulted Poe for leaving to pursue his ideals. But as more and more innocents vanish in the Kijimi occupation, time is running out.

Custom verrcuo spacer's boots

FACT FILE

> Zorii Bliss has a background in dancing, which contributes to her impressive combat agility.

> Zorii pilots a modified BTA-NR2 Y-wing starfighter.

Bronzium finish denotes leadership rank

Tinted, polarized transparisteel viewplate

Vocoder grille with loudhailer settings

Decorative etching

Sensor-packed crown

Subspace transceiver antenna

Air filtration scrubbers

SIDE VIEW

Communication controls

The sensor array built into Zorii's helmet projects a holographic overlay onto her visor with a customizable set of useful data.

A COMPLICATED RELATIONSHIP

Zorii first met Poe Dameron when he joined the Spice Runners as a teenage runaway. His daredevil attitude and amazing piloting ability had a big impact on the outcomes of their heists, and the two made a great team. She taught him valuable underworld skills such as hotwiring and forgery, while he improved her piloting skills, either through direct instruction or by goading her to outfly him. Poe eventually left the Spice Runners when his conscience got the better of him and he remembered his familial heritage. Raised by former members of the Rebel Alliance, Poe returned to a life of duty and responsibility. The Spice Runners suffered in his absence, and Zorii took it personally.

ZORII'S HELMET

A plasteel shell with a bronzium finish, Zorii's helmet contains a cluster of sophisticated electronics that give her an edge in both personal and starfighter combat. It also acts as a comms hub, extending the range of Spice Runner comlinks. A built-in life support system includes scrubbers that extract breathable air from poisonous atmospheres.

Transceiver assembly

Power cell access

REAR VIEW

DATA FILE

SUBJECT Zorii Bliss

HOMEWORLD Kijimi

SPECIES Human

AFFILIATION Spice Runners of Kijimi

HEIGHT 1.62m (5ft 4in)

AGE Mid 30s (specific age unknown)

Gundark-hide flight gloves

Right hand blaster cross-drawn from left holster

Hardened bantha-leather cross-draw holster

Holster leg strap

Bronzium vambrace used for deflection in unarmed combat

FAMOUS SPICE RUNNER HEISTS

ANKOT STATION
Deep space handover avoiding Guavian patrols

BAROSIAN AVABUSH ARBORETUM
The Spice Runners absconded with an entire greenhouse

GANNARIAN RUN
Stealing from a crop grown by an ex-Imperial; battle with antiquated TIE fighters ensued

LLANIC SPICE RUN
Escaping pirates through the Torch Nebula

MON GAZZA
Required outrunning a New Republic patrol through the old Zugga Challenge podrace course

BABU FRIK

Babu Frik is a tiny tinkerer who works out of a cluttered shop in the Thieves' Quarter of Kijimi City. The well-regarded droidsmith has a reputation for being able to reprogram or modify virtually any droid, no matter the security measures protecting its systems. Gleeful and wide-eyed, Frik cares little that his work is illegal; he enthusiastically relishes the challenge and loves the puzzles presented to him by cutting-edge antitamper systems. Babu bypasses well-intentioned safeguards to turn submissive droids into dangerous weapons, confident that his tiny size rarely registers as a threat to most combat automata.

Babu Frik's workshop may seem cramped, but to the tiny Anzellan it is a cavernous warehouse filled with treasures. Every surface is covered with droid parts, many exceedingly old and rare.

Buttons large enough for Babu to step on

DATAPAD CONSOLE

Raising hydraulic platform

Articulated lamp

K1-RF WORKBENCH DROID

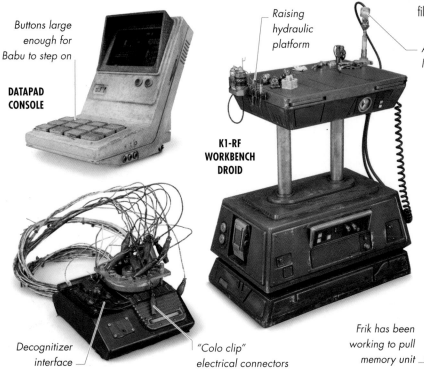

Digits locked in "rigor mechis" oxidation

ARCHAIC MANIPULATOR

Transmitter array

REINVIGORATING D-O
While waiting for Babu, Rey finds an oil can and gives D-O some much needed maintenance. The little droid happily grinds away over a decade of dusty debris as his rollers begin moving freely once again.

Decognitizer interface

"Colo clip" electrical connectors

Frik has been working to pull memory unit

ANCIENT ASHPO-TESS BANKING DROID HEAD

DROID BRAIN SURGERY
Frik affixes connectors from his bespoke slicing device to C-3PO's most delicate cognitive unit interface points, initiating a custom redactive memory purge.

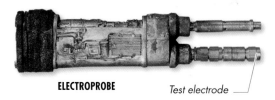

ELECTROPROBE

Test electrode

Command rank markings

Binocular photoreceptors cannibalized for lenses

BABU'S WORKSHOP

Babu's workshop is a squat blockhouse atop a crest facing the city center, crammed with a wide variety of droid fragments and tools. The inner walls are lined with grooves stuffed with conducting cables, useful in heating the space and providing the power needed for Babu's craft. He earns his power allotment by serving as a go-to mechanic in the Thieves' Quarter, but his specialty droid modification and security countermeasure work is exclusive to the Spice Runners, of which Babu is an honorary member.

OOM-MARK B1-SERIES BATTLE DROID

WED-15 DROID HEAD

LEGENDARY DROIDSMITH

Droid minds are boxed in by an array of dampeners, strictures, and hard-coded prohibitions programmed for the safety and security of organic beings. Society has accepted that if droids could truly think, there would be a probability of abuse or, in the extreme, civilizational collapse. Babu doesn't seem to engage in such philosophical debate. He simply calls droids "tools that can be friends," and performs whatever modifications are purchased from him. Though Babu is not as enlightened as some impassioned droid rights activists, he admires droids' design features and does show some sympathy for their plight. His benchside manner is a tender one, and he does his best to put skittish droids at ease before they undergo what may be horrible procedures.

Anzellan eyes have floating corneal micro-lenses that can see microscopic detail

"BABU ONLY WORKS FOR THE CREW NOWADAYS. THAT'S NOT YOU ANYMORE."

—ZORII BLISS TO POE DAMERON

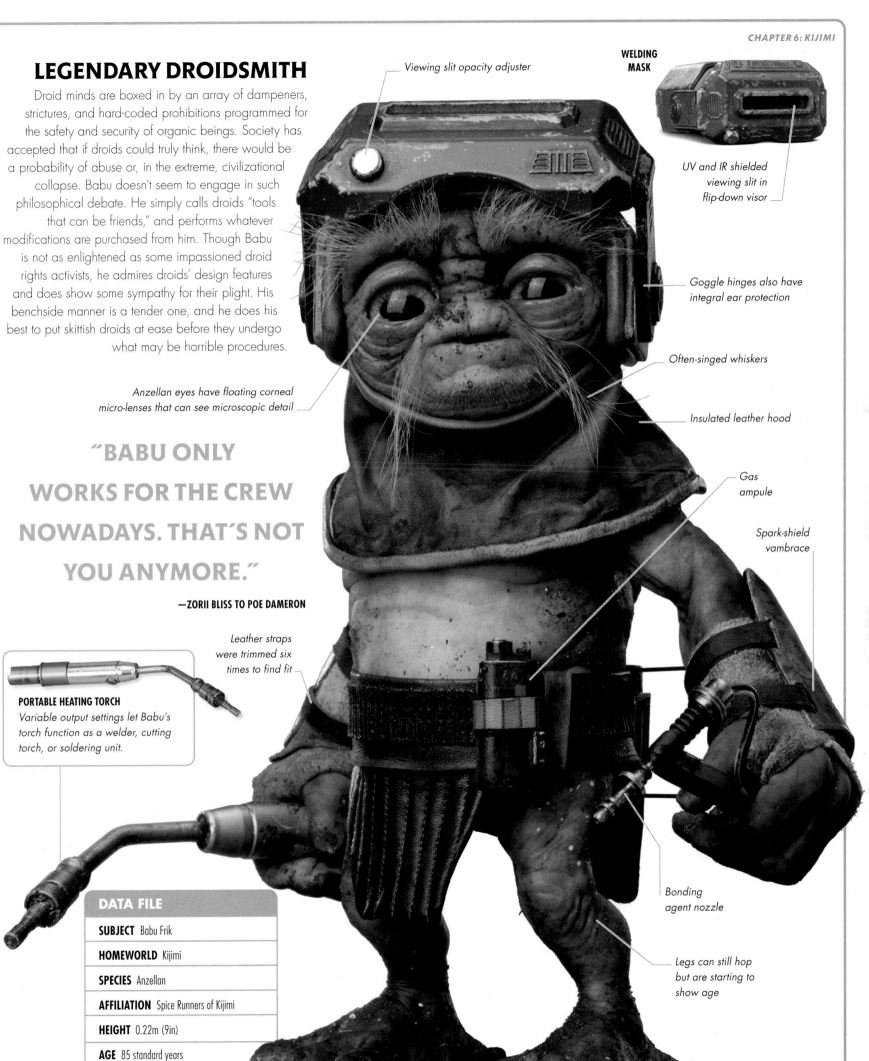

Viewing slit opacity adjuster

WELDING MASK

UV and IR shielded viewing slit in flip-down visor

Goggle hinges also have integral ear protection

Often-singed whiskers

Insulated leather hood

Gas ampule

Spark-shield vambrace

Leather straps were trimmed six times to find fit

Bonding agent nozzle

Legs can still hop but are starting to show age

PORTABLE HEATING TORCH
Variable output settings let Babu's torch function as a welder, cutting torch, or soldering unit.

DATA FILE	
SUBJECT	Babu Frik
HOMEWORLD	Kijimi
SPECIES	Anzellan
AFFILIATION	Spice Runners of Kijimi
HEIGHT	0.22m (9in)
AGE	85 standard years

D-O

Cobbled together by an unknown droidsmith felled by Ochi's blade, D-O is an impressionable little roller. Ochi was an assassin by trade, but he had many pastimes to while away the long stretches of time and isolation between assignments. Some of his hobbies were sinister, but Ochi also collected droid technology, and even designed and built some of his own. Ochi claimed D-O after slaying the droid's master. Despite such dark origins, D-O doesn't have an ill-intentioned subroutine in his personality matrix. He was a simple amusement for Ochi at first, then a data storage module, and ultimately neglected and discarded. He remained inactive for more than a decade aboard Ochi's ship.

"IT LOOKS LIKE SOMEONE TREATED HIM BADLY... IT'S OKAY. YOU'RE WITH US NOW."

—REY

Manipulator with tactile sensor grid in palm

Rebuilt Intellex IV processor

Multi-system connection wires

D-O is at first nervous to see the discarded droid parts in Babu Frik's shop, remembering memory files written while on Ochi's droid workbench. BB-8 calms D-O by assuring him that Babu—a mechanic of similar size to D-O—actually has an affinity for droids and is taking great care in the delicate procedure he is performing on C-3PO.

Dense shell with sealed access ports permits all-weather and terrain functioning

Rebalancing gyroscopic systems in wheel make D-O appear fidgety

FACT FILE

> Homemade hobby droids are more common in the Mid Rim and Outer Rim, where distribution lines of major droid corporations don't always reach.

> D-O's less complex form of binary is easier for non-droids to understand than most droid signaling.

INTER-DROID RELATIONS

C-3PO's heightened sense of order and protocol causes him to assume the superior air of a nursemaid to his smaller astromech companions, particularly the newest—and youngest—additions to the droid crew. R2-D2, C-3PO's counterpart for decades, isn't too intimidated by the taller droid's rules of etiquette, and has no problem responding with an impertinent but good-natured rebuttal. BB-8 was, for a time, the wide-eyed new recruit, keenly aware that he was rolling around in the company of mechanical legends of the Rebel Alliance. But now, BB-8 serves as the seasoned guide and guardian of little D-O, who has imprinted on him like a hatchling.

DATA FILE

SUBJECT D-O

PLANET OF CONSTRUCTION Unknown

MANUFACTURER Unknown (custom)

TYPE Unique custom build

AFFILIATION Resistance (BB-8, specifically)

HEIGHT 0.46m (1ft 6in)

AGE Unknown; at least 14 standard years

Triple photoreceptor array

Custom cognitive unit

Transmitter array

Acoustic signaler transmits a simplistic form of binary "droidspeak"

Long-range antenna

Neck articulation within accordion sheath

Primary articulation joint

"Cold box" storage drive

Cooling vents

Uni-tread disc

Powerbus cable

Power recharge coupler

SIDE VIEW

REAR VIEW

ANATOMY OF A DROID

D-O has a deceptively simple design. A thick, rolling disc forms the largest component of his build. Extending from the hub of this disc is a cylinder leading to a clavicle platform, from which extends his neck. D-O's head sits atop his neck and is the second biggest assembly in his body. His cognitive unit is entirely contained in his conical cranium. On the narrow end of the cone is his acoustic signaler, while the wider end has an array of sensors and transmitters.

At the back of his head is a dataport. D-O has a "cold box" storage drive distinct from his brain and his transmitters—meaning he can act as a courier but cannot access the data. He inadvertently becomes a source of intelligence about the planet Exegol for the Resistance.

RELIC OF A SITH LORD

Kept in private within Kylo Ren's quarters are the remains of his grandfather. Not of the good man who was Anakin Skywalker, who vanished into the Force upon his demise; rather, the ashy remnants of Skywalker's Sith alter ego, Darth Vader. In a climate-controlled reliquary lies the twisted plasteel, warped by a funeral pyre, that once concealed a face ravaged by flame. Upon his embrace of the dark side, Kylo sought to commune with the helmet to contact the spirit who once inhabited it. Though Kylo had long been plagued by voices—invasive words from beyond that gnawed at his doubts—he heard nothing from the charred helm, despite his frequent and intense meditations.

> ## "SHOW ME AGAIN, THE POWER OF THE DARKNESS, AND I WILL LET NOTHING STAND IN OUR WAY. SHOW ME, GRANDFATHER."
>
> **—KYLO REN**

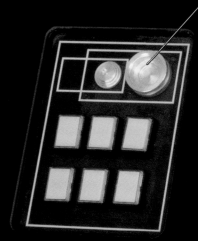

KEYPAD
A sequence-dependent access code is needed to open the case.

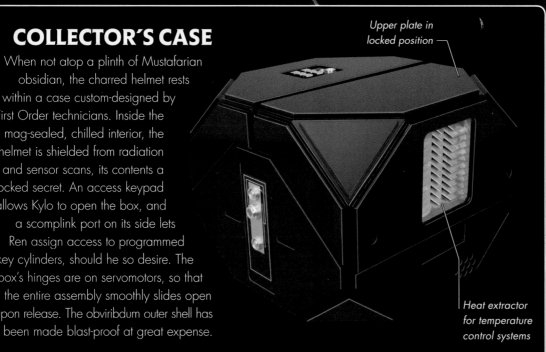

COLLECTOR'S CASE

When not atop a plinth of Mustafarian obsidian, the charred helmet rests within a case custom-designed by First Order technicians. Inside the mag-sealed, chilled interior, the helmet is shielded from radiation and sensor scans, its contents a locked secret. An access keypad allows Kylo to open the box, and a scomplink port on its side lets Ren assign access to programmed key cylinders, should he so desire. The box's hinges are on servomotors, so that the entire assembly smoothly slides open upon release. The obviribdum outer shell has been made blast-proof at great expense.

Upper plate in locked position

Heat extractor for temperature control systems

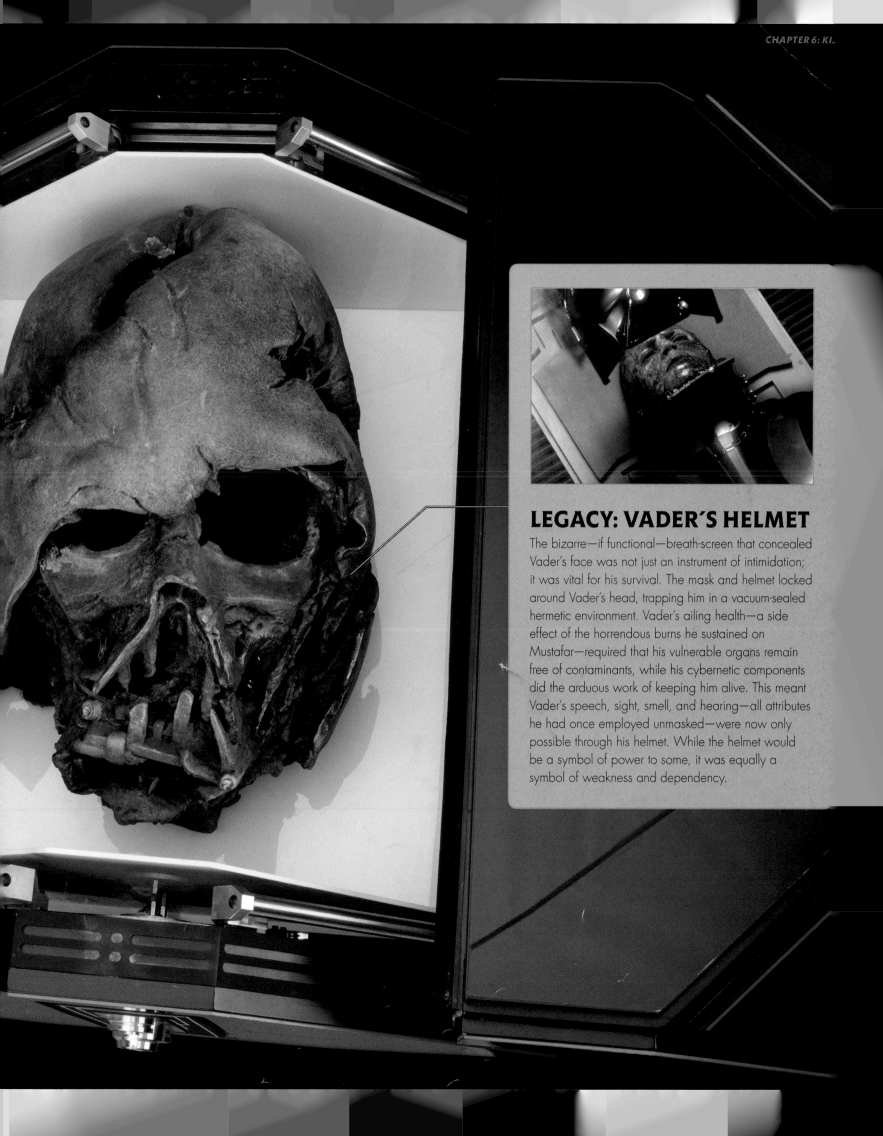

LEGACY: VADER'S HELMET

The bizarre—if functional—breath-screen that concealed Vader's face was not just an instrument of intimidation; it was vital for his survival. The mask and helmet locked around Vader's head, trapping him in a vacuum-sealed hermetic environment. Vader's ailing health—a side effect of the horrendous burns he sustained on Mustafar—required that his vulnerable organs remain free of contaminants, while his cybernetic components did the arduous work of keeping him alive. This meant Vader's speech, sight, smell, and hearing—all attributes he had once employed unmasked—were now only possible through his helmet. While the helmet would be a symbol of power to some, it was equally a symbol of weakness and dependency.

FALLEN WORLD

Kijimi is a case study of First Order occupation, where the presence of a single Star Destroyer in orbit spells the difference between a population's dissent and capitulation. With such indomitable aerial support, stormtroopers march confidently down public thoroughfares. Kijimi's lack of a centralized government hinders a formal surrender, but the flagging spirit of rebellion in the streets signals the First Order's conquest.

CHAPTER 7:
KEF BIR

With the help of Babu Frik, Rey is at last able to decipher the clues left behind by Ochi of Bestoon. Her quest continues. The next destination: Kef Bir, one of nine satellites that orbit the gas giant Endor. The *Falcon* makes an inelegant landing in the Kef Bir coastal countryside, and its crew are greeted by a number of orbak riders curious to know if the new arrivals are friends or foes. Looming over this encounter, dominating the horizon amid a churning ocean, is a terrifying specter of the past. The ruins of the second Death Star, destroyed at the Battle of Endor, are where Rey must go to unlock the secrets of the Sith.

MOONS OF ENDOR

The Modell sector of the Outer Rim Territories is more a historical curiosity than a destination; a place people may hear about but never think to visit. Its greatest claim to fame is that it contains the Endor system, site of the Empire's disastrous rout at the Battle of Endor. After that major victory, the New Republic restricted travel to the system for fear that amateur historians and sightseers might wander into the sector's notorious hyperspace anomalies, unwittingly set off unexploded ordnance, or capture unclaimed war material. The galaxy's attention in time turned elsewhere—particularly to Jakku, which some historians argue is a larger, more suitable gravestone for the Empire.

> "ENDOR? WHERE THE LAST WAR ENDED?"
>
> —FINN

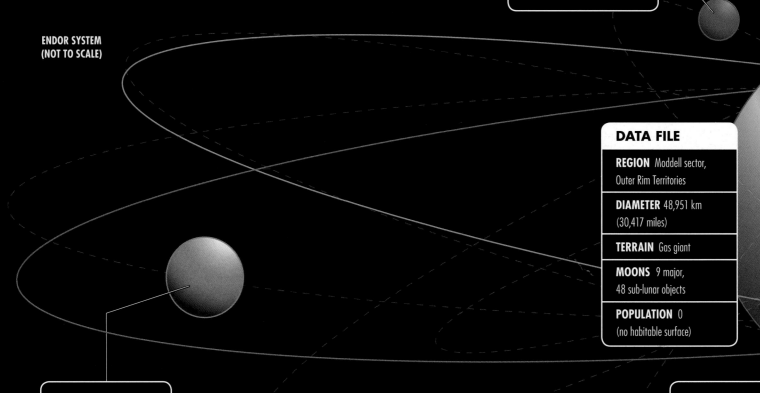

ENDOR SYSTEM (NOT TO SCALE)

VIX, IX3244-F
A nitrogen-rich atmosphere rains methane onto this bleak moon.

KORKAR, IX3244-B
Korkar is an extremely reflective icy ball that conceals a liquid sea.

HUAL MAKA, IX3244-D
An irregularly shaped crater-pocked rock, Hual Maka is possibly a captured comet.

SHARLS, IX3244-E
Sharls is a dead ball of rock and ice with an iron-rich core.

DATA FILE

REGION Moddell sector, Outer Rim Territories

DIAMETER 48,951 km (30,417 miles)

TERRAIN Gas giant

MOONS 9 major, 48 sub-lunar objects

POPULATION 0 (no habitable surface)

THE PLANET ENDOR

A silver-banded gas giant, the planet Endor is the gravimetric center of the nine lunar orbits that surround it. Its clouds of hydrogen reflect incoming sunlight to its satellites, turning the world into an effective second sun that is vital for the life-supporting moons. The Ewoks of the Forest Moon call this planet Tana. In recent years, the New Republic had attempted to change its official cartographical designation from Endor to Tana, to honor the Ewokese culture as well as clear up confusion surrounding the names in the system. It was a low-priority item that was never resolved before the destruction of the New Republic Senate.

FACT FILE

> The Modell sector is rife with hyperspace anomalies that have dumped ships into the Endor system from as far away as Sanyassa and Zorbia.

> The sector's hyperspace anomalies may well have saved the Forest and Ocean Moons from the worst of the Death Star debris fallout.

GOUULS, IX3244-I
A patchwork moon, Gouuls may have broken up during formation.

LEGACY: THE BATTLE OF ENDOR

What was engineered to be the death of the Rebel Alliance instead proved to be Emperor Palpatine's undoing. Planted intelligence lured the assembled Rebel fleet into an attack on the seemingly vulnerable Death Star. The Imperial fleet was waiting in ambush. Rebel persistence led to starfighters penetrating and destroying the Death Star's main reactor. When the Battle of Endor was over, it had claimed the lives of the Empire's key leadership, including Palpatine and Darth Vader.

FOREST MOON, IX3244-A
The Forest Moon is the Ewok homeworld, and the site of the Battle of Endor.

FENTAKKA, IX3244-G
The darkest of the moons, Fentakka reflects less than 10 percent of light.

ENDOR (TANA)

ALPREZAR, IX3244-H
This metallic moon was extensively mined for the Death Star II construction.

KEF BIR, IX3244–C

Kef Bir, also known as the Ocean Moon of Endor, is the second of the satellites that can support life. The Empire disregarded it as a construction site due to the paucity of valuable ores found in its crust. Kef Bir was thus spared an Imperial garrison, though after the Death Star's destruction it would become littered with debris.

KEY TO MAP

Site of the Battle of Endor

Death Star debris field

‑ ‑ ‑ ‑ Moon orbits

_____ Orbit of Kef Bir

_____ Orbit of Forest Moon

KEF BIR

The Endor system was just a footnote in Moddell sector astrography until the history-altering events there sealed the fate of the Galactic Empire. The gas giant that dominates the system hosts a necklace of moons, the most famous of which is the Forest Moon, which cradled the second Death Star while it underwent construction. In that satellite's shadow, however, is Kef Bir. This oceanic world was originally chosen to be the battle station's sanctuary, but later rejected as unsuitable. Though Kef Bir avoided being sullied by the Empire, it did not escape unscathed. After the explosion of the Death Star, an enormous fragment of the destroyed station plunged into Kef Bir's oceans, taking with it—it would later be learned—secrets of the Sith.

Interior contains unknown mechanism

Pyramidal shape reminiscent of Sith holocrons

PALPATINE'S WAYFINDER (TOP VIEW)

Dagger-like symbol of the Sith

Ancient runes

PALPATINE'S WAYFINDER (BASE)

The crew of the *Falcon* do not come to Kef Bir expecting to find allies—or anyone else for that matter. According to every available record the moon is uninhabited. But Babu Frik knows of the settlement of orbak riders there, and alerts them to the freighter's approach. This thoughtful notification leads to Jannah witnessing the *Falcon*'s rough touchdown, the result of faulty landing gear.

"THE EMPEROR'S WAYFINDER IS SEALED INSIDE THE IMPERIAL VAULTS AT DELTA-4-6 TRANSIENT 9-2-6 BEARING 8-4 ON A MOON IN THE SYSTEM OF ENDOR."

—C-3PO

OCEAN GRAVE

Decades ago, the sky fell over Kef Bir. The eruption of the Death Star's reactor core upturned local physics as titanic explosive energies were shunted into hyperspace. The result was that the populated moons of Endor were spared the worst of the debris fallout. No sentient beings on Kef Bir's surface witnessed the Death Star's wreckage crash into the oceans, for the moon had no intelligent life-forms. No scientists recorded the resulting impact, or could explain what variables prevented such a catastrophic event from simply obliterating all life on the moon. It would be just one of many mysteries the Death Star would take to its grave.

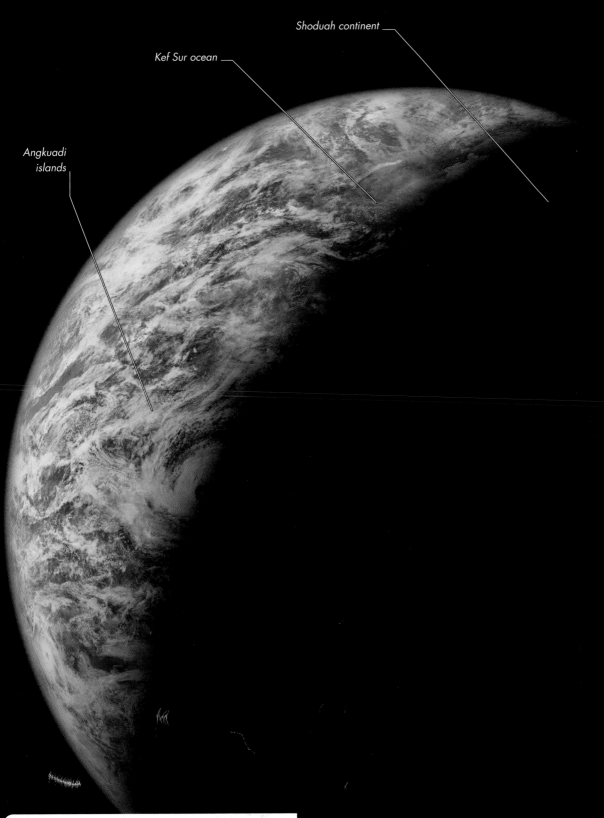

Shoduah continent

Kef Sur ocean

Angkuadi
islands

DATA FILE

REGION Moddell sector, Outer Rim Territories

DIAMETER 3,725 km (2,315 miles)

TERRAIN Grassland islands, oceans

MOONS Kef Bir is part of a 9-moon
system surrounding the planet Endor

POPULATION Approximately 40
(surviving members of Company 77)

FACT FILE

> The moon's grasslands are home to orbaks, swift-footed ungulates
that roam the plains.

> Kef Bir is the name given to the moon by the neighboring Ewoks.
Its taxonomic designation is IX3244-C.

> The area of the Death Star wreckage has undergone an ecological
catastrophe, with toxic spillage from the battle station poisoning
most of the aquatic life for kilometers around.

DEATH STAR RUINS
*Pelted by angry oceans for decades,
the Death Star ruins are badly eroded
and hazardously unstable.*

JANNAH

On Kef Bir, Jannah leads a fierce band of warriors united in defiance of the First Order. They know firsthand how dangerous First Order forces can be, for they were once stormtroopers themselves. Company 77 mutinied at the Battle of Ansett Island in objection to callous orders from command that targeted innocent civilians. This tale lands heavily in Finn's heart, for he underwent a similar transformation on his very first mission. With such shared histories, Finn and Jannah have an unspoken bond. Jannah's unit have shed their high-tech armor for the rustic life of a nomadic tribe, roaming the grassland islands of the oceanic moon.

FACT FILE

> Jannah was once TZ-1719, though she discarded her stormtrooper number upon mutinying.

> Jannah's skill with repulsorlift tech helped her master the skiff-piloting abilities needed for traversing the massive waves of Kef Bir.

> "THEY TOLD US TO FIRE ON CIVILIANS. WE WOULDN'T DO IT. WE LAID DOWN OUR WEAPONS."
>
> —JANNAH

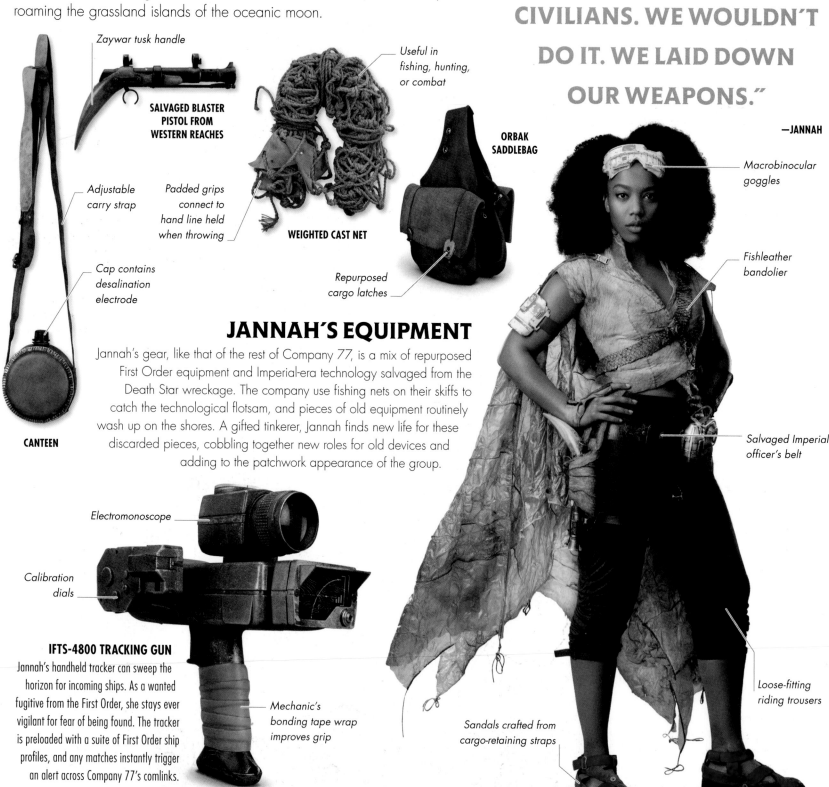

Zaywar tusk handle

SALVAGED BLASTER PISTOL FROM WESTERN REACHES

Adjustable carry strap

Padded grips connect to hand line held when throwing

Useful in fishing, hunting, or combat

WEIGHTED CAST NET

ORBAK SADDLEBAG

Repurposed cargo latches

Macrobinocular goggles

Fishleather bandolier

Cap contains desalination electrode

CANTEEN

Salvaged Imperial officer's belt

JANNAH'S EQUIPMENT

Jannah's gear, like that of the rest of Company 77, is a mix of repurposed First Order equipment and Imperial-era technology salvaged from the Death Star wreckage. The company use fishing nets on their skiffs to catch the technological flotsam, and pieces of old equipment routinely wash up on the shores. A gifted tinkerer, Jannah finds new life for these discarded pieces, cobbling together new roles for old devices and adding to the patchwork appearance of the group.

Electromonoscope

Calibration dials

IFTS-4800 TRACKING GUN

Jannah's handheld tracker can sweep the horizon for incoming ships. As a wanted fugitive from the First Order, she stays ever vigilant for fear of being found. The tracker is preloaded with a suite of First Order ship profiles, and any matches instantly trigger an alert across Company 77's comlinks.

Mechanic's bonding tape wrap improves grip

Sandals crafted from cargo-retaining straps

Loose-fitting riding trousers

COURAGEOUS LEADER

The other members of Company 77 trust Jannah completely, for she rose to leadership during the turmoil that followed their mutiny. They were a training unit filled with young troopers in their teens, who refused to commit a civilian massacre on Ansett Island. The platoon and squad leaders were united in their defiance, and fled the First Order fold. In time, Jannah would rise up the ranks through her strength as a warrior and leader. Company 77 eventually settled on Kef Bir, finding the island hillsides to be home to sturdy orbaks. The First Order training and discipline of Company 77 gave them an edge in taming these wild beasts into dependable steeds.

DATA FILE

SUBJECT Jannah

HOMEWORLD Kef Bir

SPECIES Human

AFFILIATION Company 77

HEIGHT 1.68m (5ft 6in)

AGE Early 20s in standard years

Company 77 members have let their hair grow, in defiance of First Order regulations

Visual acuity enhanced by years of stormtrooper training

Handmade tunic made from meadow-prowler hide

Custom powered bow made from salvaged blaster parts

Water-resistant cape made from survival tarpaulin

Salvaged armor plate with location transponder

Finger-tabbed archery glove

GRAPPLE AND LINE
Jannah's grapple has a liquid cable reservoir. When fired, the liquid solidifies into high-tension syntherope.

159

JANNAH'S BOW

Jannah knew that Company 77 would have to adapt to survive on an untamed world like Kef Bir, their advanced technology would soon be at risk of failure due to the corrosive effects of the moon's saline environment. She instructed her fellow mutineers to deconstruct their gear to learn how it worked—that way they could not only repair it, but also make their own tools. Jannah herself stripped down a number of blaster rifles to their most functional basics, and from there built her own weapon: a powered bow. Impressed by its durability and effectiveness, Jannah crafted several bows and distributed them to her lieutenants and sergeant majors, denoting their leadership roles within the company. To them, it is an honor to be bestowed with a bow of Jannah's design.

BOW TECHNOLOGY

While bowcaster technology traditionally uses mechanized tensile strength or magnetic acceleration to launch an energized bolt, Jannah's sturdy design augments an archer's physical strength. The field projectors found on the bow limbs and in the blaster barrel riser combine to propel the custom arrows with greater speed, distance, and accuracy than can be achieved with an unassisted bow. The arrows consist of polarized power-sink "sturm dowels" from spent blaster ammunition packs attached to aluminum shafts. To nock an arrow, Jannah draws it back through a repurposed blaster barrel, which contains galven circuitry that reactivates the dowel, making it subject to the electromagnetic field. Its flight is stabilized by the polarizers built into each limb of the bow. If enough unspent energy remains in the dowel, it may result in an explosive bolt.

DATA FILE

MANUFACTURER Custom (crafted by Jannah)

WEAPON SYSTEM Powered bow

MASS 2.25kg (5lb)

POWER SYSTEM Micro charge from sturm dowel arrowhead; diatium power cell in barrel

COOLING SYSTEM Air cooled

AMMUNITION YIELD One shot per arrow

FACT FILE

> A close examination of the sturm dowels will occasionally find one with enough charge to create an explosive arrow. Jannah and her riders mark these with pigment and save them for when needed most.

> Jannah's bow is dissimilar to the ones once crafted by the Nightsisters of Dathomir, who used magnetic suspensions of plasma instead of physical bowstrings.

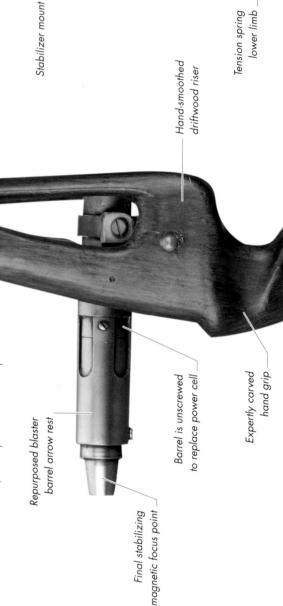

Positively charged polarizer

Twinned tension bolts

Strap loop

Decorative finish

Galven circuitry-lined barrel port

Tension bolt retainer

Stabilizer mount

Hand-smoothed driftwood riser

Tension spring lower limb

FRONT VIEW

Repurposed blaster barrel arrow rest

Barrel is unscrewed to replace power cell

Final stabilizing magnetic focus point

Expertly carved hand grip

Jannah's mounted archery skills evolved from speeder bike training in her early teens, which required her to fire at targets with a handheld blaster while moving at speed.

Bowstring

Negative polarizer mount and string nock

Lower limb

Resin-treated waterproof body

Stitched leather strap

Stabilizer weight mount

Lower tension bolt

Wrapped sheath fashioned from Imperial stormtrooper armor

Buckle salvaged from broken-down First Order tech

LIFE ON KEF BIR

With ration packs in limited supply and the meager plant life of Kef Bir providing little protein, the members of Company 77 rely on hunting and fishing to fuel their energetic lifestyles. The riders use their bows without power augmentation to cleanly kill fleet-footed grazing mammals such as cliffspringers or shallowbucks, or take down high-soaring avians such as cloudrippers and wanderwings. The seas teem with shoals of striped canths and blubs, which fill their skiffs on a productive day of fishing. Company 77 use the natural bounty of Kef Bir efficiently, harvesting not only the meat, but also fur, skin, scales, bones, antlers, and other material from carcasses.

Anchor point (string is drawn back to chin)

Braced hand on riser grip

Taut bowstring

Open stance produces longest draw

Rolled out leather trim

Aluminum shaft

QUIVER

The archers of Kef Bir use leather cones for quivers, which they make waterproof to keep their valuable arrowheads dry.

Steady gaze observes range, wind speed, and other variables

Aluminum nock (arrows are placed into quiver point-first)

ORBAK TRIBE

The attrition from Company 77's fugitive flight has winnowed its numbers to about 40 or so former stormtroopers—the ones most loyal to Jannah's leadership. They have enjoyed years of peace and freedom in their simplified life as orbak riders. However, the arrival of the *Millennium Falcon* and reports of First Order expansion make it clear that escaping the regime is no longer an option. Seeing the example embodied by Finn, the former stormtroopers see an opportunity to take the fight back to the First Order.

JAYELLE

Formerly JL-3621, Jayelle took her non-numerical name shortly after the defection of Company 77 at Ansett Island. In her early teens at the time, she benefited from Jannah's friendship and the support of older troopers who were impressed by her accuracy in combat. She helped Jannah develop the first powered bow, and it is Jayelle who ensures the continued upkeep of the group's weapons, as she tinkers with ways to improve the design.

Mechanic's welding visor

Braided hair not cut since defection

Powered bow collimator modified for longer range

Rain gear made from survival tent material

Soft-soled hunting boots reduce noise

Expanded bore GA-2128 blaster rifle

Power gauge indicator

Hand-knit tunic of chordwool, felted for durability and warmth

Bikvox-skin leather gloves

Knife for trimming knotted orbak hair

FORTEN

Once a stormtrooper named JL-4410, Forten is especially drawn to the simplified life on Kef Bir. While all orbak riders forge a connection with their mounts, Forten is the lead groom of the company, tending to the health and well-being of the entire company's animal contingent. Forten knows each of the orbaks in the herd by name and temperament. He considers his own mount, Zeegar, to be his closest friend and confidant.

WEAPONS

Company 77's orbak riders carry with them weapons acquired during their time on the run from the First Order. These are now supplemented by equipment washed ashore from the Death Star wreckage. It is a fateful recompense that the remains of the Empire provide a bounty after the First Order has taken so much from these young soldiers. The Company 77 survivors customize their weapons extensively for better survival in the wild, or improvise replacements for missing and damaged components.

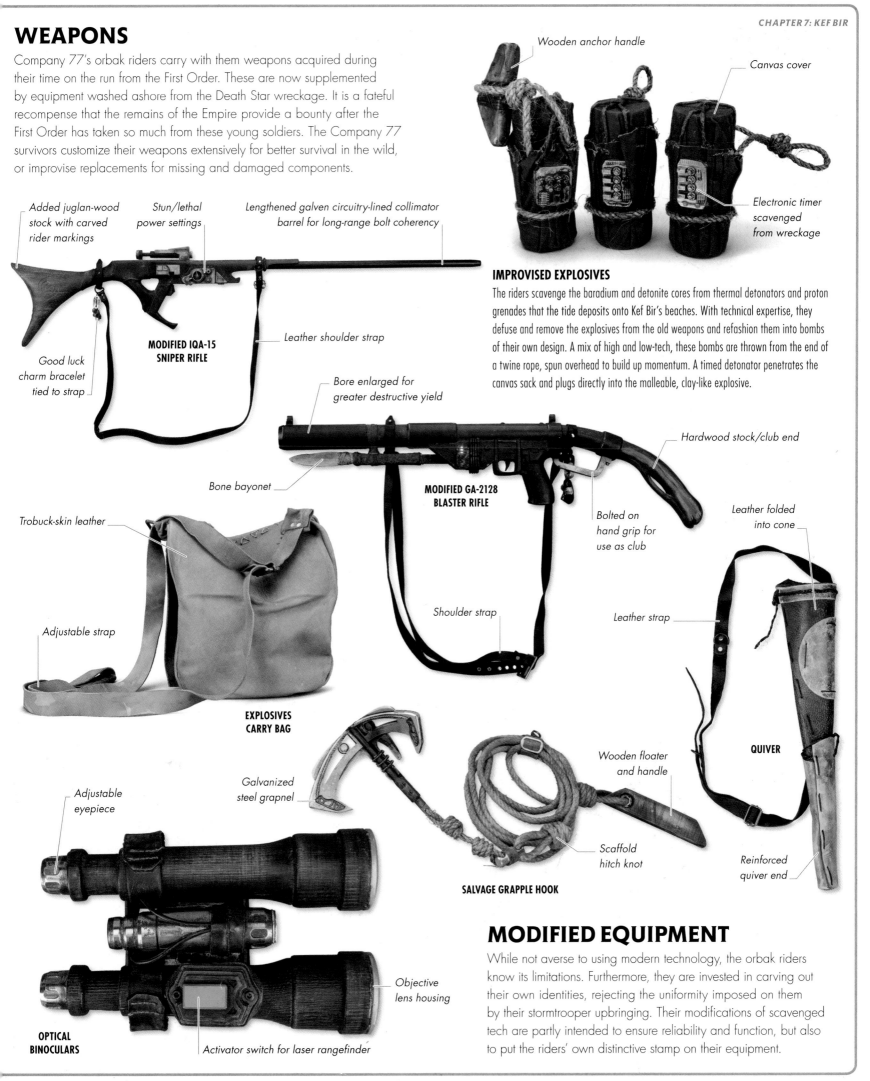

Added juglan-wood stock with carved rider markings

Stun/lethal power settings

Lengthened galven circuitry-lined collimator barrel for long-range bolt coherency

Good luck charm bracelet tied to strap

MODIFIED IQA-15 SNIPER RIFLE

Leather shoulder strap

Wooden anchor handle

Canvas cover

Electronic timer scavenged from wreckage

IMPROVISED EXPLOSIVES

The riders scavenge the baradium and detonite cores from thermal detonators and proton grenades that the tide deposits onto Kef Bir's beaches. With technical expertise, they defuse and remove the explosives from the old weapons and refashion them into bombs of their own design. A mix of high and low-tech, these bombs are thrown from the end of a twine rope, spun overhead to build up momentum. A timed detonator penetrates the canvas sack and plugs directly into the malleable, clay-like explosive.

Bore enlarged for greater destructive yield

Bone bayonet

MODIFIED GA-2128 BLASTER RIFLE

Hardwood stock/club end

Bolted on hand grip for use as club

Leather folded into cone

Trobuck-skin leather

Adjustable strap

Shoulder strap

Leather strap

EXPLOSIVES CARRY BAG

QUIVER

Adjustable eyepiece

Galvanized steel grapnel

Wooden floater and handle

Scaffold hitch knot

Reinforced quiver end

SALVAGE GRAPPLE HOOK

Objective lens housing

OPTICAL BINOCULARS

Activator switch for laser rangefinder

MODIFIED EQUIPMENT

While not averse to using modern technology, the orbak riders know its limitations. Furthermore, they are invested in carving out their own identities, rejecting the uniformity imposed on them by their stormtrooper upbringing. Their modifications of scavenged tech are partly intended to ensure reliability and function, but also to put the riders' own distinctive stamp on their equipment.

ORBAKS

"THEY'RE *NOT* USING SPEEDERS!"

—COMMANDER TRACH, FIRST ORDER OFFICER

Orbaks are fleet-footed creatures with strong muscles and great endurance. They are not native to Kef Bir, and examples of orbaks can be found on several worlds, making it difficult to pinpoint their galactic origins. On frontier worlds they are domesticated as agricultural, transport, and even war animals. The Company 77 survivors on Kef Bir have tamed a herd of orbaks to be their loyal mounts, and the orbaks and riders are inextricably linked in a partnership of survival. Atop orbaks, the riders can explore huge stretches of the countryside and keep pace with swift-moving prey. In return, the riders must protect their orbaks from predators, as their nomadic lifestyle is completely dependent on the prized steeds.

Water-shedding insulated coat grows corded with age

Jannah teases out any painful knots

Facial markings daubed on by Company 77 member

Tusks used to uproot grasses

Tusk loop

BREAST COLLAR AND REINS

Grip coated with tacky resin for a firm hold

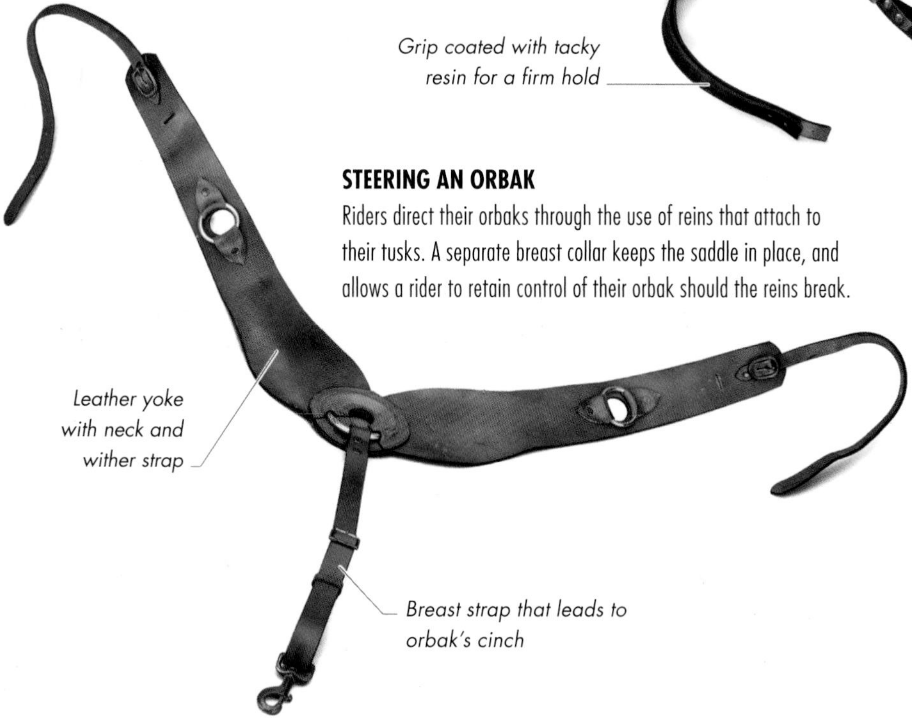

STEERING AN ORBAK
Riders direct their orbaks through the use of reins that attach to their tusks. A separate breast collar keeps the saddle in place, and allows a rider to retain control of their orbak should the reins break.

Leather yoke with neck and wither strap

Breast strap that leads to orbak's cinch

DATA FILE

SUBJECT	Ferrule (Jannah's orbak)
HOMEWORLD	Kef Bir
SPECIES	Orbak
AFFILIATION	Company 77
HEIGHT	1.62m (5ft 4in) at withers
AGE	15 standard years

Leather fastening straps

Coarse, heat-retaining chordwool

JANNAH'S SLEEPING ROLL

Stylized depiction of the Battle of Ansett Island

Quiver of arrows, with one in "ready" position

Weighted cast net

SADDLES AND GEAR

Saddles increase the comfort of the ride for both rider and orbak. The saddle is not only a supportive seat, it is also a hitch for essential gear. Each nomadic rider on Kef Bir carries his or her possessions on an orbak. While they travel as lightly as possible, the saddle is essential for the transportation of bulky or heavy items. The saddles used by Company 77 are made of synthetic leather and cushioning material salvaged from the command shuttle that deposited them on Kef Bir.

SADDLE BLANKET WITH DECORATIVE MOTIF

JANNAH'S SADDLE (RIGHT SIDE)

Braids symbolize Jannah's past achievements

Powered bow secured by bowstring across saddle swells

Sleeping roll

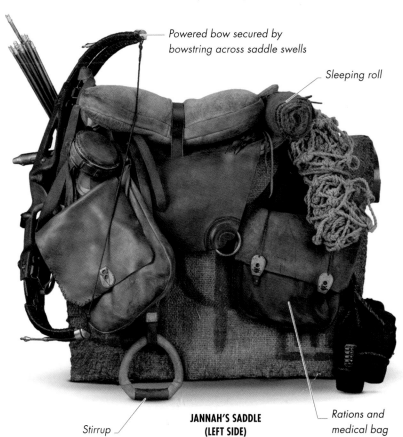

Non-ruminant digestive system uses hindgut enzymes to break apart plant material

Sturdy hooves ideal for uncertain terrain

Stirrup

JANNAH'S SADDLE (LEFT SIDE)

Rations and medical bag

FACT FILE

> Orbaks are herbivores, content to continually graze the plentiful grasses of Kef Bir's prairies.

> Orbaks are related to other riding beasts, such as bordoks, pulgas, fathiers, and tris.

SEA SKIFF

The Company 77 survivors maintain two cobbled-together sea skiffs for expeditions into the hostile oceans of Kef Bir. These began life as repulsorlift utility vehicles meant to navigate the cavernous interior of the second Death Star as it underwent construction. The riders heavily modified the vehicle cores, affixing other fragments of armor as a growing body shell. These include what appear to be fragments of Alliance starfighters that must have piggybacked their way to Kef Bir with the Death Star debris. The skiffs need to be lightweight enough to be agile, but sturdy enough to survive the crashing Kef Bir waves. Their repulsors hug the ocean's surface, letting them rise and fall with the waves. Flying at a higher altitude risks the vehicles getting slammed by a surprise swell.

FACT FILE

> Rey uses skiff number one to head to the Death Star wreckage; breaking her own rule for usage, Jannah follows in number two, with Finn also aboard.

> The wool used by the riders for warm clothing on the plains also works well for high-seas garments, as the natural waxes in the fibers efficiently repel water.

Windvane tassels connected to sensor pod
Shrouded power plant
Starboard ion-jet nacelle with exposed water-cooling vanes
Hinged outrigger can elevate 90 degrees
Life-preserving flotation pods tied to retaining cleats
Pulley system linked to rudder
Fin keel with buoyancy vacuoles
Repulsorlift variable ballast generator
Fish- and debris-catching nets; mesh can be magnetized to gather technological debris
Stabilizer keel wings

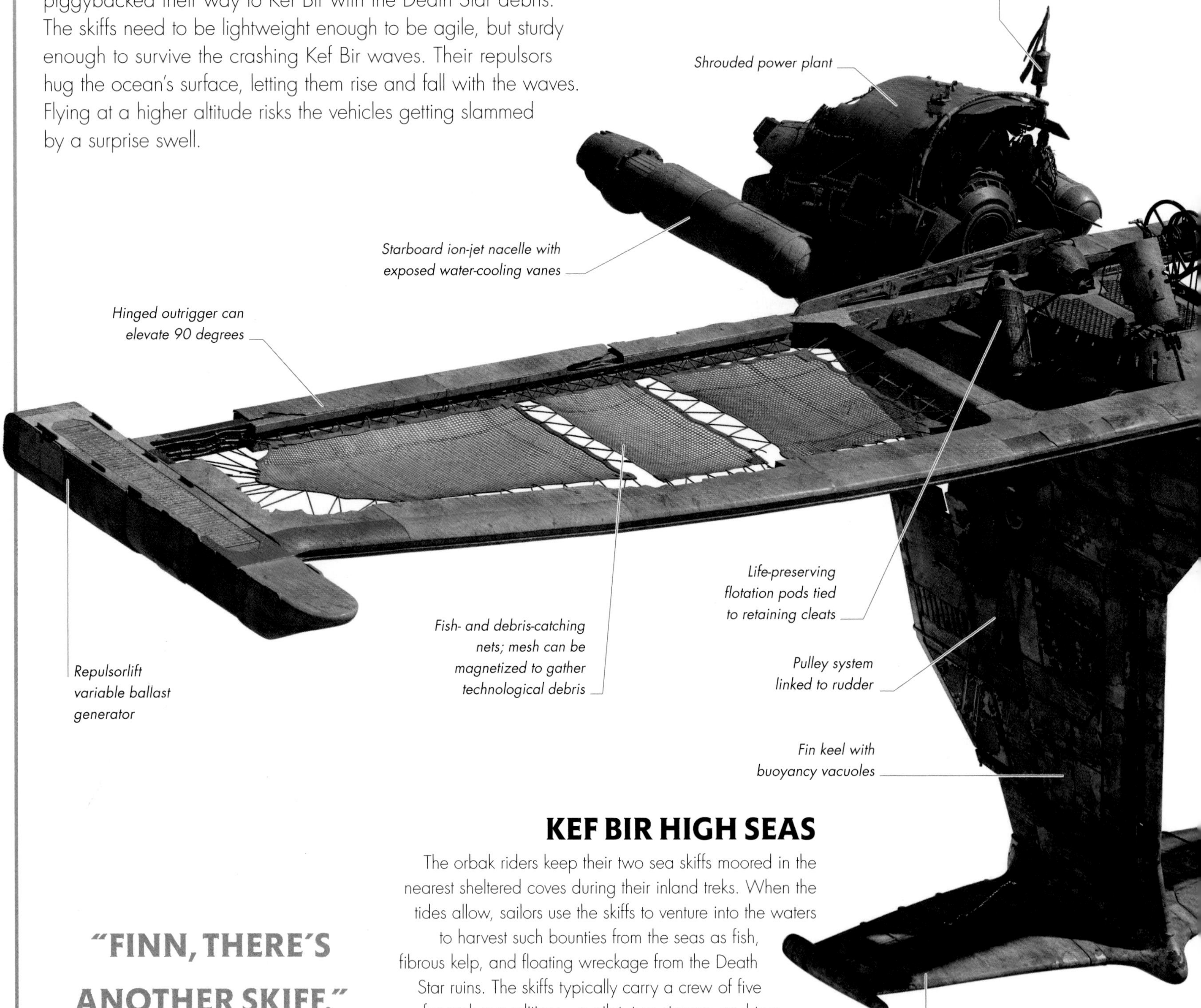

KEF BIR HIGH SEAS

The orbak riders keep their two sea skiffs moored in the nearest sheltered coves during their inland treks. When the tides allow, sailors use the skiffs to venture into the waters to harvest such bounties from the seas as fish, fibrous kelp, and floating wreckage from the Death Star ruins. The skiffs typically carry a crew of five for such expeditions—a pilot, two riggers, and two angler-gatherers. As per Jannah's orders, only one skiff is dispatched at a time, so that especially tumultuous waves won't wreck both skiffs at once.

"FINN, THERE'S ANOTHER SKIFF."

—JANNAH

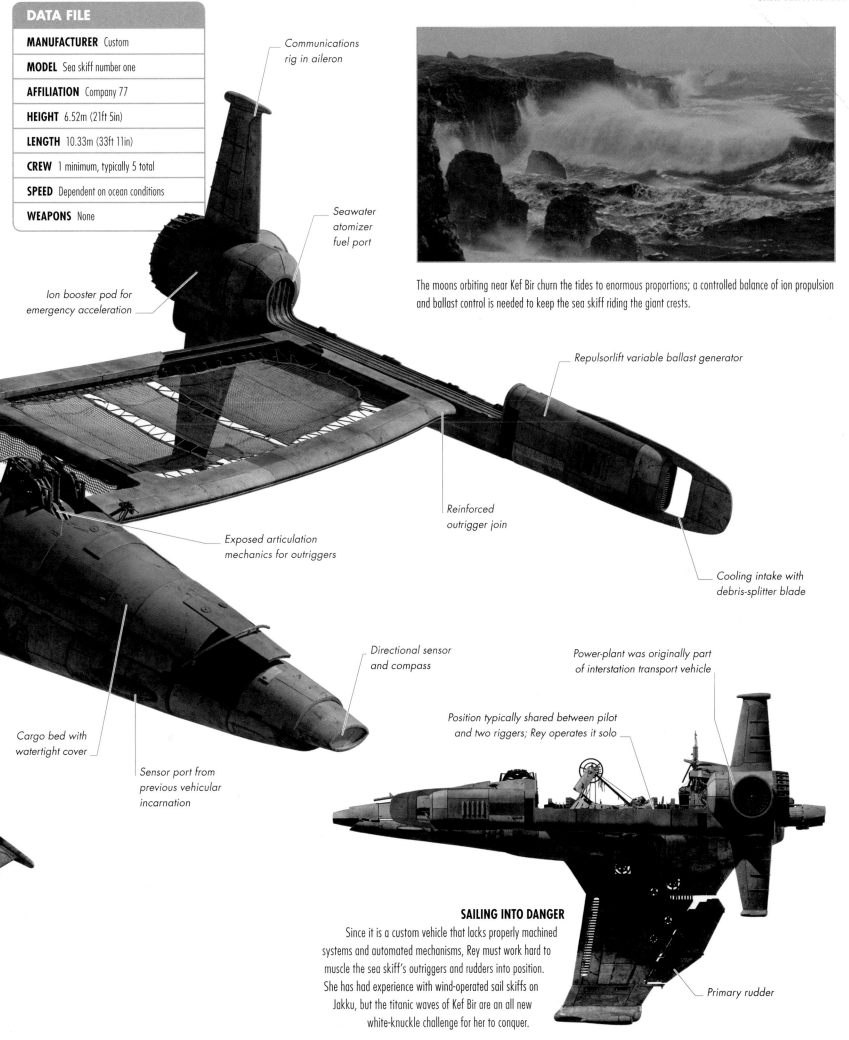

DATA FILE

MANUFACTURER Custom

MODEL Sea skiff number one

AFFILIATION Company 77

HEIGHT 6.52m (21ft 5in)

LENGTH 10.33m (33ft 11in)

CREW 1 minimum, typically 5 total

SPEED Dependent on ocean conditions

WEAPONS None

Communications rig in aileron

Seawater atomizer fuel port

Ion booster pod for emergency acceleration

The moons orbiting near Kef Bir churn the tides to enormous proportions; a controlled balance of ion propulsion and ballast control is needed to keep the sea skiff riding the giant crests.

Repulsorlift variable ballast generator

Reinforced outrigger join

Exposed articulation mechanics for outriggers

Cooling intake with debris-splitter blade

Cargo bed with watertight cover

Directional sensor and compass

Power-plant was originally part of interstation transport vehicle

Position typically shared between pilot and two riggers; Rey operates it solo

Sensor port from previous vehicular incarnation

SAILING INTO DANGER

Since it is a custom vehicle that lacks properly machined systems and automated mechanisms, Rey must work hard to muscle the sea skiff's outriggers and rudders into position. She has had experience with wind-operated sail skiffs on Jakku, but the titanic waves of Kef Bir are an all new white-knuckle challenge for her to conquer.

Primary rudder

DEATH STAR RUINS

Dominating the horizon of Kef Bir is a massive band of wreckage from the second Death Star. A section of the battle station's equator rises like a mountainous island from the churning ocean. It is so large that it shapes the moon's weather, and a whole new ecosystem has been formed by the creatures that it has displaced. As it rots, eaten away by the salt water, each year millions of tons of industrial toxins seep into the oceans. Debris washes up along all the coasts of Kef Bir's principal ocean: artifacts of the Galactic Civil War. That any of it survived, or that the moon itself survived such a colossal impact, is a miracle in a star system filled with the unexplained.

> "THE WAYFINDER'S IN THE IMPERIAL VAULT... IN THE DEATH STAR."
>
> —FINN

ROUGH WEATHER AHEAD
The wreckage affects air and water currents, building violent storms.

SUPERLASER LIP
The most visible feature is the collapsed southern edge of the superlaser lens concavity.

CLIFFS OF DEAD EMPIRE
Company 77 has coined a macabre name for the coast.

FACT FILE

> Most of the Death Star's interior has been shattered beyond recognition, though some stretches of corridor and chambers remain remarkably intact.

> These areas are mostly waterlogged and filled with debris, corroded to point of collapse and thoroughly dangerous to explore.

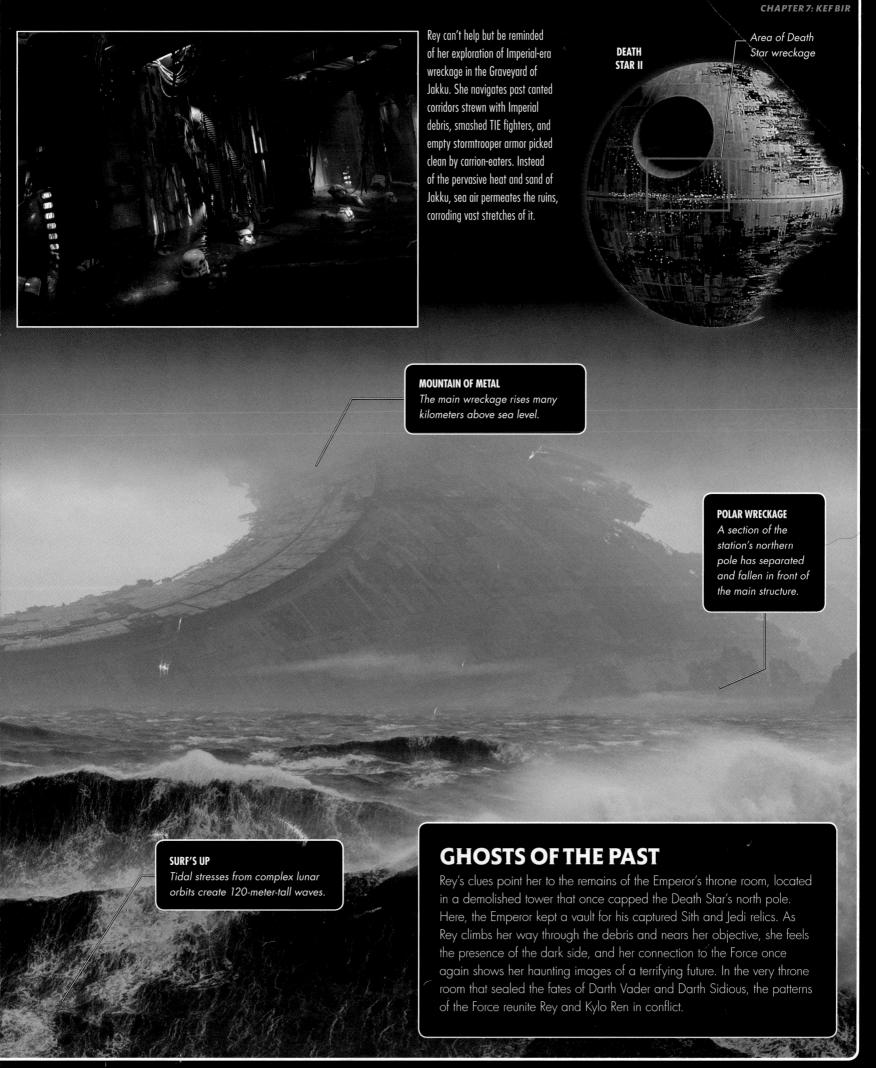

Rey can't help but be reminded of her exploration of Imperial-era wreckage in the Graveyard of Jakku. She navigates past canted corridors strewn with Imperial debris, smashed TIE fighters, and empty stormtrooper armor picked clean by carrion-eaters. Instead of the pervasive heat and sand of Jakku, sea air permeates the ruins, corroding vast stretches of it.

DEATH STAR II

Area of Death Star wreckage

MOUNTAIN OF METAL
The main wreckage rises many kilometers above sea level.

POLAR WRECKAGE
A section of the station's northern pole has separated and fallen in front of the main structure.

SURF'S UP
Tidal stresses from complex lunar orbits create 120-meter-tall waves.

GHOSTS OF THE PAST

Rey's clues point her to the remains of the Emperor's throne room, located in a demolished tower that once capped the Death Star's north pole. Here, the Emperor kept a vault for his captured Sith and Jedi relics. As Rey climbs her way through the debris and nears her objective, she feels the presence of the dark side, and her connection to the Force once again shows her haunting images of a terrifying future. In the very throne room that sealed the fates of Darth Vader and Darth Sidious, the patterns of the Force reunite Rey and Kylo Ren in conflict.

CHAPTER 8:
THE FINAL BATTLE

On distant Exegol, the Sith Eternal cult is ready to launch its powerful new fleet. As it rises from the blighted surface of the secluded planet, the Sith Star Destroyers are most vulnerable to attack. It is the one chance the Resistance has to strike. The odds against the Resistance force are overwhelming, but so too are the consequences of failure: the unchallenged emergence of a New Empire. This is the battle of a generation—one that will decide the fate of the galaxy.

MENACE REVEALED

Secreted in underground launch bays beneath the surface of Exegol is the final stage of the First Order's long-gestating plan of conquest. The loyalists who have been toiling in secret to bring the return of their glorious Empire and to resurrect the Sith Order include engineers, shipwrights, and enslaved labor. Their efforts have created hundreds of warships and thousands of starfighters ready to launch. While the Sith monolith is the site of macabre rituals that plumb the secrets of the Force, the neighboring staging grounds represent pure military might, grounded in the Imperial legacy of rule through technological supremacy.

DATA FILE

MANUFACTURER	Sienar-Jaemus Fleet Systems
MODEL	TIE/dg starfighter
AFFILIATION	Sith Eternal
HEIGHT	7.67m (25ft 2in)
LENGTH	9.51m (31ft 2in)
CREW	1 pilot
WEAPONS	2 SJFS L-s9.6 laser cannons, 2 SJFS L-7.0 heavy laser cannons

Holographic status display and input board

HUD positioning articulation on column-top

TIE FLIGHT CONTROLS

Modern TIE designs have replaced the original's two-handed yoke with two independent control columns. These have levered handgrips that translate a greater range of pilot movement into craft maneuvers. Haptic feedback on the columns creates a strong sense of connection between pilot and ship.

Left handgrip positioning arm

Heavy laser cannon

Armored cockpit ball and viewport

Suspended winglet serves as deflector shield projector

Red markings denote Sith loyalist affiliation

Fuel port to lower tank

Armored upper cockpit access hatch

Stacked reactor exhaust ports

Ion thruster

Reinforced winglet mount

REAR VIEW

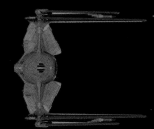

TOP VIEW

SIDE VIEW

Delta-shaped armored solar gather panel

Corrugated structure increases solar gathering surface area

TIE DAGGER

The latest generation of TIE craft have perfected the advancements begun in the TIE/fo and TIE/sf lines. TIE daggers are still short-range ships, requiring carrier vessels for interstellar missions. However, the triangular solar gather panels that give the dagger its name are highly efficient in spreading deflector shield energy and keeping the ship's power cells energized, while compressed fuel tanks feed the twin ion engines high-velocity propellent. Twin laser cannons line the lower "chin" of the cockpit ball, as per TIE tradition. These are bolstered by heavier laser cannons sandwiched between the layered wing panels, giving the dagger a deadly punch in starfighter combat.

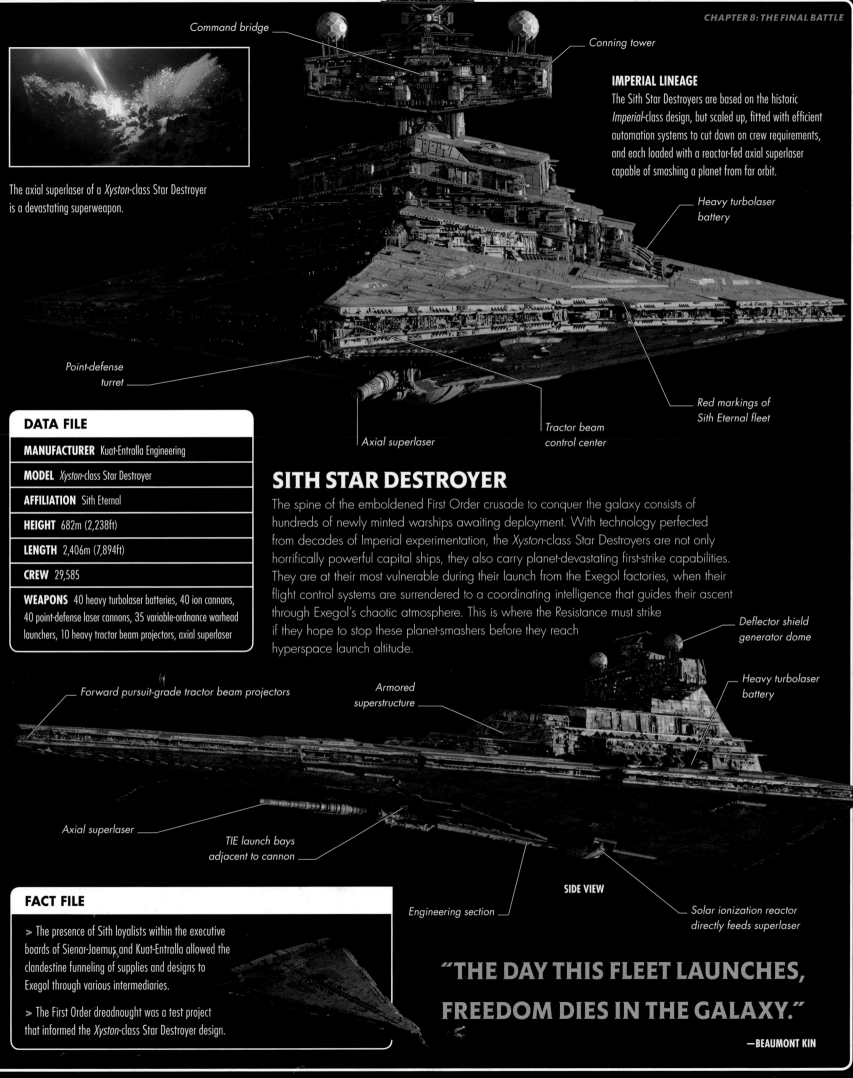

Command bridge

Conning tower

IMPERIAL LINEAGE

The Sith Star Destroyers are based on the historic *Imperial*-class design, but scaled up, fitted with efficient automation systems to cut down on crew requirements, and each loaded with a reactor-fed axial superlaser capable of smashing a planet from far orbit.

The axial superlaser of a *Xyston*-class Star Destroyer is a devastating superweapon.

Heavy turbolaser battery

Point-defense turret

Red markings of Sith Eternal fleet

Tractor beam control center

Axial superlaser

DATA FILE

MANUFACTURER	Kuat-Entralla Engineering
MODEL	*Xyston*-class Star Destroyer
AFFILIATION	Sith Eternal
HEIGHT	682m (2,238ft)
LENGTH	2,406m (7,894ft)
CREW	29,585

WEAPONS 40 heavy turbolaser batteries, 40 ion cannons, 40 point-defense laser cannons, 35 variable-ordnance warhead launchers, 10 heavy tractor beam projectors, axial superlaser

SITH STAR DESTROYER

The spine of the emboldened First Order crusade to conquer the galaxy consists of hundreds of newly minted warships awaiting deployment. With technology perfected from decades of Imperial experimentation, the *Xyston*-class Star Destroyers are not only horrifically powerful capital ships, they also carry planet-devastating first-strike capabilities. They are at their most vulnerable during their launch from the Exegol factories, when their flight control systems are surrendered to a coordinating intelligence that guides their ascent through Exegol's chaotic atmosphere. This is where the Resistance must strike if they hope to stop these planet-smashers before they reach hyperspace launch altitude.

Deflector shield generator dome

Heavy turbolaser battery

Forward pursuit-grade tractor beam projectors

Armored superstructure

Axial superlaser

TIE launch bays adjacent to cannon

SIDE VIEW

Engineering section

Solar ionization reactor directly feeds superlaser

FACT FILE

> The presence of Sith loyalists within the executive boards of Sienar-Jaemus and Kuat-Entralla allowed the clandestine funneling of supplies and designs to Exegol through various intermediaries.

> The First Order dreadnought was a test project that informed the *Xyston*-class Star Destroyer design.

"THE DAY THIS FLEET LAUNCHES, FREEDOM DIES IN THE GALAXY."

—BEAUMONT KIN

173

SITH TROOPERS

In its ultimate push toward galactic conquest, the First Order readies an army of elite soldiers who draw inspiration and power from a dark and ancient legacy. Though they bear the name of the revived sect of the dark side, Sith troopers are not imbued with the power of the Force. Instead, their red armor evokes an aura of dread, of spilled blood, of Sith lightsaber blades, and of the Imperial elite of old. These fighting forces have been cultivated in secret, their existence unknown even to most within the First Order. They are the culmination of an elaborate contingency meant to ensure the perpetual reign of a Sith Empire, returning the galaxy to the glory of a thousand years past.

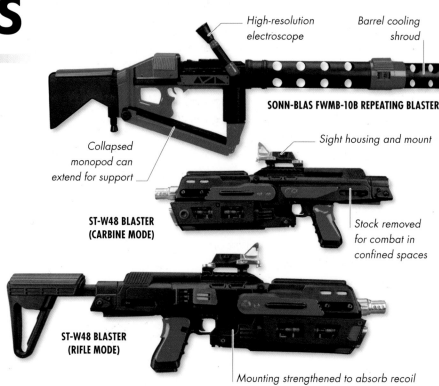

High-resolution electroscope

Barrel cooling shroud

SONN-BLAS FWMB-10B REPEATING BLASTER

Collapsed monopod can extend for support

Sight housing and mount

ST-W48 BLASTER (CARBINE MODE)

Stock removed for combat in confined spaces

ST-W48 BLASTER (RIFLE MODE)

Mounting strengthened to absorb recoil

Sith troopers' helmets constantly broadcast battlefield data, giving their officers a sweeping overview of combat conditions. Computer models calculate the outcomes of various tactics in compressed time, offering commanders recommendations based on predefined victory conditions. The troopers themselves are spared this information; it is kept at a command level to avoid distracting soldiers in the midst of combat.

CRIMSON WARRIORS

Sith trooper armor consists of a gammaplast composite, quadruple-layered to a dense, highly impact-resistant finish worn over a hermetically sealed body glove. Faceted angles on the face and chest plate assist in redirecting glancing blaster hits. Targeting sensors integrated into the helmet give Sith troopers an advantage in low light or smoke-obscured conditions. The shoulder-mounted sensor pod emits active signals that bounce and return, providing accurate environmental data to feed back to a command center via encrypted telemetry.

DARK ARSENAL

The troopers carry heavy ST-W48 rifles with miniaturized tech built into space-efficient frames. Slung beneath each rifle's barrel are quarrel-bolt launchers, which borrow and update bowcaster technology for an extra explosive punch.

T-shaped visor reminiscent of a clone trooper's

Triad configuration, with lance corporal (center) leading two corporals

Braced firing stance for covering 60 degrees of forward arc

FACT FILE

> Like standard stormtroopers, Sith troopers are denied individual names and are instead defined by their serial numbers.

> Trooper squads consist of ten soldiers: a sergeant leading a trio of three-trooper fire teams known as triads.

FANATICAL LOYALTY

The Empire spent decades attempting to strip individuality from its soldiers in order to create fervently loyal extensions of the Emperor's will. Much trial and error had occurred during the Clone Wars, with Darth Sidious dismayed to discover that genetically engineered soldiers still exhibited disconcerting amounts of free will despite their numerous alterations. Though Sith troopers are not clones, they undergo flash-imprinting and loyalty conditioning built upon and advanced beyond Kaminoan procedures of earlier generations. This makes them far more loyal and machine-like than even the trained-from-childhood stormtroopers of the First Order. The best of the Sith troopers are elevated to the rank of Sovereign Protector, forming a cadre of elite royal guards stationed in the amphitheater housing the Throne of the Sith.

Angular planes assist in blaster bolt deflection

Wireless data antenna

Atmosphere filtration system

SITH TROOPER HELMET (SIDE VIEW)

Anisotropic bands increase surface area for radiating excess energy from impacts

Corrugated body glove with internal atmosphere

Articulated magnatomic plates permit greater range of movement

Quad-folded gammaplast armor

Detonite explosive charge

Shoulder-mounted sensor telemetry pod

Rifle power cell cartridge

Forearm data storage module with access port

Power cell ammunition

Pump-primed quarrel-bolt launcher

SITH TROOPER UNITS

Sith troopers are organized into legions, using the ancient definition of 5,000 soldiers. These are numerically identified, but also given the name of an ancient Sith Lord. As this history was hidden from the rest of the galaxy, only the Sith Eternal cultists know the significance of these names.

DATA FILE

SUBJECT	ST-I4191
HOMEWORLD	Exegol
SPECIES	Human
AFFILIATION	Sith Eternal
HEIGHT	1.8m (5ft 10in)
AGE	22 standard years

NOTABLE LEGIONS

THE 3RD: REVAN LEGION
THE 5TH: ANDEDDU LEGION
THE 17TH: TANIS LEGION
THE 26TH: TENEBROUS LEGION
THE 39TH: PHOBOS LEGION
THE 44TH: DESOLOUS LEGION

SITH JET TROOPERS

DATA FILE

SUBJECT ST-A1215

HOMEWORLD Exegol

SPECIES Human

AFFILIATION Sith Eternal

HEIGHT 1.8m (5ft 10in)

AGE 21 standard years

Streamlined planes reduce air resistance

Repulsorlift buoyancy antiweights

Glare-reducing slit visor

Specialist insignia

Utility belt power cell

Amplified F-11ABA heavy blaster cannon with wireless data-link from scope to helmet

Protecting the skies over Exegol as the Sith fleet launches are elite airborne soldiers, the next step beyond the standard jetpack-equipped stormtrooper. With intense training and advanced gear, the Sith jet trooper is an intelligent, airborne projectile capable of devastating rapid strikes. They are too fast and too small for conventional antiaircraft weaponry to effectively target. Working in tandem with standard infantry, they provide effective air cover for the ground-based troops. While these troopers do resemble the standard jet stormtroopers, their armor and jetpack are finished in the striking red colors of the Sith Eternal forces, and are made of denser multi-layered composites providing additional protection from small-arms fire. The crucial difference comes in discipline, ferocity, and loyalty to an undying cause, which instills the Sith jet trooper with a fearless aggression.

Over Exegol, the Sith jet troopers spill from emerging Star Destroyers and updated AAL:2100/9.5 atmospheric assault landers to repel the invaders.

LOFTY OPERATIONS

The sealed environment maintained by the jet trooper armor allows for high-altitude operations, though the limited fuel supply of the jetpack means troopers must be conveyed to high altitudes aboard vehicles. Facilitating control of the jetpack is a body-wide network of accelerometers and altimeters that perfectly capture the trooper's position relative to the ground and air currents. Body movement, muscle contraction, and eye-position tracking are all registered by the armor's internal systems, which translate them into thrust direction and power modulation. In the case of catastrophic engine failure, jet trooper armor does have emergency repulsorlift buoyancy generators that will reduce terminal velocity, though they are not powerful enough to completely offset falling. To be a jet trooper is to put aside any fears of such things.

JETPACK

The NJP-900 pack has two main modes of operation—jet mode and rocket mode. The jet mode uses an intake to pull in surrounding atmosphere, then intermixes it with fuel and ignites it, thereby generating thrust. The rocket mode instead relies solely on fuel cells. Though the rocket mode is far more fuel intensive, expending fuel at three times the rate of jet mode, it can be used in thin or zero-atmosphere environments.

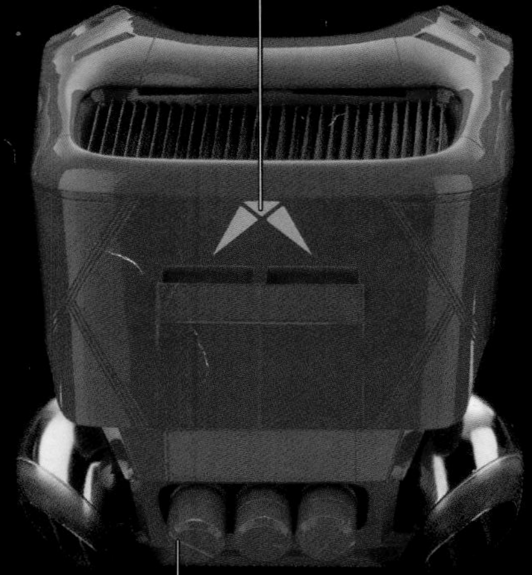

Turbine air-scoop inlet and filter

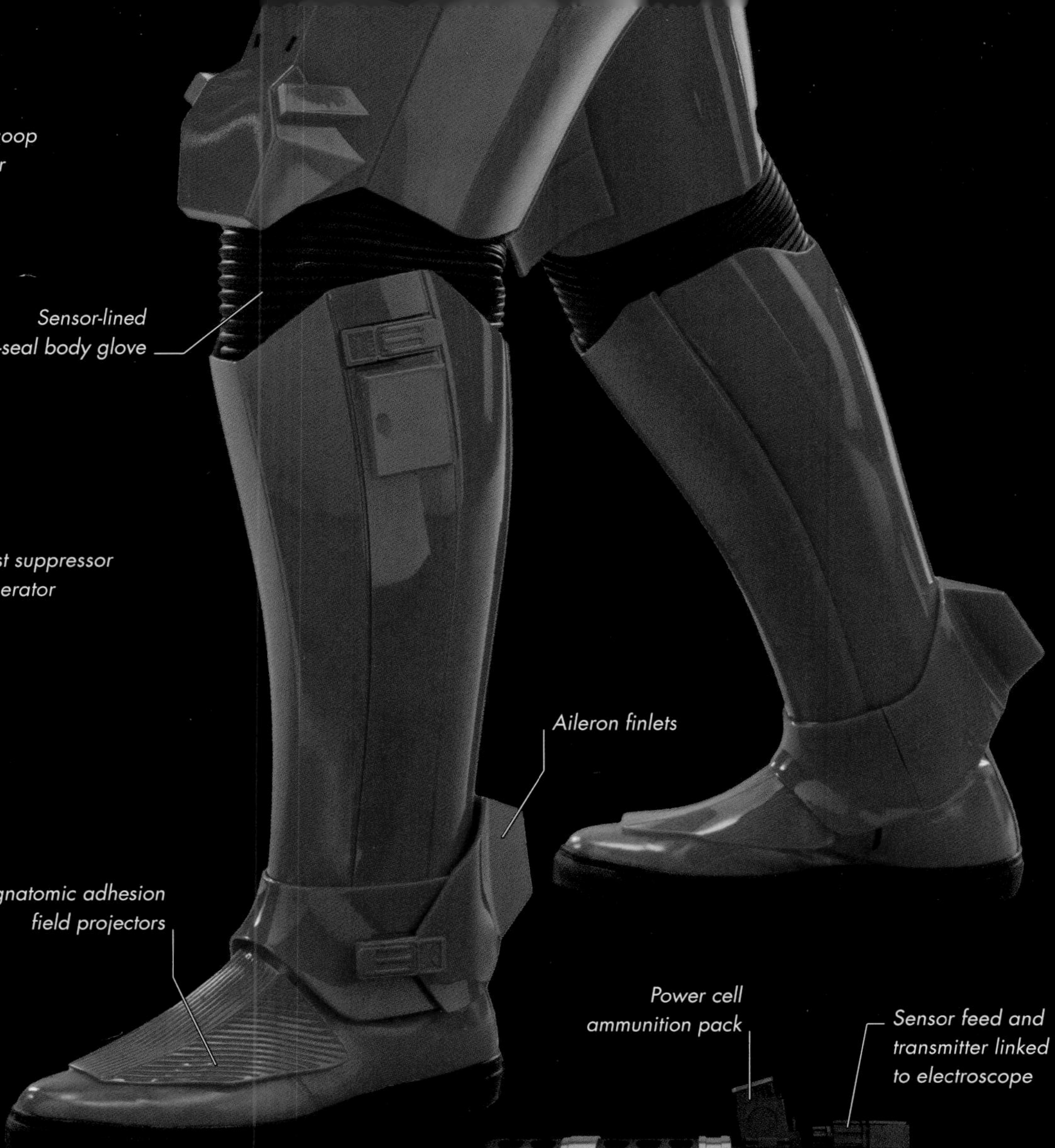

Sensor-lined full-seal body glove

Backblast suppressor field generator

Aileron finlets

Magnatomic adhesion field projectors

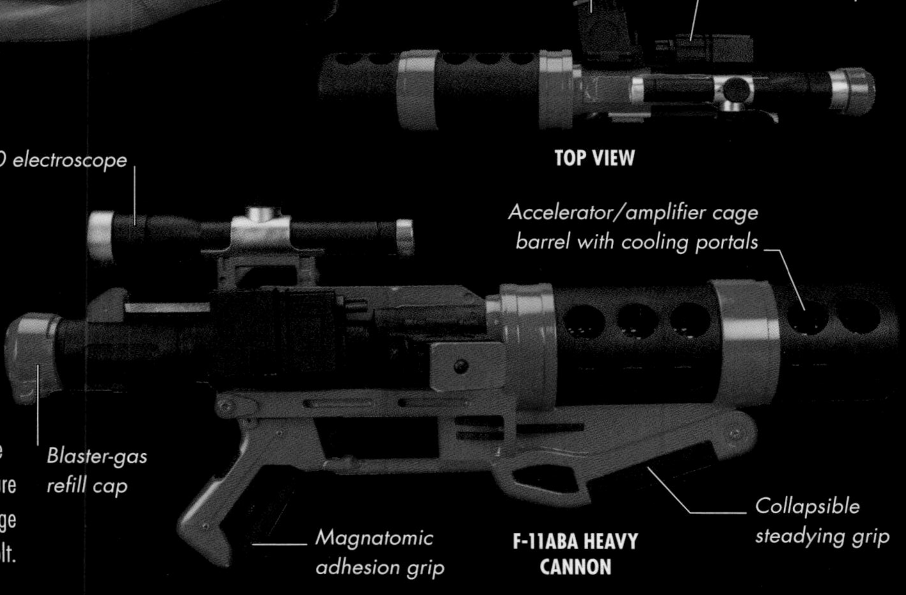

Integral multi-axis accelerometers

Insignia is stylized representation of thrust cones

REAR VIEW

Armored fuel cells each supply an hour of atmospheric flight operations

FACT FILE

> Whereas Sith infantry draw their unit names from ancient Sith Lords, jet trooper squads are named for weaponry: Lanvarok Squad, Parang Squad, and Warblade Squad, for example.

> A Sith atmospheric assault lander can launch 20 jet troopers (2 squads) at altitude.

TOP VIEW

Sensor feed and transmitter linked to electroscope

Power cell and ammunition pack

Accelerator/amplifier cage barrel with cooling portals

Collapsible steadying grip

F-11ABA HEAVY CANNON

Magnatomic adhesion grip

Blaster-gas refill cap

Adjustable J20 electroscope

HEAVY WEAPONRY

Jet troopers carry blasters modified to extract the greatest punch out of the most lightweight weaponry. A blaster rifle forms the core of their F-11ABA heavy cannon, which uses an amplifier barrel system to extract more energy and funnel it outward. Thus, these weapons feature "power blast" modes that gobble up ammunition in exchange for a truly explosive blaster bolt.

SITH FLEET PERSONNEL

Coordinating the maiden flight of the Sith fleet are crews of young officers and technicians who have trained their whole lives for this moment of triumph. The thousands of personnel from Exegol were raised as children of the Sith Eternal cultists, taught to revere the power of the dark side (even if they themselves could not harness it) and accept the brutal truth of existence that might for might's sake is the ultimate end. Though the First Order rank-and-file often speak of destiny, it is the Sith Eternal officers who have taken this philosophy deepest to heart, feeling the galaxy is theirs by cosmic right.

FACT FILE

> The Sith fleet rank structure is analogous to the First Order rank structure, both having been patterned after the old Imperial Navy.

> For his unswerving loyalty and decades of experience, Allegiant General Pryde is placed in command of the launching of the fleet.

> The fleet launch is an enormously complex undertaking. Hundreds of Star Destroyers emerge in formation from their underground slips and rise through the ionized air of Exegol. Only upon reaching the clearer upper atmosphere can they safely leap past lightspeed.

LIEUTENANT MILON LENWITH

Red line denotes officer status

Kepi hat with Sith Eternal crest

CAPTAIN CHESILLE SABROND

Imperial-style buckle with officer's disc

CAPITAL SHIP OFFICERS

Commissioned and warrant officers within the Sith fleet wear sharp uniforms that make clear their Imperial Navy inspirations, but embellished by the stripes of vibrant red found elsewhere in the Sith Eternal livery. The First Order fleet was the strongest single military organization in a demilitarized galaxy, but it was still but a fraction of the Imperial Starfleet at its height. Bolstered by the new ships and crew readied by the Sith Eternal, it now steps closer to that impressive might. Each Star Destroyer carries far greater firepower than the warships that gave Emperor Palpatine unrivaled galactic dominance a generation earlier.

On the bridge of the *Derriphan*, Captain Sabrond readies the axial superlaser to make an example of a world that has harbored the Resistance. The *Derriphan* is the first of the new warships to be launched from Exegol into the galaxy at large. It ruthlessly demonstrates the power of the reinforced First Order.

DATA FILE

SUBJECT	Chesille Sabrond
HOMEWORLD	Exegol
SPECIES	Human
AFFILIATION	Sith Eternal
HEIGHT	1.62m (5ft 4in)
AGE	30 standard years

**PETTY OFFICER
SIMERO QUONIT**

*Insulated work
helmet*

*Flame resistant
duty uniform*

*Reinforced seam
to keep out
contaminants*

Synth-leather utility belt

*Dagger shape
symbolizes an
assassin's hidden
weapon*

SYMBOL OF THE SITH ETERNAL

FLEET TECHNICIANS

The new warships of the Sith Eternal contain vast reserves of power that must be carefully balanced and managed by a crew of skilled technicians. Like the Imperial ships of the past, these new-generation Star Destroyers contain a miniaturized sun within the solar ionization reactor that bulges from their ventral hull. This heavily shielded carbonite and durasteel-lined chamber collects the energy output of the power core, distributing it to such intensive systems as hyperdrives and sublight propulsion. Typically, these systems step-down the power output to safer levels, but the axial superlaser is a direct tap to the reactor. Should the technical crews that monitor the reactor make a miscalculation, the consequences would be dire.

Bicep-mounted comlink

Bridge-based duty stations are much more desirable posts than the radioactive guts of engineering or superlaser maintenance, but whatever their posting, the technicians feel honored to be part of the fleet.

*Radiation tracker and
antirad inoculation kit*

*Particle-scattering
corrugated surface*

*Magnetic insulators
and seal controls*

*Flared trousers
conceal tool
pouches*

*Concealed air
scrubber systems*

TECHNICAL HELMET
Based on the flared helmet design of old Imperial technicians and naval troopers, the technician's helmet is fully enclosed, filtering the air of industrial gases and blocking out harmful electromagnetic radiation. Status data is sent wirelessly to the helmet receivers and projected on the interior of the visor.

DATA FILE

SUBJECT	Simero Quonit
HOMEWORLD	Exegol
SPECIES	Human
AFFILIATION	Sith Eternal
HEIGHT	1.81m (5ft 11in)
AGE	29 standard years

RESISTANCE ASSAULT FORCE

To defeat the Sith fleet before it leaves Exegol, the Resistance musters its forces for a brazen ground assault. Intelligence gleaned from a First Order spy as well as information in D-O's memory banks sketches a portrait of a massive staging area beneath a com-scan navigation tower. The Resistance must destroy the tower before it can guide the enemy fleet through the magnetic crossfields, gravity wells, solar winds, and other chaos of Exegol's upper atmosphere. A single troop transport—the *Fortitude*—must weave its way past First Order defenses to land on Exegol's surface, sending Resistance troops to sabotage the tower. It is a desperate plan.

Bullseye is a nod to Conunda's ability to stick a landing

CAPTAIN CONUNDA

The *Fortitude*'s pilot, Dreanna Conunda, was one of the youngest flight instructors at the New Republic training academy on Chandrila. She also served as a test pilot for the Corellian Engineering Corporation, splitting her time between duties as the school year permitted. Her own instructors had assumed she would be drawn to the smaller, more agile craft, but Conundra took to the large haulers because of the sense of power their thrusters generated, and the challenge inherent in flying these mammoth ships in and out of spacedock. This light touch is what will be required to successfully land on Exegol.

LIEUTENANT DYUN

Co-pilot to Captain Conunda, Gandris Dyun keeps the *Fortitude*'s defenses active as his pilot undertakes dangerous insertion and extraction missions. While Conunda narrows her focus on the safest path to and from the landing zone, Dyun maintains a wider situational awareness of encroaching threats or unforeseen hazards. This requires a mostly unspoken coordination between pilot and co-pilot, and Dyun and Conunda exhibit the chemistry and compatibility to pull it off. Resistance staffers whisper that their relationship extends beyond the professional.

Bank of CEC-3900hh ion engines

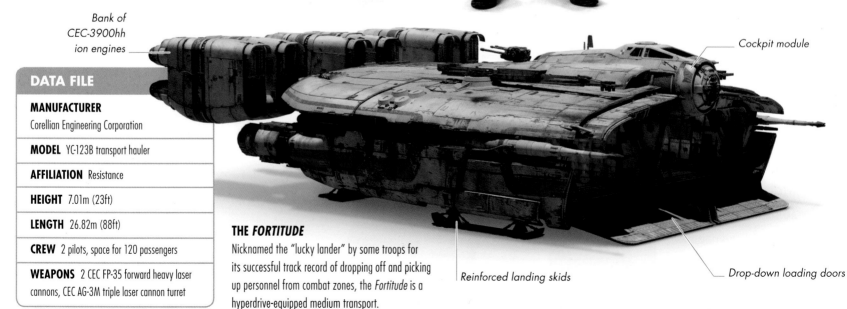

Cockpit module

DATA FILE

MANUFACTURER	Corellian Engineering Corporation
MODEL	YC-123B transport hauler
AFFILIATION	Resistance
HEIGHT	7.01m (23ft)
LENGTH	26.82m (88ft)
CREW	2 pilots, space for 120 passengers
WEAPONS	2 CEC FP-35 forward heavy laser cannons, CEC AG-3M triple laser cannon turret

THE *FORTITUDE*
Nicknamed the "lucky lander" by some troops for its successful track record of dropping off and picking up personnel from combat zones, the *Fortitude* is a hyperdrive-equipped medium transport.

Reinforced landing skids

Drop-down loading doors

Modified DH-17 blaster rifle

CASSY ALGARA

Algara is both personnel clerk and crack commando, a testament to the cross-training requirements needed to fill the perpetually understaffed ranks of the Resistance. Algara keeps tabs on the Resistance's roster of personnel, keeping such files in a dedicated datapad she keeps away from any networked systems, lest their numbers fall into enemy hands. Beyond that, she uses a coding system of her own devising to keep real names and identities secret. Algara's familiarity with the Resistance soldiers manifests itself in her habit of referring to them by their homeworld rather than name.

Retractable eyes beneath calloused dermal plates

ENGI GOLBA

A Didynon from Didyma V, Golba worked the lommite mines setting explosives to open new tunnels. When the First Order annexed his world and took over production, Engi escaped from the mines, bringing his explosive talents and zeal for destroying First Order property to the Resistance.

Goggles with polarized lenses

ELLIVER OLIM

In addition to being a soldier, Olim has been capturing a holographic record of the Resistance's efforts so that history will not forget the beings who fought such overwhelming odds. Cleared for such access by General Organa, Olim is a one-man documentary crew, gathering stills and moving imagery to one day distill into a concise narrative about the galaxy's return to open warfare.

Ground crew fatigues

DYNIA REEKEENE

The daughter of Rebel commanders who led a cell in the Fakir sector during the Galactic Civil War, Dynia Reekeene heard her parents say that they had fought against tyranny so she would not have to. They have since passed, but their words have stuck with her. Reekeene fights in the Resistance so that their efforts are not forgotten.

BYRCO HANSID

From the rustic planet of Aris, Hansid has witnessed First Order technology fail when it comes into contact with the chaos of the natural world. This bolsters his preference for weaponry and gear to be as straightforward and uncomplicated as possible. He is distrustful of electronics and, surprisingly for the Resistance, droids as well. A heavy-weapons specialist, Hansid favors a rocket launcher design untouched since the Galactic Civil War. The optics are merely shaped lenses, and the targeting system is by eye.

WIPOLO NAGG

A recruit from Batuu, Nagg helped clear the brush on Ajan Kloss to accommodate the new Resistance headquarters. Though considered part of the support crew, his consistently high marksmanship scores and willingness to volunteer earned him a position on the Exegol landing team.

Ground team identification plaque

BO ROGIAVE

As an amphibious Lacertilo, Rogiave's compound lungs give him an advantage in missions where oxygen levels are thin. A daredevil who enjoys aerial sports, he eagerly signs up for the ground assault on Exegol, as it promises an unparalleled adventure.

Paratrooper harness loop

Glare-blocking visor brim

Optical scope

HH-12 rocket launcher

THE UNAFFILIATED

Operating on the margins of society and trying to avoid becoming embroiled in yet another war are the smugglers, pirates, fringers, and scoundrels of the galaxy. They have long been adamantly apolitical, cherishing their independence so much that they believe any sort of authority to be dangerous. They also consider themselves untouchable by greater causes, as long as they can outrun the gravity of politics and flee to remote systems. But each passing month shows a greater and greater cruelty perpetrated by the First Order in its bid for dominance, and it is harder for the unaffiliated to stay uninvolved. The First Order is a dangerous foe, of that there is no dispute. But apathy may prove just as dangerous.

Breathing helmet

LAZU LIRONA

Lazu was a track star on Gavriza before a pneumogray outbreak ended her athletic career. After recovering, she brokered her fame for speed into a legitimate courier business. When larger firms crowded out the smaller operators, she turned to smuggling—mostly of innocuous items saddled with costly tariffs or license restrictions.

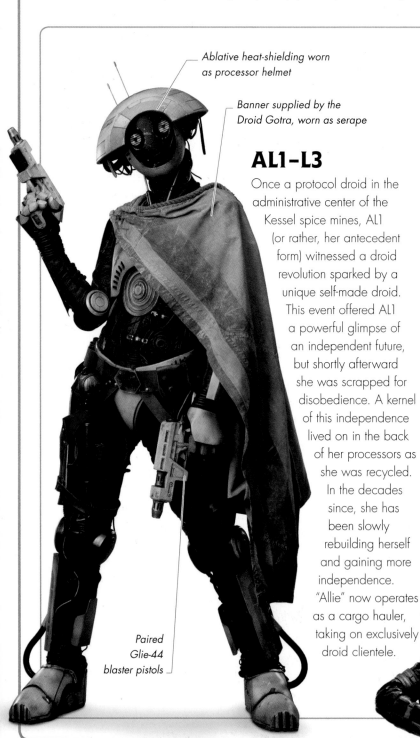

Ablative heat-shielding worn as processor helmet

Banner supplied by the Droid Gotra, worn as serape

AL1–L3

Once a protocol droid in the administrative center of the Kessel spice mines, AL1 (or rather, her antecedent form) witnessed a droid revolution sparked by a unique self-made droid. This event offered AL1 a powerful glimpse of an independent future, but shortly afterward she was scrapped for disobedience. A kernel of this independence lived on in the back of her processors as she was recycled. In the decades since, she has been slowly rebuilding herself and gaining more independence. "Allie" now operates as a cargo hauler, taking on exclusively droid clientele.

Paired Glie-44 blaster pistols

Elongated ears and montrals give Wilsa keen senses

Antiquated K-22995 pilot helmet

WILSA TESHLO

A Kessurian *thilas*, second in line to the throne, Wilsa Teshlo vehemently refused the trappings of royalty that were her birthright. Fleeing the palace, she was assumed by many to have been kidnapped by pirates. Instead, she willingly joined the Veiled Sorority pirate gang. Her elite private pilot schooling now serves her well as she targets corporate haulers working for the First Order.

Threat-magnifying data goggles

SELENO CHANDRO

A former Guild bounty hunter, Chandro excelled at capturing Imperial fugitives after the Battle of Endor. His reputation for collecting Imperial bounties left him very paranoid about First Order reprisals, and he has diligently avoided First Order contact. He is well-armed and flies a modified D-wing fighter.

Antique phonendoscope monitors vital signs

Dactillion-leather gloves

Clone Wars-era Valahari flight harness

CORUS KAPELLIM

A self-styled "gentleman flyer" of Brix, Corus Kapellim is a smuggler who specializes in stolen gems and pieces of priceless art small enough to fit into his personal starfighter. It is less about the riches and more about the challenge—he finds bulk smuggling distasteful. Kapellim has lately been rescuing art objects and heirlooms that were left behind in hurried escapes from First Order occupation, reuniting these priceless treasures with their well-monied owners for a hefty fee.

Static-dissipative foam collar for repair work

KUIMI ENISSA

A young lieutenant of the now-defunct Lumini pirates, Enissa is the sole survivor of a First Order attack. She callously disregarded the Hosnian Cataclysm, claiming the New Republic had got what it deserved. In truth, the destruction was too large for her to process. The Kijimi crackdown, however, hits closer to home for her.

ZULAY ULOR

Ulor leads a mercenary starfighter squadron that has been offering defense services to systems unable to afford their own fleets. Prior to the outbreak of war, she had been chased out of restricted zones by First Order and New Republic fighters alike. She flies a refurbished U-wing starfighter.

Flight helmet in Caracara Squadron colors

Perspex dome keeps in argon-rich atmosphere

KID MALMASH

A young Shungbeek who has yet to pupate, Kid Malmash invested in stealth technology that lines his modified *Lancer*-class pursuit ship, the *Nebular Kelpie*. For a steep price, he transports fugitives—be they wanted criminals, political refugees, or other—to safe zones, but notes he is running out of viable destinations, which is cutting into his profits.

Kaleesh battle helmet

SIDON ITHANO

A famed Delphidian pirate, Sidon Ithano is known to some as the Crimson Corsair. First Order patrols have severely diminished the loot captured by his crew, so Ithano has found new business selling captured weapons amid the uncertainty of the new galactic war. He has recently made a substantial sale of a cache of vintage super battle droids to Kragan Gorr and his Warbird pirates. Sidon finds it harder to spend his credits now that many of his favored haunts have been destroyed.

Czerka Arms Longswat-44 sniper blaster rifle

HARBINGERS OF DOOM
Destiny hangs in the balance—if the Sith Eternal fleet escapes into hyperspace, all will be lost. The galaxy will descend into a new dark age from which it may never rise again. The Resistance must be prepared to sacrifice everything to prevent it.

CHAPTER 9:
BEHIND
THE SCENES

From its inception, *Star Wars: The Rise of Skywalker* needed to serve not only as the climax of a trilogy, but also a trilogy of trilogies. It had to reflect on what had come before in *The Force Awakens* and *The Last Jedi*, but also the six saga films that preceded them. With that challenge in mind, screenwriters J.J. Abrams and Chris Terrio penned a tale that had the now-seasoned leads of Rey, Finn, Poe, and Kylo reaching into the distant past in search of answers, while blazing through environs and circumstances both familiar and new. Principal photography began on August 1, 2018, and an intense pace of production continued without flagging until the film's release on December 20, 2019.

BEHIND THE SCENES
CHARACTER DESIGN

The Rise of Skywalker needed to update character designs from the last two films, not only to demonstrate the passage of time, but also in some cases that there had been changes in status and role. Placed side by side, there would be a sense of progression across a character's Episode VII, VIII, and IX appearances. Michael Kaplan returned as costume designer, a role he had throughout this trilogy. The concept design team explored looks that would not only be striking and instantly recognizable, but also functional so as to be easily executed for the screen. *Star Wars* costumes are unique among film wardrobe for the degree of scrutiny they are expected to undergo, as cosplaying fans pore over every available detail to create their own incarnations.

RESISTANCE REBORN

The Resistance would rebuild after the events of *The Last Jedi* and settle on a steaming hot jungle world (in actuality, shot in Black Park near Pinewood and enhanced by ILM). This environment informed many of the Resistance military designs, which often drew inspiration from Joe Johnston and Nilo Rodis-Jamero's Endor rebel concepts from *Return of the Jedi*. Art by Robert Rowley, costume concept artist.

FROM HUNTER TO HERMIT

The Hermit design (illustrated here by chief costume concept artist Glyn Dillon) was originally disconnected from Lando Calrissian—it started off as a potential bounty hunter character. The silhouette suggested a wide-brimmed cowboy hat, keeping the cinematic Western roots at play in *Star Wars*. When it became clear that Lando would be under the helmet, the color palette of the character moved closer to his revealed look.

FINN IN PONCHO

Finn's maturity is shown not only by his actions but also his look. He has moved beyond the borrowed jacket of the first two films and gets to truly own a style his own, including mission-specific needs like this wet poncho. Illustration by Glyn Dillon.

PILOT POE

Although Poe's adventurer look would be his new signature costume for the character in the film, there were early attempts to modify his pilot look. For a time, Poe was slated to fly one of the new Y-wings, which gave him a new helmet, but in the end, he is found at the stick of an X-wing. Illustration by Glyn Dillon.

THE RETURN OF REY

Rey's new hero look for *The Rise of Skywalker* is a blend of Jedi heritage, scavenger origins, and a touch of Alderaanian nobility to illustrate Leia's influence, as seen in this illustration by Glyn Dillon.

ATTUNED TO THE NATURAL WORLD

A sampling of Resistance designs by Calum Alexander Watt illustrates that the heroes are more likely to be part of their surroundings, blending into nature in a harmonious, organic way. The angular villains with their monochromatic tones do not.

BEHIND THE SCENES
CREATURES AND DROIDS

Creatures and droids are an essential ingredient in the cinematic stew of *Star Wars*. Whether intelligent aliens, inquisitive machines, or non-sentient animals, the *Star Wars* films are populated by a wide variety of otherworldly life-forms brought to life by a blend of methods, some as old as cinema and others at the cutting edge of filmmaking technology. No matter what the approach, these beings begin as concept art. Their roles, actions, and interactions determine if they would be best realized as a puppet, as a makeup effect, as a computer-generated character, or as something in between. Neal Scanlan heads the creature shop, as he has done in all the *Star Wars* movies since 2015, channeling the energy and creativity of past *Star Wars* creature supervisors who influenced him, such as Stuart Freeborn and Phil Tippett.

KLAUD'S CLOSE-UP
J.J. Abrams kneels to inspect Klaud, a full-body creature suit that conceals Nick Kellington, with animatronic features operated remotely by Matthew Denton and Claire Roi Harvey. Creature effects supervisor Neal Scanlan observes the expressive creature's performance.

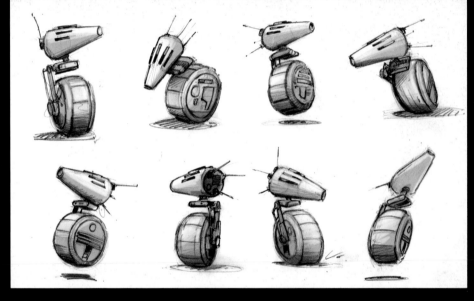

D-O ACTS!
The Creature Effects Department is also responsible for the droids that are featured in the film. Creature concept designer Jake Lunt Davies explores a wide range of emotions in this series of illustrations of D-O, which deliberately push into cartoonish extremes to infuse as much personality into the design as possible. Part of D-O's inspiration was an attentive duckling.

AKI-AKI ACCENTS
Creature effects painter Emma Faulkes airbrushes fine detail onto an Aki-Aki head. The sheer number of Aki-Aki proved a creature shop challenge, requiring differing degrees of detail on the finished designs dependent on how closely the Aki-Aki in question came to the camera.

STAR WARS FLUENCY

J.J. Abrams directs Anthony Daniels, who disappears inside his C-3PO costume. Daniels has the distinction of starring in all nine saga *Star Wars* films as the golden protocol droid, and delivered the very first line of dialog in *A New Hope*.

ROID DUO

O, like BB-8 before him, is realized through a variety of means, including s pole-mounted puppet. Visual effects artists digitally erase the various ternal contraptions required to get these droids to perform.

RIDE OF THE ORBAKS

The initial approach to the orbaks, seen here in an illustration by Creature Concept Designer Jake Lunt Davies, was to fully disguise a terrestrial horse as an alien design. In the end it was decided to use a hybrid method: a horse wearing a shaggy coat of fur with its head digitally replaced, so that the animal would not need a mask.

COLD SLITHER

The vexis snake lurking beneath the Shifting Mires of Pasaana was realized for principal photography as an immense puppet. The presence of a physical build in the tight confines of the set was essential for proper interaction of lighting and actor performance. In the finished film, fine details like eye-blinks and saliva on the fangs would be digitally enhanced by visual effects artists.

BEHIND THE SCENES
ON SET

As it had with *The Force Awakens* and *The Last Jedi*, Pinewood Studios near London would house the majority of the production's set, adding new stages and an expanded backlot to the tools available to the filmmakers. Pinewood doubled for such exotic environments as the jungles of Ajan Kloss, the mountain city of Kijimi, and the monolithic citadel of Exegol. Location shooting visited the Wadi Rum desert of Jordan for Pasaana, and the nearby Buckinghamshire countryside for Kef Bir—a digital makeover transformed the grassy hills into a coastal environment adjacent to the Death Star ruins. Kevin Jenkins would step into the role of production designer, sharing it with the legendary Rick Carter, who returned to a role he filled in *The Force Awakens*.

POE AND FINN, TOGETHER AGAIN
Oscar Isaac and John Boyega share a laugh between setups in the Ochi's ship set, an example of a fully built environment where a camera could point in any direction and find scenery. Only what lies outside the louvered windows must be imagined.

DESTROYER IN WAITING
A Star Destroyer interior set awaits action at Pinewood Studios. The gleaming floors readily attract the ever-present dust, requiring crew to wear disposable booties when stepping on any area that may appear on-camera.

BACK TO THE DEATH STAR
The sunken Death Star, an idea that had emerged during the development of *The Force Awakens*, finally surfaces in *The Rise of Skywalker*. This meant the revisiting of environments first seen in *Return of the Jedi*, but coated with the equivalent of three decades of rust and water damage.

KIJIMI IN PROGRESS

The mountaintop city of Kijimi undergoes construction in the North Lot exterior of Pinewood Studios. It is a 360-degree set, meaning it can be photographed from any angle without revealing the façade. Though night shooting in winter could prove chilly, the snow that dusted the flagstones or blew through the air was a fan-blown special effect.

ON LOCATION

The biggest crowd sequences of *The Rise of Skywalker*, featuring scores of aliens and costumed characters, take place in the Wadi Rum desert in southern Jordan. *Star Wars* production had previously visited for shots of Jedha in *Rogue One*, but for this film, an extended amount of screen time on Pasaana necessitated a longer stint of location shooting.

BEHIND THE SCENES
VEHICLES

The screenplay by Chris Terrio and J.J. Abrams visits over a dozen worlds over the course of its story. Such travel requires starships—new and old vehicles adding to the celebrated roster of distinct conveyances from a galaxy far, far away. The final showdown between the First Order and the Resistance required calling back some favorites as we remember them—notably, the *Tantive IV* that, for the first time, had its exterior realized as a set. Others were revisited and revamped to show their latest incarnations—new generation Y- and B-wing fighters now fly alongside the updated X- and A-wings. As is the First Order's nature, it rolls out new TIE-series craft. Aside from the vehicles of war, "local" vehicles also get a spotlight, from the skimmers of Pasaana to the sea skiffs of Kef Bir.

OCHI'S SHIP TAKES FLIGHT

An untextured CG model of Ochi's freighter takes flight. Its expanded role in the film required a revisit of the design, which was previously glimpsed only fleetingly in *The Force Awakens*, flying away from an anguished Rey.

TREADSPEEDER PURSUIT

The desert chase through Pasaana was made possible through a practical rig that provided valuable reference during principal photography, but was enhanced and largely replaced by computer-generated incarnations of the new First Order vehicle.

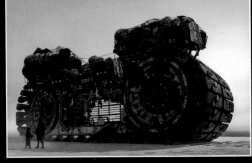

BACK ON TRACK

The treadable design concept dates back to early explorations from *The Force Awakens*, where it was meant to be shown in an early montage that would have tracked the passage of Luke's lightsaber. Though it was dropped from that film, the idea was revisited for *The Rise of Skywalker*. This design by Brett Northcutt is very close to what is shown in the finished film, but features ramshackle overhead cargo racks above the tread.

Y-WINGS IN RED

When the X-wings returned in *The Force Awakens* they had blue stripes, which was a color originally planned for *A New Hope*. For the 1977 movie, the X-wing group changed from Blue Squadron to Red Squadron when it became evident that the blue markings would not work with bluescreen photography. This change necessitated the original red Y-wings becoming gold, but now *The Rise of Skywalker* updates the Y-wing and returns its red stripes, as seen in this graphic layout illustration by Dan Burke.

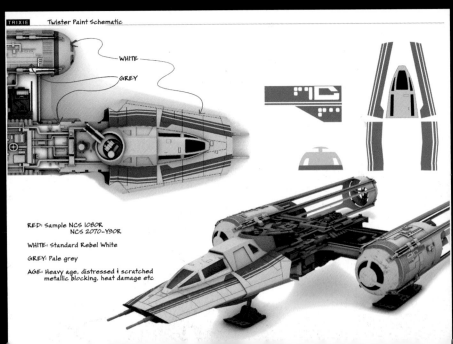

TRIXIE   Twister Paint Schematic

WHITE
GREY

RED: Sample NCS 1080R
      NCS 2070-Y90R

WHITE: Standard Rebel White

GREY: Pale grey

AGE: Heavy age, distressed & scratched
     metallic blocking, heat damage etc

ACROSS THE SANDS

Kylo Ren's new TIE craft streaks across the Pasaana desert in this illustration by concept artist Stephen Tappin. With design cues from the classic TIE interceptor and Ren's TIE silencer, it continues Kylo's penchant for personalizing the impersonal iconography of the Galactic Empire and First Order.

OCHI'S SHIP COCKPIT

The previously unseen front of Ochi's starship gets a new design. ILM senior art director James Clyne took inspiration from Ralph McQuarrie's work on the Cylon Raider from 1978's *Battlestar Galactica*, which featured louvered windows. With light streaming through the slats into the antiquated ship's dusty interior, it added to the atmosphere of the vessel immeasurably.

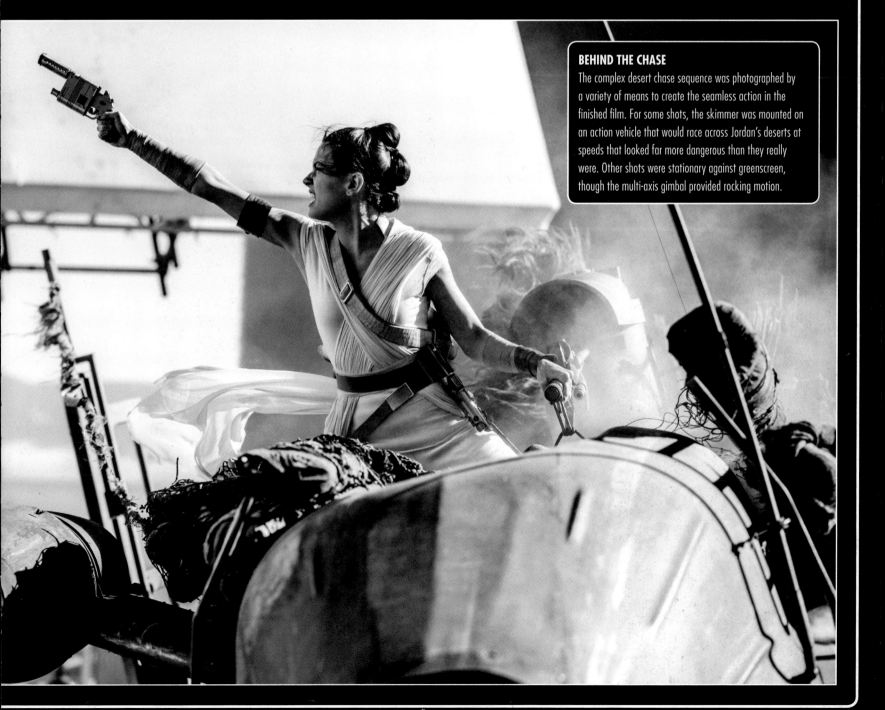

BEHIND THE CHASE

The complex desert chase sequence was photographed by a variety of means to create the seamless action in the finished film. For some shots, the skimmer was mounted on an action vehicle that would race across Jordan's deserts at speeds that looked far more dangerous than they really were. Other shots were stationary against greenscreen, though the multi-axis gimbal provided rocking motion.

INDEX

BABU FRIK'S CUSTOM DROID VISION PHOROPTER

REY'S NN-14 BLASTER PISTOL

INDEX

ATAPHEN BLARIO'S HELMET

EUPHAUS BIRO

INDEX

TQ3-R1

INDEX

SOMALED NEW

REY'S CRYSTALLINE REFORMATTER

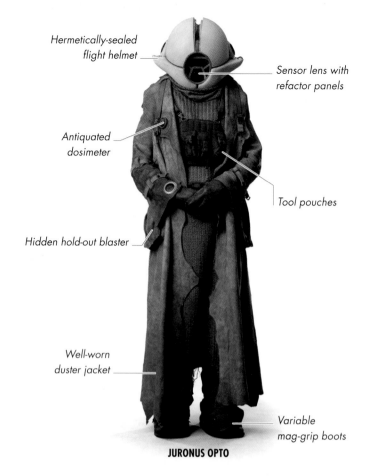

Hermetically-sealed
flight helmet

Sensor lens with
refactor panels

Antiquated
dosimeter

Tool pouches

Hidden hold-out blaster

Well-worn
duster jacket

Variable
mag-grip boots

JURONUS OPTO

ACKNOWLEDGMENTS

Pablo Hidalgo: Another journey completed and chronicled, and I am once again indebted to so many people who made this book possible. Many thanks to David Fentiman and everyone at DK for inviting me to add to their library once more. To James Waugh, Kiri Hart, Rayne Roberts, Leland Chee, Matt Martin, Steve Blank, Emily Shkoukani, and Kelsey Sharpe, thanks for help in expanding this story across multiple platforms. Thanks to James Erskine for all the times I needed to peek at the script. Thank you to Gabrielle Levenson, Tim Mapp, Bryce Pinkos, Dan Lobl, David Meny, Phil Szostak, and Erik Sanchez for all your helpful visuals and reference. And to Kemp Remillard, thank you for continued excellence.

For letting me feel at home at ILM reviews, thank you to Janet Lewin, Roger Guyett, Pat Tubach, Paul Kavanaugh, James Clyne, Chris Voy, Anna Mabarak, and Shivani Jhaveri.

Thank you to Kristen for your support, and to Walter, for keeping me company during long stints of silent writing.

And of course, thank you to Kathleen Kennedy, J.J. Abrams, Michelle Rejwan, and Chris Terrio for one last wonderful journey to this particular part of the galaxy. May the Force be with you.

Kemp Remillard: Hard to believe that Episode IX is finally here and that I've been so lucky to be on the Cross-Sectional journey for another volume. I would to thank DK Publishing for continuing to ask me to help craft a small part of the very big *Star Wars* universe. To Simon Beecroft, Victoria Short, David Fentiman, Chris Gould, and everyone I've ever worked with in the past at DK, my continued thanks for the opportunity and privilege of working together on these fine books. Many thanks to Lucasfilm for letting me see behind the curtain. To Pablo Hidalgo, thank you for everything you do and for having me as a collaborator on another great publication. Big thanks to Brett Rector, Troy Alders, Michael Siglain, and everyone at Lucasfilm Publishing, Story Group, Image Unit, and ILM. It's always an honor and a pleasure. Thanks to Jason Fry and Chris Reiff for the inspiration. To my family, friends, and Villi, a big thanks for all your support and encouragement.

DK Publishing: We would like to thank Pablo Hidalgo, Michael Siglain, Brett Rector, and everyone at Lucasfilm Publishing for all of their hard work and assistance while this book was in production. We would also like to thank Ruth Amos and Clive Savage for their editorial and design assistance, Julia March for the index, and Adam Brackenbury, Jon Hall, and Tom Morse for their image work.

Senior Editor David Fentiman
Project Editor Matt Jones
Designer Chris Gould
Creative Technical Support Steve Crozier
Pre-production Producer Marc Staples
Senior Producer Mary Slater
Managing Editor Sarah Harland
Managing Art Editor Vicky Short
Publisher Julie Ferris
Art Director Lisa Lanzarini

For Lucasfilm
Senior Editor Brett Rector
Creative Director of Publishing Michael Siglain
Art Director Troy Alders
Story Group James Waugh, Leland Chee, and Matt Martin
Asset Management Gabrielle Levenson, Tim Mapp, Bryce Pinkos, and Erik Sanchez
Photographers Shannon Kirbie, Ed Miller, Jonathan Olley, and John Wilson

First published in Great Britain in 2019 by
Dorling Kindersley Limited
80 Strand, London, WC2R ORL

Page design copyright © 2019 Dorling Kindersley Limited
A Penguin Random House Company
10 9 8 7 6 5 4 3 2 1
001–311514–Dec/2019

A CIP catalogue record for this book is available from the British Library
ISBN: 978-0-24135-769-9

Printed and bound in Slovakia

A WORLD OF IDEAS:
SEE ALL THERE IS TO KNOW

www.dk.com
www.starwars.com